CURRICULUM DEVELOPMENT IN THE POSTMODERN ERA

Patrick Slattery

GARLAND PUBLISHING, Inc.
New York & London / 1995

Grateful acknowledgment is made to the following for permission to reprint material.

Excerpt from "Choruses from 'The Rock'" in *Collected Poems 1909–1962* by T.S. Eliot, copyright © 1964, 1963 by T.S. Eliot, reprinted by permission of the publisher.

Excerpt from "Little Gidding" in *Four Quartets,* copyright © 1943 by T.S. Eliot and renewed 1971 by Esme Valerie Eliot, reprinted by permission of Harcourt Brace & Company.

Excerpts from *A Lesson Before Dying,* copyright © 1993 by Ernest J. Gaines, reprinted by permission of Alfred A. Knopf.

Figure 8.1 on page 181 is taken from figure 8.2 in Donald Oliver and Kathleen W. Gershman, *Education, Modernity, and Fractured Meaning: Toward a Process Theory of Teaching and Learning* (Albany: State University of New York Press, 1989).

Figure 9.1 on page 202 is taken from figure 7–3 in William H. Schubert, *Curriculum: Perspective, Paradigm, Possibility* (New York: Macmillan, 1986).

Library of Congress Cataloging-in-Publication Data

Slattery, Patrick, 1953–
    Curriculum development in the postmodern era /
Patrick Slattery.
        p.   cm. — (Garland reference library of social
science ; vol. 929. Critical education practice ; vol. 1)
    Includes bibliographical references and indexes.
    ISBN 0–8153–1509–0 (hardcover : acid-free paper). —
ISBN 0–8153–1926–6 (pbk. : acid-free paper)
    1. Curriculum development.   2. Curriculum change.
3. Education—Curricula—Philosophy.   4. Postmodernism.
I. Title. II. Series: Garland reference library of social
science ; v. 929. III. Series: Garland reference library of
social science. Critical education practice ; vol. 1.
LB2806.15.S63   1995
375'.001—dc20   94–33596
                                     CIP

Paperback cover design by Patti Hefner

Printed on acid-free, 250-year-life paper
Manufactured in the United States of America

For
Cheryl, Michelle, Katie, and Joshua

The fundamental human quest is the search for
meaning and the basic human capacity for this
search is experienced in the hermeneutic process, the
process of interpretation of the text (whether artifact,
natural world, or human action). This is the search
(or research) for greater understanding that
motivates and satisfies us. . . . The act of theorizing is
an act of faith, a religious act. . . . It is an expression
of the humanistic vision in life.

James B. Macdonald (1988, pp. 105, 110)

Contents

Series Editors' Introduction

Recently we were fortuitous in finding ourselves dining at a Portuguese restaurant in Boston, discussing love with Paulo Freire. Along with our friends Donaldo Macedo and Connie Titone, we carefully listened to Paulo describe his *loves*: his wife, and the relationship between his love and his work. At one point, the conversation turned to the nature of *radical love*—the combustible spirit behind Freire's pedagogy and the passion that fuels our lives as teachers. Paulo was poetic as he described a radical love's ability to transcend traditional social expectations. A radical love, he said, is unencumbered by strings and is freely given by a teacher to his or her students. In the weeks that have passed since that unforgettable conversation, we have often thought about the nature of radical love in our own relationship, in our work, and in the work of our friends in a variety of vocations and life settings. It is in this context that we think of Patrick Slattery.

Curriculum Development in the Postmodern Era sets the standard for the postmodern "textbook." The modernist textbook was typically a cold, impersonal compilation of factoids to be inserted into the passive minds of students. In order to achieve distinction in its field of disciplinary knowledge the cold and impersonal nature of the book needed to be emphasized—no need for contamination by the realm of the personal, the subjective. The idea of radical love in forming the spirit of a textbook was unthinkable. Patrick Slattery has escaped the boundaries of the modernist force field. Like Patrick McGoohan in *The Prisoner* TV series of the 1960s, Slattery has negotiated the obstacles devised by regressive modernism's "Number Two." Gaining asylum in the domain of the postmodern, Slattery is free to inject his radical love into his work. The book that emerges is an autobiographical document that views knowledge within a context that reflects human interests and values. And, confidentially, we find a personal book on what could be the stuffy topic of curriculum development much more interesting and meaningful than the traditional approach.

As the editors we hope that scholars in the field will read this book, but, like Slattery, we hope that classroom teachers, university students, and school district supervisors will find it relevant to their concerns. As the gap between curriculum scholars and classroom practitioners has widened into a chasm, analysts like Slattery are needed to seal the break. As one who has extensive experience as a teacher, a principal, and a scholar, Slattery brings a seasoned eye to the book. When this experience combines with both his Louisiana-bred facility as a raconteur and his understanding of William Pinar's autobiographical method, a unique text is created. What emerges is a textured analysis of schooling. It is an examination that views curriculum as what Peter McLaren calls a "contradictory terrain," an arena that can be used for social control and/or democratic empowerment.

Plunging headfirst into the postmodern maelstrom, Slattery engages global traditions and long-suppressed knowledges in the debate over curriculum development. Chief Seattle, Toni Morrison, Jackson Pollock, Francis of Assisi, Lau Tsu, Jesus, Friedrich Nietzsche, Alice Walker, and T. S. Eliot are all players here, voices that engage and question those scholars more typically identified with discourse of curriculum. In a postmodern cosmos turned upside down, Slattery echoes Walker Percy's call to look at the world afresh through the eyes of one newly arrived. Here rests the key to Slattery's postmodern critiques: to rethink curriculum from the bottom up. In the process he urges us to consider T.S. Eliot's question to modernity: "Where is the wisdom we have lost in knowledge?" At times Slattery's prose suggests Maxine Greene's travel journal after Scotty beamed her into Tennessee Williams' New Orleans. Indeed, Patrick's southern "take" on postmodernism engages us all.

Slattery wants curriculum students to understand that the world is far more complex and ambiguous than the positivists would have us believe, that teacher education is more than well-formatted lesson plans, behavioral objectives, and anticipatory "sets." Taking his readers on a walking tour of the twilight zone of postmodern uncertainty, Patrick exposes the folly of modernist standardization. School people need to enter into the conversation about curriculum, he implores. With style he exhorts his colleagues to consider curriculum as if it were a human question. As a human question, curriculum development becomes a process of meaning making. When educational scientists divided knowledge into byte-sized chocolate morsels, meaning was destroyed; it is Slattery's contention that the postmodern charge involves the restoration of meaning and the demolition of Pink Floyd's *wall* that separates bricks of truth and virtue, values and facts, and curriculum and social justice.

As the consummate postmodern eclecticist, Slattery draws upon phenomenology, existentialism, pragmatism, deconstruction, chaos theory, multiculturalism, poststructuralism, feminism, theology, hermeneutics, and critical theory. Within this amalgamation he never strays too far from his passion for aesthetics and its direct line to meaning making. Via this link Slattery pounds the modernists and the failure of their rationalistic vision. Connecting the aesthetic to the spiritual, Patrick reclaims spirituality as a progressive issue. Using religious texts to connect modernist rationalism and religious fundamentalism, Slattery explains to students the importance of hermeneutics, of interpretation, in the act of curriculum development. Teachers must build a postmodern community of interpreters that seeks to understand lived experience and the self in relation to others. It is this very attempt to interpret or understand that sabotages the modernist "fundamentalists." The hermeneutic teacher violates the confines of the traditional lesson plan with her or his celebration of the unexpected question and the throwaway comment. The insurrection is out of control—Slattery and the postmodern hermeneuts will no longer obey the curriculum authorities, passively execute the official methodologies of instruction, or accept the radical orthodox interpretations of the canonical texts. Slattery revels in his hermeneutical life outside the law.

Patrick knows that meaning is made—it does not hibernate in the snug warmth of a text. In the context created by this epistemological assertion, Slattery sees curriculum development as an effort to prepare a space that is conducive to students constructing a series of synthetical moments. Bill Pinar has referred to these moments as time when self-understanding results from the synergistic unification of intellect, body, spirit, and cosmos. Time, place, and meaning collide in an aesthetic harmony that provides the motivation to learn that educational scientists have futilely tried to contrive. If not for the jolt of such synthetical moments, many of us would have abandoned the academy years ago. This jolt, this earthquake of the spirit plays out daily in the lives of our students, in their awakenings and subsequent escapes from the arms of cyber-Morpheus. It is here that the challenge Slattery presents us reveals itself: Are we prepared to develop a postmodern curriculum that critically examines our students' (and our own) autobiographies in the context of social and historical realities?

Slattery's postmodern autobiographical curriculum is not warm-fuzzy, let's-all-feel-good-about-ourselves, self-indulgent, pseudo-academic course of study. Missing are the pop psychologists, the self-concept lessons, the motivational speakers who threaten slackers/students with a future of life in a "van down by the river," and the equation of white, middle-class values with definitions of personal success. Slattery's curriculum is a bold invitation to students to "enter history rather than simply observe history from a distance," to become participants in a quest for meaning on which the survival and emancipation of the species depends.

Exploration is central—of the world, of different cultures, of outer space, of quantum reality, of course. But in the process of the journey, we return to where we started. Here we are empowered so that we understand our "place" and thus ourselves, as Eliot put it, "for the first time." Understanding our place, our selves, allows us to take our place within the web of reality—to comprehend our own consciousness construction and what it means. Such insight can be gained only with a knowledge of the world, an appreciation of difference, and a confrontation with the "other." The journey is difficult and ambiguous—Slattery is an able guide. His radical love is omnipresent.

Shirley R. Steinberg
Joe L. Kincheloe

Preface

Curriculum and instruction are the very heart and soul of schooling. Elliot Eisner, professor of education and art at Stanford,
writes: "Clearly, there are few issues that are more central to the
experience that students have in schools than the content of the
curriculum and the ways in which it is mediated" (1993, p. 38).
While this may seem to be an obvious understatement to some, it
is, nonetheless, more complicated and controversial than initially
apparent.

Let me begin with an analogy. I suspect that there would
be little disagreement among physicians, nurses, medical school
personnel, and patients that the primary function of the contemporary health care professions is healing and wellness.
Insurance, hospital construction, computerization, and record
documentation, although important and often cumbersome,
should be peripheral to the primary purpose of healing in the
medical field and allied services. As current debates about the
reform of the health care industry unfold in the United States
and comparisons to international health care delivery methods
are discussed in the media, we are beginning to recognize the
barriers and limitations that restrict our ability to focus on the
healing and wellness of individuals.

The education profession has borrowed much terminology
from the medical profession (despite the fact that the analogy is
problematic). We "test" and "diagnose" students in order to apply appropriate "treatments." Students who are "deficient" are
sent to a "lab" for "prescriptive" remediation. The lab staff per-
forms further tests to ascertain more accurately the extent of the
deficiency. If the treatment in the lab works, students are declared "well," and further visits to the lab occur only for

"relapses." Teachers participate in "clinical" supervision programs to evaluate instruction. Some educators have proposed a form of "triage" through alternative schooling, tracking, tech-prep schools, or promotion exams, while others resist triage in favor of "holistic" approaches (Books, 1992). Eisner (1993) calls curriculum and teaching the "systole and diastole" of schooling when he writes that curriculum and teaching, like the heart, reside within a "body," the school. Eisner continues:

> The school's structure and its function influence the way in which systolic and diastolic operations occur. In turn, the school inhabits an environment and like the body itself, is not immune to the quality of that environment. . . . The educational health of the classroom is intimately related to the school in which it is nested and the health of the school to the environment within which it resides. (1993, p. 38)

Like the medical profession, the education profession has also struggled to remain focused on its primary purpose of learning and instruction for students. Donald Schon (1983, 1987, 1991) in several popular books has challenged all professions to examine their purpose and function in society. Particularly, he has encouraged professionals to overcome the debilitating effects of bureaucracy, disconnectedness, and inertia by becoming "reflective practitioners" who promote learning from, in, and through experience. In this book I will support Schon's call for reflection and action in the professions. Particularly, I believe that educators must focus on a renewed understanding of curriculum and instruction in the postmodern global society that is emerging in the 1990s.

My twenty years of experience in education at various levels of instruction from elementary classrooms to high school administration and to graduate school seminars in several different states leads me to believe that understanding curriculum and instruction in our profession, like wellness and healing in the health care field, must move to the forefront of our thinking and action.

This is not to imply that gallant efforts have not been made to improve curriculum development, design, implementation, and evaluation. The field of educational administration expends much energy promoting administrators as "instructional lead-ers" and "curriculum innovators." The field of educational psy-chology has worked for decades evaluating the validity, reliabil-ity, and effectiveness of tests, textbooks, and teaching methods. The field of curriculum and instruction has taught methods courses to several generations of teachers. However, all these efforts, no matter how important or how noble they may have been, must now be reevaluated for three reasons: first, schooling in the 1990s is in the midst of a debilitating crisis; second, a postmodern worldview is emerging; and third, a reconceptual-ization in the field of curriculum and instruction has occurred. Rather than panic over these events, I embrace our contemporary social and educational milieu and look for hope and renewal in the midst of the turmoil and chaos.

This book is meant to serve as an introductory guide to the field of curriculum and instruction for university students, school district supervisors, curriculum specialists, classroom teachers, and others interested in understanding curriculum de-velopment as it relates to emerging postmodern education paradigms. As the book proceeds, terms such as curriculum de-velopment, postmodernism, hermeneutics, paradigm, chaos the-ory, poststructuralism, and critical theory will be discussed in the context of the educational milieu of the 1990s. However, these terms defy self-evident definitions. Readers may have to reevaluate their preconceived notions of the meaning of curricu-lum development and postmodern education and allow new and sometimes startling understandings to emerge.

I hope that the process of reading this book about curricu-lum and postmodernism, two concepts that are very significant in my own personal and scholarly growth, will challenge, affirm, and refresh, and sometimes even jolt, those who explore the ideas in this book. I often tell my graduate students that if my seminars are successful, then we should all leave class with con-cerns, doubts, and questions rather than certainty. The disequi-librium and complexity, I contend, provide an opportunity for further clarification and exploration, which in turn will lead to the emergence of a deep ecology of the schooling process.

This book is divided into three sections. Part one explores curriculum development as a field of study and situates curriculum and instruction in a postmodern context. Particular emphasis will be placed on the Reconceptualization of curriculum studies that occurred in the late 1970s but that has yet to be fully explored in elementary and secondary schools and even some graduate classrooms. Additionally, historical and theological conceptions of curriculum will be introduced. Part two explores many of the issues associated with contemporary curriculum discourses in areas such as hermeneutics, race, gender, culture, philosophy, politics, democracy, ecology, aesthetics, autobiography, and cosmology. Because of the complexity of the research in all these areas, the purpose of the chapters in part two is to introduce the themes, provide examples, and point the reader to areas of possible further study. In this sense, part two is designed to appeal to curriculum specialists, teachers, professors, and beginning students who are interested in an overview of curriculum theory or a short supplementary introductory text. Part three of this book presents a proposal for rethinking curriculum development for the postmodern era. The two chapters in this final section of the book present reflections on the multiple levels of understanding the issues presented in part two.

Taken as a whole, this book challenges professors, students, and curriculum specialists to transcend traditional approaches to curriculum development and incorporate various postmodern discourses into our reflection and action. However, I acknowledge the contribution of traditional curriculum development in part one in order to remind us that as we explore postmodernism we carry the past and the future within us.

I would like to thank my mentors and teachers who have shared not only their wisdom but also their souls with me. I carry your wisdom within me. Particularly I thank Bill Pinar, Bill Doll, Mary Minella, Mary Aswell Doll, Louis Welker FSC, John Burke, and Pattie Cotter Burke, my mother. I also thank my colleagues who have offered valuable criticism and support through many hours of stimulating dialogue, especially Shirley Steinberg, Joe Kincheloe, Elizabeth Willis, Hilly Bernard, Sue Books, Kevin Daigle, and Janet Miller, who reviewed drafts of the manuscript, as well as Jeanie Bernard, Wen-Song Hwu, David Ray Griffin, John Cobb, Angela Lydon, Susan Edgerton,

Judy Konikoff, Carol Whelan, Sally Dobyns, Joe Riehl, Spencer Maxcy, Joe Green, David Purpel, Jim Henderson, Don Guenther, Roy Graham, Denise Knapik, Vic Devalcourt, John St. Julien, Bill Reynolds, my students and colleagues at the University of Southwestern Louisiana, Ashland University, and the University of St. Thomas, and friends at Louisiana State University. My family has been most generous to encourage my writing. I have also had the privilege of watching my wife, Cheryl Friberg Slattery, develop her own feminist voice through the publication of her children's stories. We have also collaborated together by writing about our work in the *Journal of Childrens' Books in Ireland*. Our own children, Michelle, Katie, and Joshua, remind us of the very tangible importance of our curriculum theorizing.

Technical details in the production of this manuscript could not have been completed without the generous support of many friends, including Elizabeth Langlinais, Linden Bercegeay, Jr., Bonnie Belsome, Dawn Guidry, Ardy Bass, James Davis, and Richard Chachere. I am truly grateful to these friends and colleagues. I also thank all of the editors and staff at Garland Publishing, who were very supportive, especially Marie Ellen Larcada and my series editors, Shirley Steinberg and Joe Kincheloe. Finally, I cite professor James B. Macdonald, now deceased, at the beginning of this book. His writing has been a rich source of reflection for me. In this sense, Professor Macdonald has also been a mentor, for his words continue to inspire. He has reminded me that what is required in education is a profound faith that there is meaning to our lives. As educators we ultimately must affirm visions of that meaningful life for ourselves, our students, and our planet. The hermeneutic process of discovering this meaning inspired Macdonald. We, too, must believe that our work has the potential for redemptive consequences and a cosmological vision of hope, justice, and compassion.

The front cover photograph of Piazza D'Italia in New Orleans was taken by Anne E. Pautz, a graduate student in curriculum studies at Louisiana State University. Piazza D'Italia, designed by James Sterling, is a stunning example of the eclecticism, irony, and playfulness of postmodern architecture. While the Piazza stands in stark contrast to the linear and functional modern skyscrapers of downtown New Orleans, it is also inti-mately integrated into the modern milieu of the financial district on Poydras Street. In recent years Piazza D'Italia has fallen into disrepair. Located near the proposed site of the largest land-based casino in the nation, Piazza D'Italia is currently scheduled to be destroyed to make way for another major building.

Introduction

Graduate courses such as elementary and secondary curriculum development, curriculum supervision, curriculum evaluation, and curriculum planning are often required as part of advanced degree programs in university departments of curriculum and instruction. Traditionally, a synoptic (comprehensive) textbook with an emphasis on quantitative research methodologies and practical application of curriculum goals, objectives, lesson plans, scope and sequence guides, and evaluation instruments has been used by professors to provide an overview of the areas of policy, planning and design, implementation, and supervision of the school curriculum. Most synoptic textbooks in the past have been consistent with the dominant philosophical approach to curriculum development called the Tylerian rationale after Ralph Tyler's influential book *Basic Principles of Curriculum and Instruction*, which has dominated the curriculum field since its publication in 1949. In fact, Tyler's handbook itself has often been used as a supplementary reading by those professors committed to the rationale, and at times in the past forty years it has almost taken on the stature of an icon of the field. Thus, several generations of graduate students, teachers, supervisors, administrators, and curriculum specialists have been influenced by the Tylerian rationale and sometimes indoctrinated to believe that this is the only viable conception of curriculum development available for schooling. While acknowledging the historical contribution of Ralph Tyler to curriculum development in the modern era, contemporary curriculum discourses challenge the assumption that the Tylerian rationale should be the basis of all curriculum studies. In fact, postmodern philosophies are emerging that transcend and often replace the traditional model of curriculum development itself.

Since the Reconceptualization of the curriculum field in the late 1970s and early 1980s, Tyler's handbook is often used by those who teach historical, political, or theoretical education courses to critique the impact of the rationale paradigm on the curriculum field and classroom practice. In the 1990s major battles over the meaning, purpose, and function of curriculum are raging in the universities, in school districts, among parent groups, in churches, and in political organizations. Various constituencies, some of them local groups concerned about particular programs or books used in their district schools and others committed to national or international paradigm changes in educational philosophies, have brought curricular concerns to the forefront of national debates.

In 1988 William Pinar, one of the leading contemporary curriculum scholars, described the Reconceptualization this way:

> The field of curriculum has undergone an enormous change—a reconceptualization if you will—during the past twenty years. From a field concerned with the development and management of curriculum it has evolved into a field more concerned with scholarly understanding of several dimensions of curriculum. These dimensions include issues of development and management; however, these are explored through political, gendered, phenomenological, and other means. (1988a, p. v)

This reconceptualized field has resulted in much discussion on the university level, but until now it has not begun to filter into elementary and secondary schools.

This book is intended to bridge many gaps that currently divide various stakeholders in the curricular debates of the 1990s: traditionalists who cling firmly to the Tylerian rationale and reconceptualists who insist on a new understanding of curriculum; university professors of curriculum and school district personnel in elementary and secondary schools; modernists and postmodernists; promoters of cultural literacy and advocates of revisionist history; curriculum planners and critical theorists; curriculum specialists and lay observers of curriculum practices; educational administrators and political special interest groups; and even teachers and students. There is a definite need for all these stakeholders to consider carefully the historical and contemporary curriculum discourses that can inform and sometimes mediate the contentious debates that currently exist in the United States and other nations concerning curriculum development. Those involved with schooling in the 1990s, including parents, teachers, students, school board members, professors of education, university graduate students, politicians, and school administrators are all intimately familiar with the volatility of curricular debates. While many outstanding textbooks have been published in recent years which present summaries of curriculum research in order to clarify the various contemporary perspectives on curriculum (e.g., Schubert, 1986; Jackson, 1992; and Pinar et al., in press), these textbooks and the themes they discuss are not always accessible, and sometimes not easily comprehensible, to many teachers, curriculum specialists in school districts, beginning graduate students, and even professors of education who have not yet studied the contemporary research and therefore remain committed only to traditional textbooks with a focus on the Tylerian rationale.

Before commenting on the approach that this book will take to address the curricular debates described above, it is necessary to review briefly the various synoptic textbooks that have influenced the curriculum field. Without a sense of this historical perspective it will be difficult to understand why a book on curriculum development and postmodern education is even necessary. However, it is hoped that this book will introduce elements of contemporary curriculum research in such a way that curriculum discourses will become accessible to many more of the stakeholders in the curriculum field today, especially those who are involved in the daily struggle to implement curriculum theories in schools as well as graduate students who will one day be the curriculum specialists responsible for such implementation in the universities and in classrooms.

Some of the popular synoptic textbooks that the traditionalists in the field are using in the 1990s include the following texts that have dominated the field since their first editions appeared between 1954 (Saylor) and 1982 (Oliva):

Ronald C. Doll (1992, 8th ed.) *Curriculum Improvement: Decision Making and Process*; J. D. McNeil (1990, 4th ed.) *Curriculum: A Comprehensive Introduction*; Peter F. Oliva (1992, 3rd ed.) *Developing the Curriculum*; J. Galen Saylor et al. (1981, 4th ed.) *Curriculum Planning for Better Teaching and Learning*; Daniel Tanner and Laurel Tanner (in press, 3rd ed.) *Curriculum Development: Theory Into Practice*; J. Wiles and J. C. Bondi (1993, 4th ed.) *Curriculum Development: A Guide to Practice*; and R. S. Zais (1976) *Curriculum: Principles and Foundations*. These texts provide an approach to curriculum development that is compatible with the philosophy of those professors who are interested in curriculum policy making and the construction of model curriculum guides, scope and sequence charts, and lesson plans with behavioral goals for evaluation as the central focus of their curriculum course requirements. Synoptic texts have a long history in the curriculum field dating back to the publication in 1935 of Hollis L. Caswell and Doak S. Campbell's *Curriculum Development,* which established the tradition of synoptic texts in the American curriculum field. Caswell was a pioneer of statewide programs of curriculum development in the 1930s.

Since the Reconceptualization of the field of curriculum and instruction in the 1970s (Jackson, 1992; Pinar et al., in press), there has been a virtual explosion of new theoretical constructs that have moved the field beyond the traditional Tylerian rationale and beyond the scope of behavioral curriculum planning in the traditional synoptic texts. New textbooks address issues of race, gender, politics, critical pragmatism, phenomenology, poststructuralism, aesthetics, ecology, deconstructionism, philosophy, social theory, autobiography, ethnography, hermeneutics, literary theory, historicity, multiculturalism, theology, international global education, and, of course, postmodernism. Additionally, all the traditional structural disciplines of the curriculum field have been reconceptualized as well. This is exemplified by the following: *educational evaluation* is seen as "expressive," "imaginative," "metaphorical," and "connoisseurship" by Elliot Eisner (1985, 1991) rather than objective and scientific; *supervision of instruction* is described as "theatrical and image constructive" by Edward Pajak (1989), "shared and empowering" by Carl Glickman (1992), and "interpretive inquiry" by Nelson Haggerson and Andrea Bowman (1992) rather than "bureaucratic, inspectional, and clinical" as in the traditional supervision models; *policy making* is viewed as "less deterministic" by Elmore and Sykes (1992) and as "a complex appreciation of relations among school, individual experience, and public life" by Page (1990) rather than exclusively a "rational process of instrumental intervention and analyzable negotiation guiding educational practice" (Wise, 1979); *curriculum theory* is described as "a postmodern process of richness, recursion, relations, and rigor" by William Doll (1993) rather than "concrete elements of a program of instruction" (Tyler, 1949); and finally, *curriculum planning and design* is seen as "interdisciplinary" (Sizer, 1984) and "opening up possibilities that enable learning rather than as management of expected outcomes" (Carson, 1989).

The traditional texts in the curriculum field tend to ignore the Reconceptualization and reject the new theoretical understandings of curriculum and instruction identified above. This is reflected in the fact that the textbooks by Oliva, McNeil, R. Doll, Tanner and Tanner, Saylor, Zais, and Wiles and Bondi either omit or criticize in passing (often in a footnote) the reconceptualized curriculum discourses. The traditional texts simply do not include issues of race, gender, hermeneutics, autobiography, critical theory, phenomenology, poststructuralism, ecology, theology, and global education in their concept of curriculum development.

Despite the dramatic changes (some claim a paradigm shift) in the curriculum field since the 1970s, a critical dilemma has developed within the reconceptualized field of curriculum and instruction itself. In the 1970s and early 1980s, curriculum scholars who were writing specifically about race, gender, ethics, politics, empowerment, autobiography, and phenomenology were relatively small in number. Their voices were usually excluded from mainstream discourses, professional journals, and curriculum textbooks and virtually nonexistent in the curriculum development programs of elementary and secondary education. These scholars remained united in their opposition to the Tylerian rationale and other quantitative and behavioral approaches to curriculum studies. (See, for example, Giroux, Penna, and Pinar, 1981.) By the 1980s this coalition broke down as each group began to claim that their mode of analysis was either superior or normative for the reconceptualized field. Marxist and feminist analyses initially appeared to gain ascendancy by 1980 and 1985, respectively.

Thus, in the climate of the 1990s curriculum professors committed to political analysis use texts in the political genre, for example, Bowles and Gintis (1976), Apple (1979, 1982, 1985, 1993), Giroux (1981, 1988, 1992), Aronowitz (1992), Kincheloe (1993), Freire (1970, 1985), Freire and Macedo (1987), Stanley (1992), McLaren (1989), Willis (1977), Wexler (1992), and Kozol (1975, 1991), and those committed to feminist gender analysis use texts in the feminist genre, for example, Lather (1989, 1991), Grumet (1988a, 1988b, 1988c), Noddings (1984, 1989, 1992), Miller (1987, 1990), and Pagano (1990). Those whose work is rooted in phenomenology reference Aoki (1985, 1988, 1992), Aoki et al., (1987), Greene (1978), van Mannen (1982, 1984, 1986, 1988, 1990, 1993), Husserl (1964), Merleau-Ponty (1962), Carson (1987, 1992), Jardine (1992), and Pinar and Reynolds (1992). Process philosophers of education cite Whitehead (1929, 1933), Dewey (1899, 1938, 1985), Bergson (1946), James (1958), Griffin (1988a, 1988b), Griffin et al. (1993), W. Doll (1993), Huebner, (1975), and Oliver and Gershman (1989). Scholars who focus on race and curriculum reference West (1988, 1990), McCarthy (1990, 1993), Castenell and Pinar (1993), and Watkins (1993). This scenario is repeated in each of the areas of specialization of the field.

In this milieu, very few curriculum scholars have written comprehensive synoptic textbooks that attempt to bridge the growing gap between the various sectors of the field, much less one that attempts to expose practitioners in the schools to the growing body of scholarship that could support efforts to reconceptualize teaching and learning. However, there are some excellent books that discuss both the traditional and the reconceptualized field with practical and theoretical scholarship included. For example, Joe Kincheloe and Shirley Steinberg's (1992) edited *Thirteen Questions: Reframing Education's Conversations* includes a variety of voices from the reconceptualization with an emphasis on accessibility to practitioners in the schools. Additionally, the work of Elliot Eisner (1985, 1991), William Pinar (1975, 1988a, 1992, 1994), and

Henry Giroux (1988, 1991, 1992, 1993) is often used to provide alternative and reconceptualized approaches to evaluation, curriculum theory, and social theory, respectively. One of the only comprehensive synoptic textbooks that has been available in the field that includes scholarship from the Reconceptualization is William Schubert's (1986) *Curriculum: Perspective, Paradigm, Possibility*. While the structure of Schubert's text has been criticized for its artificial constructs, the comprehensive scope of the book has made it the only option available for graduate students and curriculum specialists in recent years who wish to understand curriculum from various perspectives and not just the Tylerian approach.

Two new publications since 1992 will expand on the work begun in Schubert's 1986 textbook: Philip Jackson's (1992) edited *Handbook of Research on Curriculum* and William F. Pinar et al.'s (in press) *Understanding Curriculum: An Introduction to the Study of Historical and Contemporary Curriculum Discourses*. Both Jackson and Pinar are leading scholars in the curriculum field. The commitment of their publishers, Macmillan and Peter Lang, respectively, to publish these two major textbooks (each over 700 pages in length) and the sponsorship by the American Educational Research Association (AERA) for Jackson's text, indicate that contemporary curriculum discourses have entered the mainstream scholarship of the field in the 1990s. Since this new scholarship has gained ascendancy in the major universities of the United States and Canada, among other countries, it is only a matter of time before a new generation of curriculum specialists brings this scholarship into the schools. William Pinar (1988a) alludes to the movement of the Reconceptualization from the universities to the elementary and secondary schools when he writes about the "second wave" of the Reconceptualization from the university scholars, to graduate students, and finally to elementary and secondary school teachers. As of this writing many curriculum scholars continue to wait for the "second wave" to break.

Jackson's *Handbook of Curriculum Research* and Pinar's *Understanding Curriculum*, along with the texts by Schubert, Eisner, and Giroux, will certainly serve as primary references in the 1990s for advanced graduate courses in curriculum theory and curriculum development. Additionally, professors committed exclusively to the Tylerian rationale will continue to lose influence in the field, and there will be a gradual decline in the use of the R. Doll, McNeil, Oliva, Saylor, Tanner and Tanner, Zais, and Wiles and Bondi textbooks. This points to the need for concise introductory texts that will provide access to the major themes and resources of the emerging postmodern curriculum field for professors, graduate students, and curriculum specialists who do not yet feel comfortable with the theories, movements, and philosophies of the contemporary curriculum discourses. *Curriculum Development in the Postmodern Era* is an attempt to provide one such resource.

It is now necessary to see how *Curriculum Development in the Postmodern Era* can help to create a dialogue between the traditional and reconceptualized curriculum field, particularly in elementary and secondary schools. Many teachers and scholars are interested in exploring the reconceptualized field, but they often feel compelled to conform to traditional practices in the schools. This book provides concise and accessible material on the history of curriculum development, the various dimensions of understanding curriculum development, and the major sectors of the reconceptualized field, each with specific examples applicable to elementary and secondary schools in our postmodern society that will help to make such exploration possible.

The introduction of the Jackson and Pinar texts, in 1992 and 1995 respectively, will satisfy the need for comprehensive synoptic texts on the advanced level for curriculum theorists. Additionally, these two textbooks will impact the field significantly by firmly establishing the Reconceptualization as a dominant paradigm for understanding curriculum. However, there remain many professors and most curriculum specialists in the schools who have used the traditional texts for years and are unwilling to replace these books or abandon the Tylerian rationale completely. Some of these professors are open to new developments in the field and willing to explore them on a limited basis. It is these professors and specialists whom this book is intended to serve.

Additionally, there are professors of graduate and undergraduate courses who are interested in contemporary curriculum theory, but they have not yet been exposed to all the various philosophical paradigms prominent in the 1990s literature. Thus, they are uncomfortable with the comprehensive synoptic texts. They simply need general information that introduces the complexities of the field for their undergraduate and beginning graduate students in curriculum theory as well as those in allied fields. It is hoped that these professors and students will find this book useful and informative.

Indeed, the scope of the issues involved in contemporary curriculum theory is so immense, and the language in many of the texts is so specialized, that some professors, graduate students, and curriculum specialists are frustrated by the theoretical discourses—and at times they should be! There is a definite need on the part of many practitioners for a concise introduction to historical and contemporary curriculum discourses and the implication of these discourses for the school curriculum in the emerging postmodern global society. Much more needs to be written for these practitioners that will make the contemporary curriculum proposals accessible and defensible.

There is another intended audience for this book. Unlike many professors in large research universities, educators in smaller liberal arts colleges, teachers and curriculum specialists in public elementary and secondary schools, and private school educators have been exposed to some of the possible applications of the Reconceptualization on a grass roots level in their schools. While not universally accepted, and in some school districts quite controversial, curricular philosophies such as whole language instruction, integrated language arts, interdisciplinary studies, curricular immersion, authentic assessment, peer coaching, team teaching, autobiographical and narrative portfolios, mentorship, critical thinking, aesthetic evaluation, community thematic learning, and nongraded primary schools are the focus of much discussion in the 1990s. Educators who have incorporated these philosophies into their pedagogy or who would like to explore similar curricular themes desperately need support to situate these proposals within a wider theoretical framework. The opposition to change and innovation in schools is pervasive, and many curriculum leaders abandon their efforts to reconceptualize teaching and learning for lack of support. Additionally, the misapplication of many philosophies and innovations exacerbates public suspicion of some programs. John Dewey (1938) wrote one of his later books, *Experience and Education*, in part to disassociate himself from the misinterpretation of his educational philosophy by some in the progressive education movement in the 1930s. While the curriculum field of the 1990s has many philosophical connections to the progressive education movement, curriculum theorists are aware of the excesses and abuses that led to the repudiation of progressive ideas by 1957 with the launch of the Soviet Sputnik satellite and the conservative political reaction of those like Admiral Hyman Rickover. Curricular programs in the 1950s, for example the "new math" developed by Max Beberman, exemplified the political and social reaction not only to progressive philosophies but also to the cold war politics of the time.

Today, the reconceptualized curriculum field provides the necessary grounding for reflection, renewal, and innovation to move beyond both progressive and conservative curriculum development models of the past, and this book provides access to these postmodern curriculum theories. However, we must be aware that a variety of understandings and interpretations exists, lest we repeat the same misapplication that John Dewey warned against.

Innovative practitioners are often attacked by entrenched bureaucrats and political factions resistant to change. Support for these educators currently exists in journals such as *The Journal of Curriculum Studies*, *Curriculum Inquiry*, *JCT: An Interdisciplinary Journal of Curriculum Studies*, *Teaching Education*, *Journal of Curriculum and Supervision*, *Journal of Teacher Education*, *Social Education*, *Educational Theory*, *The International Journal of Qualitative Studies in Education*, *Taboo*, and *Holistic Education Review*, as well as books like *The Holistic Curriculum* by John P. Miller (1988), *A Post-Modern Perspective on Curriculum* by William E. Doll, Jr. (1993), *Education, Cultural Myths, and the Ecological Crisis: Toward Deep Changes* by Chet A. Bowers (1993), *Teaching and Thinking about Curriculum: Critical Inquiry* , edited by James T. Sears and J. Dan Marshall (1990), and *Curriculum for Utopia: Social Reconstructionism and Critical Pedagogy in the Postmodern Era* by William B. Stanley (1992). In the field of philosophy of education Spencer J. Maxcy's (1991) *Educational Leadership: A Critical Pragmatic Perspective,* Maxcy's (1993) edited *Postmodern School Leadership,* Nicholas Burbules' (1993a) *Dialogue in Teaching: Theory and Practice,* Donald Oliver and Kathleen Gershman's (1989) *Education, Modernity, and Fractured Meaning: Toward a Process Theory of Teaching and Learning,* James Henderson and R. D. Hawthone's (1995) *Transformative Curriculum Leadership,* and Joe Kincheloe's (1993) *Toward a Critical Politics of Teacher Training: Mapping the Postmodern* all address these themes as well. We can also anticipate the publication of the proceedings of the three-year symposium *Education for the Good of the World: Curriculum and Higher Education* in 1995. David Ray Griffin, John B. Cobb, Jr., and the Center for Process Studies at Claremont will sponsor this symposium for scholars in the field of postmodern process education. These examples of contemporary publications indicate that there is an immense interest in political, philosophical, ecological, holistic, and reconceptualized contemporary educational discourses. These discourses must not remain concealed in the exclusive domain of professional journals and university scholarship. It is important to make curriculum theory accessible and inspirational for educators and students throughout the field.

The attempt to make such a vast body of research and writing accessible in a short introductory text without being encyclopedic and superficial is a challenge. Even the references to many authors and theories in this introduction may seem overwhelming to those unfamiliar with the literature. Additionally, the need to balance direct citations, reflective commentary, references, autobiographical experiences, and practical examples in such a text is crucial. I recognize that this book cannot be inclusive or comprehensive, and I therefore encourage readers to explore the Jackson and Pinar texts as well as the many other works cited. However, I hope that this book will uniquely contribute to the "second wave" of curricular reconceptualization in American education. I also hope that my colleagues in the fields of curriculum and instruction and foundations of education will enjoy reading my perspective, for we all recognize the importance of each contribution to the tapestry that is becoming curriculum development in the postmodern era.

PART ONE

Postmodern Curriculum Development as a Field of Study

CHAPTER ONE

Introduction to Curriculum Development and Postmodernity

There has been a virtual explosion of the use of the word *postmodern* in recent years: deconstructive postmodernism, constructive postmodernism, eliminative postmodernism, cultural postmodernism, postmodern art, postmodern society, postmodern theology, postmodern architecture, and so on. Postmodernism can be understood from at least eleven different perspectives, all of which will be explored further throughout this book: an emerging historical period that transcends the modern industrial and technological age; a contemporary aesthetic style in art and architecture that is eclectic, kaleidoscopic, ironic, and allegorical; a social criticism of unified systems of economic and political organization such as liberalism and communism; a philosophical movement that seeks to expose the internal contradictions of metanarratives by deconstructing modern notions of truth, language, knowledge, and power; a cultural analysis that critiques the negative impact of modern technology on the human psyche and the environment while promoting the construction of a holistic and ecologically sustainable global community; a radical eclecticism (*not* compromise or consensus) and double-voiced discourse that accepts and criticizes at the same time because the past and the future are both honored and subverted, embraced and limited, constructed and deconstructed; a movement that attempts to go beyond the materialist philosophy of modernity; an acknowledgment and celebration of otherness, particularly from racial and gendered perspectives; a momentous historical period marked by a revolutionary paradigm change that transcends the basic assumptions, patterns of operation, and cosmology of the previous modern age; an ecological and ecumenical worldview beyond the modern obsession with dominance and control; or finally, a post-structural movement toward de-centering where there is an absence of anything at the center or any overriding embedded truth at the core, thus necessitating a concentration on the margins and a shift in emphasis to the borders.

Cynics often maintain that the term *postmodern* is irrelevant because its meaning is elusive and contradictory, and thus it can be defined in multiple ways to suit the needs of any author. The philosophy of modernity espoused by these critics is so committed to Cartesian binary and dualistic thinking, as well as rational and structural explanations of reality, that postmodern eclecticism, inclusiveness, and irony become incomprehensible for them. However, one thing is abundantly clear in the 1990s: there is a burgeoning belief in scientific, philosophical, political, artistic, literary, and educational circles that a radically new global conception of life on the planet and existence in the cosmos is underway. Charles Jencks (1992) — describes this worldview:

> In the last ten years post-modernism has become more than a social condition and cultural movement, it has become a world view. But its exact nature is strongly contested and this has helped widen the debate to a world audience. The argument has crystallised into two philosophies—what I and many others call Neo- and Post-Modernism—both of which share the notion that the modern world is coming to an end, and that something new must replace it. They differ over whether the previous world view should be taken to an extreme and made radical, or synthesised with other approaches at a higher level. . . . Not a few people are now suspicious of [this] attendant confusion, or bored with the fashion of the term. Yet I cannot think of an adequate substitute for summarising the possibilities of our condition. (p. 10)

Jencks continues by reminding us that the modern period—from about the 1450s to the 1950s and from the Renaissance when the West became ascendant to the point where it was incorporated within a larger global culture—is on the wane and must be replaced. Whether the postmodern shift is attached to the date

1875, 1914, 1945, or 1960 (each of these dates has its defenders), Jencks insists that a period "out of the Modern" needs to be defined. Jencks (1992) continues: "The forces of the modern movement—modernisation, the condition of modernity, and cultural Modernism—have not ended. Indeed, they are often the goals of the Second and Third Worlds. . . . But the uncontested dominance of the modern world view has definitely ended" (p. 11). Whether critics like it or not, society has become a global plurality of competing subcultures and movements where no one ideology and *episteme* (understanding of knowledge) dominates. There is no cultural consensus, and—cultural literacy programs notwithstanding—there is no curriculum development consensus either. Even if the fragmentation of culture and education into many subcultures has been exaggerated, the shift to a postmodern worldview is evident.

This postmodern shift involves rethinking some very sacred beliefs and structures that have been firmly entrenched in human consciousness for at least the past five hundred years. This is not unlike the trauma that was caused in the sixteenth century by the discoveries of Copernicus and Galileo. Many astronomers were silenced, imprisoned, or excommunicated because their theories challenged the premodern worldview of the religious and political leaders of the European society. Postmodern social, aesthetic, religious, and scientific visionaries have sometimes met the same fate. For this reason, postmodern thinkers will turn to Thomas Kuhn (1970) in his text *The Structure of Scientific Revolutions* to support the belief that the global community is entering into a radically new understanding of politics, art, science, theology, economics, psychology, culture, and education. Along with Kuhn, postmodern writers call this change a paradigm shift because humanity is moving to a new zone of cognition with an expanded concept of the self-in-relation.

There have been at least two previous paradigm shifts in human history: first, the move from isolated nomadic communities of hunters and gatherers to feudal societies with city-states and agrarian support systems, and second, the move from the tribal and feudal societies to a capitalist industrial-based economy relying on scientific technology, unlimited resource consumption, social progress, unrestrained economic growth, and rational thought. The first is called the premodern period or the neolithic revolution and is dated from about 1000 B.C.E. (before the common era) to 1450 C.E. (common era). The second is called the modern period or the Industrial Revolution and is dated from about 1450 C.E. to 1960 C.E. The neolithic period is characterized by a slow-changing and reversible concept of time rooted in mythology and an aristocratic culture with integrated artistic styles. The industrial period is characterized by a linear concept of time, called the arrow of time, with a bourgeois mass-culture of dominant styles. The postmodern paradigm shift is characterized by fast-changing and cyclical concepts of time with sundry cultures and many genres of expression and is sometimes called the global information revolution.

Of course, there have been many movements in the past five hundred years that have sought to challenge the dominance of the modern concept of culture, time, and economics. The Romantics and the Luddites of the early nineteenth century are perhaps typical. However, these movements sought to return to a previous premodern existence. The contemporary postmodern worldview is different because it is more than an antimodern movement; postmodernism seeks to transcend the ravages of modernity with a radically new concept of society, culture, language, and power. Likewise, postmodern educators are committed to a new concept of curriculum development that will complement the social and cultural milieu of this new era in human history.

While there are many concepts of postmodernism, and thus much confusion about its meaning, there are some common characteristics. David Ray Griffin et al. (1993) explain:

> The rapidity with which the term *postmodern* has become widespread in our time suggests that the antimodern sentiment is more extensive and intense than before, and also that it includes the sense that modernity can be successfully overcome only by going beyond it, not by attempting to return to a premodern form of existence. Insofar as a common element is found in the various ways in which the term is used, *postmodernism* refers to a diffuse

> sentiment rather than to any set of common doctrines—the
> sentiment that humanity can and must go beyond the
> modern. (pp. vii–viii)

Humanity must transcend modernity, according to the Center
for a Post-Modern World (1990), in ways that include the
following features: a post-anthropocentric view of living in
harmony with nature rather than a separateness from nature that
leads to control and exploitation; a post-competitive sense of
relationships as cooperative rather than as coercive and
individualistic; a post-militaristic belief that conflict can be
resolved by the development of the art of peaceful negotiation; a
post-patriarchal vision of society in which the age-old religious,
social, political, and economic subordination of women will be
replaced by a social order based on the "feminine" and the
"masculine" equally; a post-Eurocentric view that the values and
practices of the European tradition will no longer be assumed to
be superior to those of other traditions or forcibly imposed upon
others combined with a respect for the wisdom embedded in all
cultures; a post-scientistic belief that while the natural sciences
possess one important method of scientific investigation, there
are also moral, religious, and aesthetic intuitions that contain
important truths that must be given a central role in the
development of worldviews and public policy; a post-
disciplinary concept of research and scholarship with an
ecologically interdependent view of the cosmos rather than the
mechanistic perspective of a modern engineer controlling the
universe; and finally, a post-nationalistic view in which the
individualism of nationalism is transcended and replaced by a
planetary consciousness that is concerned about the welfare of
the earth first and foremost. In short, postmodernism regards the
world as an organism rather than as a machine, the earth as a
home rather than as a functional possession, and persons as
interdependent rather than as isolated and independent. This
introduction to some of the concepts of postmodernism reveals
not only the scope of the issues involved in this movement but
also the dramatic paradigmatic shift in thinking that must
accompany postmodern consciousness. Therefore, the intensity
of resistance to postmodernism should not be surprising.

This description of postmodernism has immense implications for education, particularly the way that curriculum is understood in the postmodern era. For this reason, I have selected postmodernism as the theoretical construct from which to explore contemporary curriculum development. Curriculum scholars have much to gain from engaging in the postmodern dialogue, and they also have much to lose by ignoring the postmodern movement. This first chapter begins with an exploration of postmodernism in order to frame the discussion of the various approaches to contemporary curriculum development in part two.

The postmodern worldview allows educators to envision a way out of the turmoil of contemporary schooling that too often is characterized by violence, bureaucratic gridlock, curricular stagnation, depersonalized evaluation, political conflict, economic crisis, decaying infrastructure, emotional fatigue, demoralization of personnel, and hopelessness. This is not to imply that every teacher and every school is paralyzed by these problems. There are many outstanding teachers, programs, and curricular innovations. There are even some postmodern practices emerging in schools in the 1990s, albeit with resistance from those entrenched in modernity. However, the evidence of crisis is abundantly documented on both the political left and right. The solutions proposed may be dramatically different, but the recognition of the crisis in schooling is virtually unanimous.

Postmodernism provides an option for understanding the current crises in education and society. While it is certainly not the only theoretical framework being explored by contemporary social scientists and educational researchers, it is one that is pervasive in the scholarly literature of the 1990s. Additionally, I am convinced that postmodernism offers the best theoretical paradigm for exploring curriculum development. This is especially true when time is viewed as a cyclical process where the past and future inform and enrich the present rather than a linear arrow where events can be isolated, analyzed, and objectified. From this perspective, we cannot simply rely on the improvement of past curricular methods in order to solve the complex schooling problems of the 1990s. We must have a more integrated view of time and history. In chapters two and three a historical analysis of curriculum development will be explored as a prelude to the postmodern reflections in part two. But we are ahead of our discussion of postmodernism. Let us return to our investigation of the relationship between postmodernism and curriculum.

Walker Percy's essay entitled "The Delta Factor" from his book *The Message in the Bottle* is an excellent place to continue our exploration of curriculum and postmodernism. Percy (1954) writes the following:

> What does a man [*sic*] do when he finds himself living after an age has ended and he can no longer understand himself because the theories of man of the former age no longer work and the theories of the new age are not yet known, for not even the name of the new age is known, and so everything is upside down, people feeling bad when they should feel good, good when they should feel bad? What a man does is start afresh as if he were newly come into a new world, which in fact it is; start with what he knows for sure, look at the birds and beasts, and like a visitor from Mars newly landed on earth notice what is different about man. (p. 7)

Postmodernism begins by recognizing, along with Percy, that the education profession, elementary and secondary schools, preservice teacher training programs, and institutions of higher education are all "upside down." The world of schooling is in transition, and people are "feeling bad" about the condition of education. If there is any hope of understanding the confusion and malaise that grip not only society but especially our schools, it will be found in the emerging discourses and practices in the curriculum field to be introduced in this book.

Walker Percy was not the only writer in the 1950s to challenge some of the underlying assumptions of modernity. The sense of a paradigm shift in the modern age has its roots prior to contemporary educational and literary criticism in the fields of architecture, art, and philosophy. An excellent introduction to the movement can be found in two important books by Charles Jencks (1986, 1992): *What Is Post-Modernism?* and *The Post-Modern Reader*. (Note that some authors omit a hyphen in postmodern to emphasize the end of modernity; others use the hyphen to emphasize a continuity from the modern to the post-modern or the doubly-coded irony of the post-modern movement. In literary criticism the hyphen is omitted to indicate a deconstructive intent. However, the hyphen may represent a variety of symbolic, ironic, and/or playful intentions.) Jencks reviews the historical development of postmodernism, and he dates the beginning of the concept with the Spanish writer Federico de Onis. Additionally, Arnold Toynbee (1947) in his *A Study of History* established postmodernism as an encompassing category describing a new historical cycle that, he contended, started in 1875 with the end of Western dominance, the decline of individualism, capitalism, and Christianity, and the growing influence of non-Western cultures. Jencks (1986) writes that Toynbee "referred to a pluralism and world culture" (p. 8) in a positive tone but still remained skeptical of the "global village" concept. This skepticism remained with postmodern thinking well into the 1960s. Jencks (1986) describes what happened next:

> Ihab Hassan became by the mid 1970s the self-proclaimed spokesman for the Postmodern (the term is conventionally elided in literary criticism) and he tied this label to the ideas of experimentalism in the arts and ultra-technology in architecture . . . in short, those trends which I, and others, would later characterize as Late Modern. In literature and then in philosophy, because of the writings of Jean-François Lyotard (1979) and a tendency to elide Deconstruction with the Post-Modern, the term has often kept its association with what Hassan calls "discontinuity, indeterminacy, immanence." Mark C. Taylor's *ERRING: A Postmodern A/Theology* is characteristic of this genre which springs from Derrida and Deconstruction. There is also a tendency among philosophers to discuss all Post-Positivist thinkers together as Post-Modern whether or not they have anything more in common than a rejection of Modern Logical Positivism. Thus, there are two quite different meanings to the term and a general confusion which is not confined to the public. (pp. 8–9)

While Jencks acknowledges the confusion experienced by the general public as well as university scholars, he continues to explore his question, "What is Post-Modernism?" It is a question, he believes, that can be answered only by recognizing that postmodernism is in continual growth and movement, and thus no firm definitions are possible—at least until it stops moving. This may be frustrating to educators who want to understand postmodern curriculum development. However, as I often remind graduate students and school district personnel, we have been conditioned to believe that our goals, objectives, lesson plans, and educational outcomes must all be "measurable" and "behaviorally observable" in order to be valid. In my career I have met very few teachers who actually believe this philosophy of education, but even the majority who do not ascribe to this educational ideology have allowed themselves to be conditioned to behave as though they do. Postmodernism challenges educators to explore a worldview that envisions schooling through a different lens of indeterminacy, aesthetics, autobiography, intuition, eclecticism, and mystery. In this sense, a concrete definition of postmodern education with universal goals, behavioral objectives, and predetermined outcomes is an oxymoron. As you continue to read about postmodern curriculum development it will be less frustrating if you keep this thought in mind.

In its infancy in the 1960s in art and culture, postmodernists were radical and critical: pop artists and architects who argued against elitism, urban destruction, bureaucracy, and simplified language. By the 1970s, as these traditions strengthened and evolved, the movement became more conservative and academic. Jencks (1986) describes one of the inevitable results: "Many protagonists of the 1960s, such as Andy Warhol, lost their critical function altogether as they were assimilated into the art market or commercial practice" (p. 9).

In the 1980s postmodernism continued to evolve and was finally accepted by professors, academics, and society at large. Thus, postmodernism ran the risk of becoming part of the modern establishment. Jencks (1986) concludes: "[Postmodernism] became as much part of the establishment as its parent, Modernism, and rival brother, Late-Modernism, and in literary criticism it shifted closer in meaning to the architectural and art traditions" (p. 9).

While the evolution of the term *postmodern* in art, architecture, literary criticism, and philosophy is a fascinating phenomenon, our concern here is primarily with contemporary implications of postmodernism for curriculum development. In the 1990s, postmodernism is an integral dimension of many political, social, and educational analyses that have a direct impact on schooling. If we are truly at the end of the modern era, the systems of meaning that have supported curriculum development as a field of study for the past 150 years must all come under rigorous scrutiny. A similar reevaluation is occurring in politics that can be instructive for educators.

Vaclav Havel (1992), president of the Czech Republic, explains: "The end of Communism is, first and foremost, a message to the human race [that] a major era in human history [has come] to an end. It has brought an end not just to the 19th and 20th centuries, but to the modern age as a whole" (p. E15). Havel explains further that the modern era has been dominated by the belief that the world is a wholly knowable system governed by a finite number of universal laws that humans can comprehend by rigorous analysis and rationally direct for the personal benefit of men and women. The modern era from the Renaissance to the Enlightenment to socialism, from positivism to scientism, from the Industrial Revolution to the information revolution, has been characterized by rational, structural thinking. Communism, for Havel, was the perverse extreme of this trend because it attempted to organize all of life according to a single model and to subject people to central planning and control regardless of whether it was life affirming. (The parallel to modern curriculum development is unmistakable!) Havel (1992) concludes:

> The fall of Communism can be regarded as a sign that modern thought—based on the premise that the world is objectively knowable, and that knowledge so obtained can be absolutely generated—has come to a final crisis. . . . It is a signal that the era of arrogant, absolutist reason is drawing to a close . . . and that we have to see the pluralism of the world, and not bind it by seeking common denominators or reducing everything to a single common equation. . . . Sooner or later, politics will be faced with the task of finding a new, postmodern face. (p. E15)

The postmodern political clarion call of Vaclav Havel, the banished playwright turned president, beckons educators in the field of curriculum theory to also envision a new worldview. Thus, understanding curriculum in light of the fall of Communism and other contemporary social and political events is not irrelevant, it is essential. Political studies have become central to curriculum studies in the postmodern era. Postmodern curriculum development recognizes the necessity of incorporating a new consciousness that transcends the modern categories of metaphysics, epistemology, and axiology. A reconceptualization of this classical philosophical trinity must emerge that understands existence, knowledge, and ethics in the context of postmodern political, cultural, and social upheaval. Perhaps, the end of Communism in the political realm may foretell an end to curriculum development as we have known it for so many decades. The end of the modern era is not simply a vague theoretical construct, it is a challenge to all fields of study—indeed the entire global community—to reconceptualize their understanding of the deepest meaning of life in contemporary society. This is the challenge of the postmodern era for educators and curriculum specialists in the 1990s.

While there are many outstanding texts available that explore the postmodern challenge to reconceptualize curriculum development, the beginning student of postmodernism should be careful to identify an author's ideological perspective as described at the beginning of this chapter (i.e., historical, aesthetic, political, philosophical, theological, cultural, or a combination of two or more of these emphases). Understanding an author's ideological orientation can prevent a single concept of the postmodern curriculum from becoming a new positivistic rationale, behavioral goal, or ultramodern master narrative. Postmodernism promotes eclecticism rather than comprehensive systems of explanation and universal laws. There are many recent books that deserve attention from those interested in curriculum development in the postmodern era. I will introduce the central tenets of some of these books as examples of the various postmodern perspectives presented at the beginning of this chapter. However, it is important to remember that these texts are representative and not normative. As we have seen throughout this chapter, postmodern texts defy rigid categorization.

Joe Kincheloe (1993) in *Toward a Critical Politics of Teacher Thinking: Mapping the Postmodern* begins with a historical reflection on the development of postmodernism as a basis for proposing that teacher education and teacher thinking are not politically neutral activities. Kincheloe (1993) writes: "Critical postmodern teachers are not politically neutral, as they identify with a critical system of meaning and all of its allegiances. . . . On a daily basis teachers choose to include some forms of knowledge while excluding others from the curriculum, they legitimate particular beliefs while delegitimating others" (p. 39). Following his historical, political, and theoretical analysis, Kincheloe presents a description of a postmodern vision for teacher training and classroom practice called post-formal thinking. One of the most important features of post-formal thinking involves the production of one's own knowledge. The post-formal teacher helps students to reinterpret their own lives and uncover new talents as a result of their encounter with schooling. Post-formal thinking and teaching also promote metanalysis, that is, thinking about thinking and exploring the inner world of psychological experience. Kincheloe (1993) explains: "Post-formal thinking about thinking draws upon the boundary trespasses of Hermes and the playful parody of postmodernism to transgress the official constraints of our consciousness construction, to transcend modern convention by exposing its ironic contradictions" (p. 147).

Kincheloe's proposal for postmodern curriculum development as post-formal thinking includes the following concepts: seeing relationships between ostensibly different things, which he calls metaphoric cognition; connecting logic and emotion by stretching the boundaries of imagination; seeing facts as parts of a larger process of connecting the holographic mind to holographic reality; perceiving different frames of reference in order to develop the cognitive power of empathy; attending to the particular place and context of the educative event; understanding the interaction of the particular and the general; transcending simplistic notions of cause–effect to create nonlinear holism; seeing the world as a text to be interpreted rather than explained; and finally, uncovering various levels of connection between the mind and the ecosystem to reveal larger patterns of life-forces (as in Carl Jung's concept of synchronicity) for meaningful connection between causally unconnected events. Kincheloe's concept of curriculum development moves from a concern with mapping the postmodern terrain historically and politically to the construction of a philosophical and aesthetic theory of post-formal thinking. In this sense, Kincheloe is perhaps typical of the eclectic postmodernism that explores alternatives to modern curriculum models of formal analysis and cognition.

Kincheloe mediates the postmodern debate by establishing a middle ground between those who either completely accept or completely reject Western modernism. Kincheloe and Shirley Steinberg (1993) explain: "In our work, we have sought a middle ground that attempts to hold onto the progressive and democratic features of modernism while drawing upon the insights postmodernism provides concerning the failure of reason, the tyranny of grand narratives, the limitations of science, and the repositioning between dominant and subordinate cultural groups" (p. 296). In short, the challenge of postmodernism is to move to post-formal thinking as a new zone of cognition.

Another recent book that presents a postmodern paradigm shift in the understanding of curriculum development is William E. Doll, Jr.'s *A Post-Modern Perspective on Curriculum*. Doll (1993) investigates an open systems cosmology and proposes an educational matrix intended to rival the closed system of seventeenth-century notions of a stable universe. Doll contends that the stable universe became the philosophical foundation of modernity as well as the scientific principle on which the American curriculum, epitomized in Tyler's rationale and Taylor's scientific management, was developed. His postmodern educational vision flows from his analysis and "reinterpretation" (p. 13) of Piaget and living systems, Prigogine and chaotic order, Bruner and the cognitive revolution, and Dewey and Whitehead and process thought. He juxtaposes John Dewey and Alfred North Whitehead from the perspective of post-structuralism and hermeneutics in order to negotiate passages "between Whiteheadian process thought and deconstructive post-structural thought" (p. xiii). Doll's educational matrix describes a process of curriculum experience rooted in "richness, recursion, relations, and rigor" (p. 174) whose order is dependent upon disequilibrium, indeterminacy, lived experience, and chaos rather than a rigid structuralism. This is the major distinction between Doll's postmodern curriculum and other poststructural, feminist, political, and deconstructionist postmodernisms that we will investigate in more detail in chapters six, seven, and nine.

Central to Doll's postmodern perspective on curriculum is his belief that just as physics led society into the modern age, physics—particularly as evidenced in chaos theory—will lead society out of modernity and into postmodernism. However, the humanities will also join science in the postmodern process. A literal centerpiece of Doll's book is a color plate illustrating the Lorenz attractor, originally used to show unpredictability in long-term weather patterns. This geometric construct of a chaotic process brings into sharp focus the author's view that "self-organization becomes the pivotal focus around which open systems work" (p. 98). In postmodern education the curriculum itself may derive whatever form and substance it will ultimately possess from the referred-to "crossing over" points on attractors. Curriculum must not be forced to these central positions lest we lose the necessary meanderings inherent in the process. The modernist might contend that the postmodern is taking a circuitous route when the shortest distance between two points is the straight line. In postmodernism, this seemingly divergent path is simply one of many acceptable routes where even minuscule changes that are brought about in an open-ended process "will grow into major transformations over time" (Doll, p. 98). In the research of contemporary curriculum theorists working within such a context one comes to feel that the free-form processive dance of postmodernism is indeed preferable to the lock-step progressive control of modernity.

While Doll attempts to forge a path between the constructive and deconstructive postmodern theories, others are adamant in their commitment to one or the other of these two perspectives. Patti Lather (1991) in her book *Getting Smart: Feminist Research and Pedagogy With/In the Postmodern* is perhaps typical of curriculum theorists who support deconstruction, a postmodern philosophy that explores the contradictions within modern paradigms and symbols (especially language) for the purpose of exposing the injustices that emerge from the modern relationship between power and language. Lather contends that society is in the midst of a shift away from the concept of an objective, knowable, factual world "out there" toward a concept of constructed worlds where knowledge is contested and partial. Lather agrees with Michel Foucault (1972, 1980), who wrote that knowledge is an "effect of power" (cited in Lather, 1991, p. 86) and shaped by the interplay of language, power, and meaning. Lather uses feminist research in the postmodern tradition to promote self-understanding and self-determination so that an emancipatory concept of language and power will emerge in education. Lather's book exposes the difficulty of building a liberatory curriculum within existing institutions for those who are involved in unequal power relations, especially women.

An example of Lather's deconstructive approach to postmodernism is found in her critique of modernity. Lather (1991) writes:

> To position oneself in the twilight of modernity is to foreground the underside of its faith in rationality, science, and the human will to change and master: Auschwitz, Hiroshima, My Lai, Three Mile Island, Chernobyl. It is not that the dreams of modernity are unworthy; it is what they render absent and their conflictual and confusing outcomes that underscore the limits of reason and the obsolescence of modernist categories and institutions. Not only positivisms, but also existentialisms, phenomenologies, critical theories: all seem exhausted, rife with subject-object dualisms . . . the lust for certainty. . . . All seem no longer capable of giving meaning and direction to current conditions. . . . The exhaustion of the paradigms of modernity creates an affective space where we feel that we cannot continue as we are. The modernist project of control through knowledge has imploded, collapsed inward, as the boundaries between ideology and science disintegrate. (p. 88)

The deconstruction of modernity and its system of power, language, and meaning becomes the starting point for Lather in her attempt to build an empowering approach to the generation of knowledge for both researchers and classroom teachers. Lather envisions a democratized process of inquiry characterized by negotiation, collaboration, and reciprocity where knowledge is constructed from self-understanding. In this sense, postmodern curriculum development begins with the deconstruction of master narratives that impose knowledge through unequal power relations where students must be subordinate and submissive to teachers, and then moves to the emancipation of both teachers and students who have been disempowered by this structure. Thus, Lather's understanding of postmodernism emphasizes the political and philosophical perspective.

In contrast to Lather's political and deconstructive emphasis, David Ray Griffin (1993) promotes a constructive postmodernism in *Founders of Constructive Postmodern Philosophy*. For Griffin and his coauthors, the postmodernism of political and feminist writers who have been inspired by Martin Heidegger, Jacques Derrida, and Michel Foucault is really an anti-worldview because it deconstructs and eliminates the elements necessary for a worldview, such as God, self, purpose, meaning, and truth as correspondence. Griffin admits that the ethical concerns of deconstructionists to forestall totalitarian systems and unequal power relations are laudable. However, he sees the potential result of deconstruction as relativism and nihilism. Griffin even charges that deconstructionism can be called ultramodernism because its eliminations result from carrying modern premises to their logical conclusion. (Of course, Lather and other feminist researchers with political and deconstructionist emphasis would argue that Griffin is an ultramodernist because he attempts to reconstruct a worldview that includes modernist categories such as truth and God.)

Griffin seeks to overcome the modern worldview not by eliminating the possibility of worldviews, but by constructing a postmodern worldview through a revision of modern premises and traditional concepts. Griffin (1993) writes, "This constructive or revisionary postmodernism involves a new unity of scientific, ethical, aesthetic, and religious intuitions. It rejects not science as such but only that scientism in which the data of the modern natural sciences are also allowed to contribute to the construction of our worldview" (p. viii). In this respect, postmodernism is seen as a constructive social paradigm. It seeks to integrate the best features of premodern rural, agrarian societies (e.g., spirituality, cosmology, family/tribal community values) and the best features of the modern urban, technological societies (e.g., advances in health care, global communication, transportation) in order to construct a more balanced and ecologically sustainable global community. Constructive postmodernism recognizes that the world community cannot return to a premodern existence and that the negative features of the modern world (e.g., destruction of the ecosphere, spiritual bankruptcy, greed, and the depletion of resources) threaten to destroy civilization.

There are many debates about the meaning of postmodernism in educational research that expand on the distinctions made by Lather and Griffin above. Further insights can be found by contrasting *Postmodernism, Feminism, and Cultural Politics: Redrawing Educational Boundaries* edited by Henry Giroux (1991) and *Border Crossings: Cultural Workers and the Politics of Education* by Giroux (1992) with *Elements of a Post-Liberal Theory of Education* written by Chet Bowers (1987) and *Education, Cultural Myths, and the Ecological Crisis* by Bowers (1993). Both these professors have written texts that propose variations on the postmodern curriculum dialogue, thus reinforcing the contention that there is no unified conception of the postmodern. Giroux employs the post-structural term *border crossings* to emphasize the importance of political solidarity between critical theory, feminist thought, multiculturalism, and antiracist theory. Giroux exposes the porous nature of the modern boundaries that have attempted to compartmentalize knowledge and colonize cultures. In curriculum theory, crossing the border necessitates a commitment to postmodern democratic reform where subject-area disciplinary boundaries are traversed. Border crossings allow educators to reject modern academic privilege in favor of honest intellectual exchanges committed to justice and liberation. Giroux's inclusive political theory affirms the democratic, eclectic, and empowerment dimensions of postmodern thought.

Like Giroux, Chet Bowers promotes interconnectedness across boundaries. Bowers (1993) writes: "Classroom activities [must] foster a sense of connectedness across generations and between human and other members of the biotic community. Both are required as part of a change in consciousness if we are to achieve genuine sustainability" (p. 7). Bowers frames the postmodern educational discussions around ecological concerns rather than political solutions. He questions whether the political process will be effective in getting people to move beyond the modernist paradigm. Cultural, spiritual, and ecological themes permeate Bower's postmodernism.

One recent book that graduate students have found to be most instructive in the postmodern debates is Donald Oliver and Kathleen Gershman's *Education, Modernity, and Fractured Meaning: Toward a Process Theory of Teaching and Learning*. Oliver and Gershman (1989) present a process vision of postmodern curriculum as ontological knowing: "We distinguish between two kinds of knowing: *technical* knowing and *ontological* knowing. Technical knowing refers to adaptive, publicly transferable information and skills; ontological knowing refers to a more diffuse apprehension of reality, in the nature of liturgical or artistic engagement" (p. 3). Oliver and Gershman emphasize the common belief of many researchers that in order for ontological knowing to become part of the curriculum, postmodern metaphors must evolve to challenge and transform the machine metaphor of modernity. Ontological knowing requires metaphors of "organic life and transcendent dance" (p. 3) so that we can come to know with our whole bodies as we move from imagination and intention to critical self-definition, satisfaction, and finally to perishing and new being. Oliver and Gershman's book contains elements of Lather's self-understanding, Griffin's process philosophy, Giroux's border crossings, and Bowers' ecological sustainability. However, their approach to curriculum development moves beyond the distinction between constructive and deconstructive postmodernism to an ontological and cosmological process curriculum that may offer a possible reconciliation of various antagonistic factions in postmodern curriculum studies.

While there are many other perspectives and several important books that could be investigated in this introduction to the concept of postmodern curriculum development, it is not necessary to be comprehensive at this time. Postmodernism will frame the discussion of curriculum development throughout this book, and each of the perspectives introduced here will be included in further discussions in part two. Hopefully, this introduction to the complex philosophical discussions on postmodernism will provide a framework within which to evaluate a new vision of curriculum development for the post-modern era. Postmodernism is an emerging concept that elicits much debate in political, social, literary, artistic, and, in recent years, educational circles. Although the evolution of the meaning of postmodernism may be an obstacle for some readers, I believe that the possibility of a renewed understanding of curriculum development that will have a positive impact on teachers and students in schools will make the effort to explore these emerging concepts worthwhile.

CHAPTER TWO

Historical Perspectives on Curriculum as a Field of Study

Chapter one introduced the concept of historical interpretation from two different perspectives: a progressive series of distinctly separate and chronological events on a linear timeline, or a processive experience of interrelated occasions with the past and future embedded in the existential present reality. The first perspective is committed to the objective analysis and categorization of discrete parcels of information. These events become quantifiable objects of study. In this case history attempts to logically explain events according to a grand narrative of human progress through the centuries. On the other hand, the second perspective is committed to ongoing reinterpretation, the primacy of subjective experience, the indissolubility of meaning and context, the social construction of knowledge, and the interdependence of events within time and place. In short, history is understood either as events separated by time and space or as the integral interrelationship of events unified with time and space. Logical positivism and analytic philosophy are generally committed to the first perspective. Either these philosophies tend to ignore historical analysis because of the subjectivity inherent in the interconnectedness of contextual realities, or they objectify and segment history in order to control reality so that all events will conform within the paradigm of modernity. Postmodern curriculum scholars will challenge the assumption that historical interpretation must be directed toward the validation of the knowledge and values of the dominant modern paradigm. Postmodernism celebrates the eclectic, innovative, revisionist, ironic, and subjective dimensions of historical interpretation.

Curriculum development in the postmodern era will challenge the traditional approach of modern logical positivism to the study of history as a linear timeline of events. Postmodern curriculum will encourage autobiographical reflection, narrative inquiry, revisionist interpretation, and contextual understanding. Knowledge will be understood as reflecting human interests, values, and actions that are socially constructed. Herbert Kliebard (1992b) explains:

> We often make half conscious decisions as to what knowledge is most appropriate to include in the curriculum then afterwards devise the plausible-sounding reasons for so deciding. Those half-conscious decisions are tied in many instances to such matters as social class allegiances and to self-interest generally. As such, curriculum history is not so much involved with traditional epistemological questions as with questions closely associated with sociology of knowledge. History of curriculum is, in other words, critically concerned with what is *taken* to be knowledge in certain times and places rather than what is ultimately true or valid. . . . A fundamental question imbedded in the history of curriculum, then, is not simply one of who went to school and who did not, but the way in which the social machinery may be constructed to differentiate access to certain forms of knowledge. [This is] significant not just in a pedagogical sense but in terms of status attainment and social relations, if not social justice. (p. 158)

In effect, the curriculum will seek to understand history contextually rather than delineate a coherent metanarrative of selective events and artifacts. Just as the curriculum is affected by social conditions and values, so too can the curriculum help to reshape or preserve those conditions and values. The relationship between society and the curriculum is reciprocal. This chapter will introduce the historical dimension of curriculum development from this perspective, which contains many elements of postmodern theory.

Integral to postmodernism is the critique of reason, totality, universal principles, and metanarratives. As Charles Jencks posited in chapter one, this critique is clearly articulated in the work of Jean François Lyotard. In the text *The Postmodern*

Condition, Lyotard (1984) challenges Enlightenment notions of totality and argues that postmodernism is inseparable from an incredulity toward metanarratives. What are these metanarratives? For Lyotard, they are unified historical narratives and overarching philosophies of history. Examples would be the Enlightenment concept of the gradual but steady progress of reason and freedom, Georg Wilhelm Friedrich Hegel's dialectic of spirit coming to know itself, and Karl Marx's drama of the forward march of human productivity and class conflict resulting in proletarian revolution. The postmodern era will reject these and other modern metanarratives because their moral and epistemological theories propose that knowledge, truth, and justice exist independent of contingent, historical practices. In short, Lyotard critiques metanarratives because they privilege one historical analysis without acknowledging their own contextuality and without acknowledging the validity of other discourses. Therefore, metanarratives do not problemitize their own legitimacy, and thus attempt to logically order history according to the preconceived modern notions of totality as reflected in patriarchical, technological, colonial, anthropocentric, rationalistic, militaristic, and Eurocentric paradigms. These modern paradigms deny the historical and social construction of their own first principles. As a result, Lyotard concludes, modern metanarratives ignore particularity, contingency, irony, and difference. Henry Giroux (1993) summarizes Lyotard's postmodern perspective succinctly:

> Lyotard argues that appeals to reason and consensus, when inserted within grand narratives that unify history, emancipation and knowledge, deny their own implications in the production of knowledge and power. More emphatically, Lyotard claims that within such narratives are elements of mastery and control in which "we can hear the muttering of the desire for a return of terror, for the realization of the fantasy to seize reality." Against metanarratives, which totalize historical experience by reducing its diversity to a one-dimensional, all-encompassing logic, Lyotard posits a discourse of multiple horizons, the play of language games, and the terrain of micropolitics. (p. 52)

Postmodern curriculum discourses understand history as contextual, multidimensional, ironic, proleptic, contingent, evolving, and autobiographical. Because modern notions of logic are actually ahistorical, the postmodern curriculum effectively resuscitates an authentic historicity. Educators in the post-modern era will no longer be able to simply "teach" history as facts to be memorized. Because the autobiographical, local, and particular are essential in order to understand history, teachers will now have to listen to students and their life stories. As feminist scholars insist, history is not simply "his story," that is, the master narratives of Anglo-Saxon European Protestant heterosexual male warriors. Rather, "her story" is also integral to history. Especially, history is understood as a recursive contextual experience or, from Lyotard's perspective, "differ-ence, contingency, and particularity." History is thus the mystery of autobiography, "my story."

While this introduction to curriculum history may initially seem difficult and controversial for those beginning the journey toward understanding postmodern curriculum discourses, the challenge for curriculum scholars in the 1990s is to examine critically their own story in the context of the history of curriculum development. If the postmodern curriculum chal-lenges students to enter history rather than simply observe history from a distance, then teachers must begin historical studies by entering this process themselves. This participatory view of history is what Jonathan Kozol has proposed for social studies classrooms. Kozol argues against schooling that is not transformative and against schooling that does not participate in history. Kozol (1975) writes:

> School teaches history in the same way that it teaches syntax, grammar, and word-preference: in terms that guarantee our prior exile from its passion and its transformation. It lifts up children from the present, denies them powerful access to the future, and robs them of all ethical repossession of the past. History is, as the sarcastic student says, an X-rated film. The trouble is that everyone we know, love, touch, hold, dream to be, or ever might become, has first to be told: I cannot enter. (p. 83)

History, therefore, from the postmodern perspective must not be seen as a series of events to be memorized but rather as an opportunity to inform the present and provide access to the future. Kozol challenges curricularists to adopt a transformative pedagogy in order to recover a participative mode in history education.

Another contrast between the modern and postmodern view of the function of the social studies curriculum in schools is portrayed in a popular classroom poster entitled *Occupations to Which Interest in History May Lead*. The poster lists the occupations of archaeologist, curator, writer, critic, archivist, anthropologist, librarian, or teacher. It is interesting that nowhere on this type of list will there be words to suggest the possible goal of being one who enters history. In contrast, the postmodern curriculum challenges both teachers and students to enter into the historical process as participants rather than as observers.

Schools in the 1990s are inundated with textbooks and curriculum materials that promote "critical thinking." Examining critical thinking materials carefully reveals that some programs establish boundaries around thinking in which the parameters of knowledge are limited by specific interpretations of human history. However, some educators encourage freedom of interpretation from an existential perspective. The conflict centers on the question of whether language and social studies teachers, for example, should encourage or even allow subjective interpretation of literature and history, or whether critical thinking should be directed toward a range of legitimate interpretations established by scholarly authorities. Postmodern curriculum historians insist that authoritative metanarratives cannot present politically, theologically, racially, gendered, and culturally neutral perspectives. History, like knowledge, is socially and culturally constructed. Curriculum in the postmodern era includes a more eclectic and subjective understanding of hermeneutic interpretation and critical thinking. This will be denounced as heresy by those committed to the modernist paradigm. For example, *Civitas* (Bahmueller, 1991), a new national framework for civics education, cautions:

> Citizenship training, if it means anything at all, means
> teaching students to think critically, listen with
> discernment, and communicate with power and precision.
> If students learn to listen, read, speak, and write more
> carefully, they will not only be civically empowered, but
> also they will know how to distinguish between the
> authentic and the fraudulent in human discourse. . . . Civic
> education for a new century also must provide students
> with a core of basic knowledge about social issues and
> institutions, to allow them to put their understanding of
> democracy into perspective. (p. xvi)

Civitas, like conservative calls for cultural literacy, core
knowledge, and facts-based curriculum, is concerned with
teaching basic information so that students will have the ability
to make informed decisions that advance status quo political
arrangements and will be socialized into the American political
structure. However, the assumption is that students left to their
own interpretation or subjective analysis without assistance and
authoritative guidance and reason will be unable to participate
effectively or appropriately. The modern approach to science
and history contends that knowledge builds on itself through
progressive stages. Thus, students must know an objective past
before attempting to apply critical thinking in the present. This
perspective involves applying the truth of past scientific
discoveries and historical analysis in order to build new
knowledge.

Curriculum development in the postmodern era will
challenge this concept of time and linear scientific progress.
Albert Einstein provides a case in point. Joe Kincheloe, Shirley
Steinberg, and Debbie Tippins (1992) have written a biography
that investigates Einstein's difficulty as a young man with formal
schooling. Einstein's vision of the physical universe in his theory
of relativity initiated a search for a unified foundation of physics
beyond the modern worldview of Newtonian physics. Einstein's
theories called into question traditional understandings of time
and space, and by extrapolation the concept of context-free
knowledge accumulation outside time and space, that dominated scholarship in the nineteenth century. The postmodern
rejection of chronophonism, a modern notion that time is
chronological and linear, was thus initiated. Was it important for

Einstein to challenge classical physics, which dominated formal schooling of his time? The authors of *The Stigma of Genius: Einstein and Beyond Modern Education* answer in the affirmative, and they contend that the conception of curriculum and chronology that pervade modern schooling actually inhibits the creative genius of the Einsteins in our schools today.

Richard Rorty (1979) has effectively demolished the analytic and formal thinking exemplified in the linear approach to history by logical positivism and by the systematic philosophy of Locke, Descartes, Kant, Russell, and Husserl in his book *Philosophy and the Mirror of Nature*. Logical positivists have ignored historical interpretation and relegated the study of history to linear events that may be used to explain and support the modern progress of philosophic thought. Rorty argues that the investigation of correspondences between language or thought and the natural world must be abandoned, as well as theories of representation in philosophy. Rorty's philosophy is utilized by many curriculum scholars in the postmodern era to support the belief that the analytic thinking of modernity must be replaced by critical historicity in education.

Students often complain about the boredom they experience in social studies classes, especially history. If there is one discipline in the school curriculum that exemplifies Rorty's exposure of the failure of the modern behavioristic and analytic approach to education, it is certainly history classes. History is often limited to a series of events on the linear timeline to be memorized and evaluated in the context of artificially contrived epochs of sociopolitical or cultural development. The linear model divides time into the past, present, and future, and as a result removes any autobiographical connection to the historical events being discussed in textbooks or classroom lectures. In short, history has been decontextualized by the modern curriculum, and as a result, ironically, an ahistorical and anti-historical attitude has emerged in the modern school. In desperation, teachers address this problem by echoing George Santayana's warning that those who do not remember the past are doomed to repeat it. Frustrated students ignore these pleas from their equally frustrated teachers. And then, to compound the problem, national reports condemn educators because students cannot place the American Civil War in the nineteenth century or identify the president responsible for the New Deal. Typical is Chester Finn's complaint in *We Must Take Charge: Our Schools and Our Future* that students are unable to demonstrate competency in subject matter areas. Finn (1991) writes: "Today we want evidence of learning, not just of teaching. We look at outcomes. Unsatisfactory results were what led the Excellence Commission to exclaim that we were threatened by a 'rising tide of mediocrity'" (p. 3). The conservative response in the 1980s was a series of reform proposals that increased standards, objectified evaluation, and measured predetermined outcomes in education. The purpose of these standards was to ensure that American students could demonstrate recall of information that was determined by the reformers to be essential for cultural literacy, the socialization of American students, and the reproduction of the dominant values of American society.

Teachers often agree that their students do not know the factual information required for progressing through the school system and passing standardized tests, but they throw up their hands in desperation, blaming disinterested parents, boring textbooks, overcrowded classrooms, drugs, self-esteem programs, television, ineffective elementary classes, or any other convenient target. However, social studies teachers continue to use the same methods of teaching and evaluation that have dominated curriculum development for over one hundred years. Is the problem that educators have not perfected the modern methods? Or is the problem that the modern methods are no longer appropriate in a postmodern era? The latter possibility is the focus of contemporary curriculum discourses.

Obviously, the history of American education, specifically curriculum development in schooling, cannot be reviewed comprehensively in this short introductory chapter. Indeed, the preceding discussion would obviate the very effort to present a definitive chronology of curriculum development in a linear sequence. However, many excellent books have recently been published that review the history of American curriculum with sensitivity to this postmodern perspective. The following books would provide such insights into postmodern curriculum history: Herbert Kliebard's (1986) *The Struggle for the American*

Curriculum: 1893–1958; Kliebard's (1992a) *Forging the American Curriculum: Essays in Curriculum History and Theory*; Joel Spring's (1990) *The American School: 1642–1990*; George Willis et al.'s (1993) *The American Curriculum: A Documentary History*; Barry Franklin's (1986) *Building the American Community: The School Curriculum and the Search for Social Control*; and William Pinar's (1988a) *Contemporary Curriculum Discourses*. These six books provide an insightful introduction to the study of curriculum history and theory for those interested in detailed analyses.

Herbert Kliebard (1992a) reports: "When I was a graduate student there was no such thing as curriculum history as an identified area of scholarship. Of course, elements of what we now think of as curriculum history were commonly incorporated into the general history of education, but no one was identified as a curriculum historian" (p. xi). Although the field of curriculum history is relatively young, there are already many research methodologies evolving in the field: narrative inquiry, hermeneutics, autobiography, ethnography, revisionist analysis, and primary source exploration. William Schubert (1986) writes that the predominant research methodologies include the following: "surveys of thought, surveys of practice, analyses of movements, case studies, revisionists critiques, and biographies" (p. 88). Schubert provides an example of the postmodern critique of traditional historical methodologies:

> In the early 1970s, a number of books offered a challenge to standard histories of education, the early paragon of which is Cubberley's *Public Education in the United States* (1934) and *The History of Education* (1920). These new histories came to be known as *revisionists*, and they argue that it is a myth that schools will integrate the poor, oppressed, and racially and ethnically diverse. They point out that far from building the traditional "American Dream" of democratic participation, schools effectuate social control in the service of a corporate state. Against this powerful force, they argue that educational change has been illusory. (1986, p. 91)

Schubert introduces not only the variety of methodologies utilized to study the history of curriculum but also one of the postmodern concerns with the traditional approaches to historical analysis. Revisionist historical methodologies will critique and deconstruct master narratives that have not only been repeated for generations but that also form the basis of the curriculum that perpetuates the modern ideology and reproduces its inequities.

An example from the social studies curriculum that exemplifies this problem is reported by historian Carl Brasseaux. Brasseaux (cited in Konikoff, 1993) explains:

> Malcolm Muggeridge, in a short essay entitled *The Eyewitness Fallacy*, shows that even so-called authoritative eyewitness documents are subject to all sorts of errors, primarily errors of perception. To give you just one example, one of the best known diaries to come out of the Civil War Era was the one written by Mary Chesnut. Her husband was a member of Jefferson Davis' staff. It has been proven fairly recently that she rewrote the diary several decades after the Civil War . . . and this, research has shown in the last few decades, was a fairly commonplace event among people who were very influential, people who were shaping the course of history. It's fairly commonplace for writers of diaries to go back and rewrite them purposely to cast themselves in a good light, and the people they disliked in an even worse light. (p. 15)

Brasseaux demonstrates the problems associated with the modern reliance on metanarratives in historical analysis. The list of absolute uncontestable facts is actually very limited, and eventually all accounts and artifacts are influenced by subjective memory. Therefore, postmodern historical analysis will not only deconstruct traditional historical methodologies, but they will also validate and encourage autobiographical and revisionist approaches. This must also be the focus of our study of curriculum history itself.

Additionally, developments in literary criticism, philosophy, anthropology, and curriculum theory have led historians to rethink how they read and examine sources. Historians Page Putnam Miller and David Thelen (1993) contend that some scholars "no longer confidently read 'texts' from the past as guides to what actually happened" (p. B3). They argue that most historians no longer contend that the views of the past constructed today, or even documents created contemporaneously with past events, are final statements. Miller and Thelen continue: "We see them as products that reflect the political and personal dynamics and needs of those who created them. The analysis of the context of sources has become as significant as their content" (p. B3). In curriculum studies, likewise, understanding the context of curriculum development models now rivals the content of guides, plans, and models for the focus of study. Postmodernism takes this a step further and incorporates the concept of *différance* as a structuring principle that suggests definition rests not on the source itself but in its positive and negative references to other texts. Meaning changes over time and "ultimately the attribution of meaning is postponed and deferred forever" (Derrida, 1981, pp. 40).

As we discuss historical analysis, it is important to remember that the boundaries between fields and disciplines are fading in postmodern scholarship. While new historical research methodologies will be important elements of the postmodern curriculum, especially in social studies, they are not limited to the field of curriculum history. Curriculum and instruction, like so many other fields, have become interdisciplinary, inclusive, eclectic, and kaleidoscopic. As an example of the postmodern application of these methodologies, I will relate a personal story to frame a further discussion of historical curriculum development perspectives.

As a child I often visited my grandmother's home in Shreveport, Louisiana. There was an unusual tradition in the family that had been passed down to each new generation. The children would gather around to listen to stories about the Civil War while my grandmother would rub the side of her head and say "The damn Yankees shot Aunt Dora!" The story was told with passion, and even though I did not understand all the implications of the Civil War, I still grew up hating the elusive but evil "damn Yankees" who shot my aunt.

Dora Navra was the eight-year-old daughter of my great-great-great-great grandparents, Abraham Navra and Ellen Kinney, who settled in Vicksburg, Mississippi, in the 1840s. During the siege of Vicksburg in the summer of 1863 Dora was hit in the head by shrapnel from a cannon fired by Union soldiers as she rushed into town from a cave on the outskirts of the city. Dora had been sent to look for the local doctor to assist in the care of her infant brother who was ill. Dora survived; Samuel died. And ever since that fateful day members of my family have been remembering the hardship caused by the federal soldiers who surrounded Vicksburg in 1863 and inflicted such misery on the citizens.

I do not remember studying the Civil War in any detail in elementary school, high school, or college, even though my transcripts indicate that I have credit for several courses in American history. Not once do I remember studying anything about the siege of Vicksburg, and unfortunately no teacher ever encouraged me to share my family tradition. In fact, I am not sure that I ever made any connection between my unusual family tradition and the study of American history. Even as a college graduate I could not have placed the date of the siege of Vicksburg on a timeline, named the generals, or analyzed the reasons for the strategic importance of this event in American history, despite the fact that I took honors history courses in high school and graduated summa cum laude from a traditional liberal arts college. What went wrong? Even though I success-fully completed a traditional core curriculum and apparently memorized all the assigned facts about the Civil War, I did not retain this information beyond my exams. Additionally, it was years later when I took up the hobby of genealogical studies that I finally made the connection between my family history and American history. Why did my social studies education and family traditions never intersect during my twenty-four years of formal schooling?

I am convinced that my ignorance of Civil War history specifically, and American history generally, despite the fact that I memorized the information presented in my classes and passed my American history tests in school, is the result of having never been encouraged or directed to make connections between the past and the present, between my relatives who were shot by Union soldiers and my life as a student studying the Civil War.

Traditionally, curriculum development has been concerned with Ralph Tyler's four basic questions in his syllabus for Education 360 at the University of Chicago and published in

1949. These four questions have so dominated the study of curriculum for the past forty-five years that they have, in effect, become a curriculum metanarrative called the Tylerian rationale. Tyler (1949) asks the following four questions:

> 1. What educational purposes should the school seek to attain? 2. How can learning experiences be selected which are likely to be useful in attaining these objectives? 3. How can learning experiences be organized for effective instruction? and 4. How can the effectiveness of learning experiences be evaluated? (pp. v–vi)

Ever since Tyler categorized these four principles of the curriculum, most school districts and educators—whether consciously or unconsciously—have aligned their thinking about schooling experiences with this rationale. Tyler's questions have been codified as the goals and objectives, lesson plans, scope and sequence guides, and mastery of learning evaluations. The influence of Ralph Tyler on the history of curriculum development in American education cannot be underemphasized.

However, postmodern curriculum development is challenging the traditional curriculum development model of Ralph Tyler. Postmodern curriculum development is concerned with biographical and autobiographical narrative that will not only enhance the study of history but also make connections for long-term memory. One recent book that provides theoretical support for this postmodern position is *Making Connections: Teaching and the Human Brain* by Renate Nummela Caine and Geoffrey Caine and published by the Association for Supervision and Curriculum Development. Donna Jean Carter, ASCD president in 1991, makes the following important comment in her introduction to the book:

> Intuitively, I have known for some time now that many capable youngsters are either so bored with their education or so stressed out by their experiences, that optimum learning cannot take place. I have also seen many students "flower" in a learning environment that builds on their current knowledge base and personal experiences. The authors not only explain why this is so but also show how a reconceptualization of teaching, based on knowledge of brain functioning, can enhance

> student learning. . . . Teachers must become facilitators of
> learning, and they must expect students to go beyond the
> surface knowledge frequently achieved through rote
> memorization and unconnected content. By integrating
> the curriculum, we can assist students in their search for
> deeper meaning and thus enhance the brain's quest for
> patterning. The implications of this seminal work for
> teaching, testing, and remediation are far reaching.
> Repeated practice on isolated skills becomes inappropriate
> as an option for acquiring knowledge. It becomes obvious
> that skills and content must be presented in a context that
> is familiar to the learner. This contextual approach also
> supports authentic modes of assessment. (cited in Caine
> and Caine, 1991, p. v)

Carter's introduction to the central theme of Caine and Caine's
book helps to explain the problem with my formal history
education described above. My study of the Civil War never
created an atmosphere where I could make connections to my
personal historical context. Caine and Caine challenge another
strongly held belief of educators that teaching can be separated
into cognitive, affective, and psychomotor domains of learning.
Such artificial categorization may be helpful in designing
research projects, but it can actually distort our understanding of
learning. Caine and Caine contend that the brain does not
separate emotions from cognition, either anatomically or
perceptually. (Cognitive theorists are exploring the concept of
the intuitive and nonrational dimension of learning, contending
that learning is not a logical progressive sequence. This research
supports postmodern understandings of curriculum as
multidimensional, autobiographical, kaleidoscopic, and ironic.
This concept will be discussed further in chapter eight.)

　　During the nineteenth century an influential movement
called faculty psychology (or mental discipline) emerged as the
result of the findings of many scholarly reports, including *The
Yale Report on the Defense of the Classics* in 1828. The Yale Report
expressed two key concepts in faculty psychology: discipline and
furniture. The aim of the curriculum was to expand the powers
of the mind and store it with knowledge. This philosophy of
curriculum sought to arrange the information that the memory
gathers like furniture in a room. Additionally, it proposed that

the muscles of the brain should be exercised routinely like other body parts. The faculty psychology movement, therefore, contended that the brain is a muscle in need of rote memorization exercises and mental drills in order to enhance the functioning of the mind which could then accumulate more information, rearrange the data, and expand the knowledge base. Caine and Caine (1991) establish the foundation for the postmodern arguments against faculty psychology in their book:

> A physiological model of memory also calls into question the notion that learning must take place through rote memorization. In addition, by understanding properties of our spatial memory system, educators can understand that teaching behavioral objectives ignores other functions of the brain and other aspects of memory and learning. Indeed, we have come to the conclusion that educators, by being too specific about facts to be remembered and outcomes to be produced, may prohibit students' genuine understanding and transfer of learning. (p. vii)

Caine and Caine's work demonstrates that learning and teaching involve multifaceted human beings in complex interactions. The postmodern curriculum will acknowledge this complexity and move beyond narrow definitions and practices. Thus, Caine and Caine provide support for the postmodern curriculum that embraces complexity, tolerance of ambiguity, acceptance of uncertainty, and authentic, situated assessment. Evaluation becomes contextualized for individual teaching environments. The postmodern curriculum will reject formal, standardized evaluation instruments designed for universal application. These dimensions of curriculum and evaluation were not included in the classical curriculum in my formal schooling in the 1950s and 1960s. This inhibited me from making the connection between the rote memorization of facts about the Civil War and my personal family context in relation to the siege of Vicksburg.

The first time I brought my three children to Vicksburg, I retold the family history and visited all the historical landmarks, as well as our family grave sites. We made tomb rubbings and explored the public library to make copies of microfilm newspaper articles about our ancestors. We even took a picture with our three children rubbing their "injured" heads at the grave of Aunt Dora. Everywhere we went in Vicksburg we thought about Aunt Dora and her family. We explored the history of the siege of Vicksburg from the perspective of our family, including a visit to the location of the old Navra home. In short, we experienced history autobiographically in our family context. The children wanted to buy books and read about the battle as we toured every museum in town. Future visits are planned to refurbish the family burial plot and erect a historical marker.

The climax of the Vicksburg trip occurred while we were visiting the old courthouse museum, an elegant Greek revival antebellum stone building that houses many of the artifacts of the Civil War era in Vicksburg. We had never visited the museum before. As we moved from room to room, our nine-year-old daughter Katie ran ahead. Suddenly, we heard her scream in the next room, and we rushed to her side. Katie was standing in awe before a glass case. She could not contain her excitement. Katie had discovered a display of mannequins with clothing of the citizens of Vicksburg from the 1800s. Katie proudly shouted out the inscription on the case for the entire museum to hear: "This dress was a gift to Ellen Kinney Navra on her wedding day. The shawl was worn by her daughter, Dora Navra." History came alive before Katie's eyes, and as she gazed at the shawl the echo of five generations of stories about the Civil War reverberated in her ears. The siege of Vicksburg became her story, never to be forgotten because it was now indelibly imprinted in her psyche. Interestingly, Katie now tells this story to her fourth grade classmates, who are fascinated about the Civil War and want to visit Vicksburg.

The history of curriculum development in the postmodern era must also be recounted and understood from this autobiographical perspective. The content of the events in the history of curriculum development are meaningless outside the autobiographical context of individual educators engaged in the exploration and excavation of the meaning of the events and the people, both famous/infamous and anonymous, who have been part of this history. Therefore, chapter three will continue our discussion of the historical dimension of curriculum development incorporating an autobiographical methodology.

The Reconceptualization of Curriculum and Instruction

Chapter two proposed that postmodern curriculum scholars should critically examine the history of curriculum development in the context of their own educational autobiography in order to establish a participatory perspective. This concept of personal historical contextualization is rooted in my own experience as a graduate student in curriculum theory at Louisiana State University in the 1980s, when I was introduced to postmodernism and exposed to autobiographical, ethnographic, and phenomenological methodologies. This was an exciting time for curriculum professors and students alike. Professor William Pinar arrived at LSU as chair of the Department of Curriculum and Instruction from the University of Rochester, where he had nurtured a movement in the curriculum field that had come to be known as the Reconceptualization. Pinar also brought many scholars associated with the Reconceptualization to the department at LSU, including semiotician Tony Whitson, race scholar Camron McCarthy, feminist ethnographer Leslie Roman, postmodern scholar William Doll, and Canadian deconstructionist Jacques Daignault, among others. Additionally, an international array of visiting professors and speakers regularly interacted with students and faculty. Graduate students and faculty traveled together to the JCT conference (*Journal of Curriculum Theorizing*, now *JCT: An Interdisciplinary Journal of Curriculum Studies*) held at the Bergamo Center in Dayton, Ohio every October. This conference can be traced back to the University of Rochester conference in 1973, which signaled that the Reconceptualization of American curriculum studies was underway. In 1978 publication of *JCT* began with William Pinar and Janet Miller serving as editor and managing editor of the journal. The 1978 conference was held at the Rochester Institute of Technology and chaired by Professor Ronald Padgham. The conference moved to the Airlie Conference Center in Virginia from 1979 to 1982. With the support of the University of Dayton, the *JCT* Conference found a home at the Bergamo Center in Dayton in 1983. (As a result of the influence of Canadian scholars, the conference was held in Alberta at the Banff Conference Center in 1994.) Since 1978 William Reynolds of Oklahoma State and Jo Anne Pagano of Colgate University have also served as editors of *JCT*.

In the milieu established by *JCT* and its annual conference, the Reconceptualization became for me a dynamic experience of sharing emerging concepts of curriculum with a wide array of international educators rather than a remote event that occurred in the 1970s to be studied in a textbook. (An excellent review of the Reconceptualization can be found in chapter four of William Pinar et al.'s forthcoming text *Understanding Curriculum* for those interested in a more detailed analysis of these events.) The Reconceptualization continues to have an impact on curriculum development investigations in the 1990s.

As a beginning doctoral student I was unfamiliar with many of the scholars and theories associated with the Reconceptualization. In fact, before entering the program at LSU, I had never heard the word *reconceptualization* used in a curriculum context. I had worked as a high school English teacher and as a principal prior to beginning my doctoral work. I was a member of ASCD (Association for Supervision and Curriculum Development), NASSP (National Association of Secondary School Principals), and NCEA (National Catholic Educational Association). Since the mid-1970s I had attended the annual conventions of many national organizations, occasionally presented formal papers, and faithfully read the publications *Educational Leadership, Education Week, NASSP Bulletin,* and *Momentum.* As a principal I also subscribed to several other journals, including *Kappan* (the Journal of Phi Delta Kappa), *ASCD Update,* and *Principal.* However, my involvement in state and national professional associations focused on practical concerns about classroom management, testing, and staff development, as well as innovative curricular programs that might effectively raise test scores and improve instruction. There was seldom any reflection on the theoretical underpinnings, sociological impact, or political implications of such programs. Despite my dissatisfaction with many aspects of school bureaucracy in the 1970s and 1980s, I was unaware of the theoretical challenges to the dominant concept of curriculum development that were emerging in the universities. Even while studying for a master's degree in school administration in the early 1980s at Arizona State University and LSU, I was never challenged to question the Tylerian paradigm, which I had learned in my undergraduate teacher training program in New Mexico and the subsequent application of this philosophy in the schools where I taught in the 1970s.

During my tenure as an administrator in several different schools, I was constantly bombarded with innovative reforms, new technology, district programs, and packaged curricular materials designed to solve all my educational problems. I intuitively realized that these reform proposals would not ameliorate the local or the national schooling crises of the time. However, I seldom strayed very far from the Tylerian model, either out of fear of change, ignorance of alternatives, or sheer determination to make the reforms work. In the process, I was Hunterized (Madeline Hunter's *Master Learning* and *Mastery Teaching*) and Canterized (Lee Canter's *Assertive Discipline*). Later I "Bloomed" (Allan Bloom's *Cultural Literacy*), and then I was "Bushed" (George Bush's *America 2000*). I learned how to build an effective school, an essential school, a drug-free school, a James Madison School (William Bennett, 1987, 1988), and a Paedeia School (Mortimer Adler's *Paedeia Proposal*, 1982). One company even wined and dined me until I agreed to start a Renaissance School. I explored 4Mat training, Osiris training, and time management training. I learned to manage by objectives (MBO) and develop an outcomes-based curriculum (OBE).

All my efforts finally paid dividends in 1986 when I reached what I thought at the time was the pinnacle of educational achievement: Excellence in Education. William Bennett, then secretary of education under President Reagan, was about to publish a new book entitled *First Lessons*, a prescription for improving the elementary school curriculum. In conjunction with the publication, the Department of Education initiated an elementary school competition similar to an already popular high school program that began in 1983 entitled "Excellence in Education." Two hundred American elementary schools that exemplified the highest caliber curriculum and instruction would win the award and be invited to a reception at the White House with President Reagan and Secretary Bennett.

I was the principal of a rural elementary school at the time the new competition was announced, and the staff, teachers, and school board were all thrilled to participate. I was vacationing in Orlando, Florida, with my family on July 4, 1986, when the winners of the competition were announced. I was reading *USA Today* in the hotel restaurant when I discovered the article listing "America's Best Elementary Schools" state by state. I was jubilant to see my school on the list, convinced that it was indeed the best!

When I returned home from vacation, I discovered that there was tremendous pride in the local community. This award brought state and national media coverage as well as affirmation for parent volunteers, dedicated teachers, and especially the children. However, during the next school year bitterness and jealousy surfaced among a few educators and parents from other schools. An award designed to promote excellence also had the effect of generating distrust and friction. Later, I began to question the value of comparing schools in national competitions. Although I did not realize it at the time, this question helped to prepare me to understand one of the central premises of postmodern thinking: the importance of cooperative models to replace rampant competitiveness. Additionally, in the years since receiving William Bennett's excellence award, I have had the opportunity to teach, administer, and observe on many more campuses. I have discovered some truly remarkable schools that have never been recognized, despite the fact that they have completed all the requirements necessary for the Excellence Award (now called the Blue Ribbon Schools). I have also served as principal or evaluator at other schools that have received the Blue Ribbon Award even though there existed extreme divisiveness and malaise in the school community at the time of the competition. My experience with this program has allowed me to evaluate critically the shortcomings of competitive curriculum models and see the wisdom of postmodern alternatives.

The one thing that traditional curriculum development programs and reforms have in common is a commitment to organized goals, measurable objectives, and mastery evaluation to achieve a specified educational outcome. While the focus of the proposals may be different, the curricular philosophy undergirding the methodologies remains committed to the modern paradigm. The Reconceptualization exposed me to critical analyses of curriculum development theories and programs, and it has provided a postmodern alternative to the reforms and programs that dominate educational practice today.

One of the central features of the Reconceptualization is attentiveness to autobiographical and phenomenological experience. This is described by William Pinar and Madeleine Grumet in the text *Toward a Poor Curriculum*, where the authors outline some of the early thinking about a change of focus in curriculum studies. Pinar and Grumet (1976) challenge the field to focus on internal experiences rather than external objectives. The writing of existentialists such as Jean-Paul Sartre, Friedrich Nietzsche, Martin Buber, and Søren Kierkegaard, as well as the psychoanalytic work of Sigmund Freud and Carl Jung, is integral to their curriculum theory. The imaginative literature of stream-of-consciousness authors such as James Joyce, Marcel Proust, Virginia Woolf, and William Faulkner and the painting of artists like Jackson Pollock also had a major influence on Pinar and Grumet. It is important to note the authors' intention in using the fields of philosophy, psychology, literature, and art to inform a reconceptualized curriculum theory. Pinar (1976) explains:

> The sort of inquiry I want shares the focus of these fields but not their methods of looking. We cannot solely rely on the imagination, however artful its expression, or reports of psychological problems or philosophic accounts of experience. Some synthesis of these methods needs to be formulated to give us a uniquely educational method of inquiry, one that will allow us to give truthful, public and

> usable form to our inner observations. It is this search for a
> method I am on now. (p. 5)

Pinar (1994) recently published a retrospective collection of essays that trace this search entitled *Autobiography, Politics, and Sexuality: Essays in Curriculum Theory, 1972–1992.*

The method that Pinar describes is committed to an etymological understanding of curriculum as *currere.* The problem with traditional curriculum development, according to Pinar, is that the meaning of curriculum has been misinterpreted. *Currere* is derived from the Latin infinitive verb that means "to run the racecourse." Curriculum is a verb, an activity, or for Pinar, an inward journey. The modern curriculum development rationale has truncated the etymological meaning and reduced curriculum to a noun, the racecourse itself. Thus, generations of educators have been schooled to believe that the curriculum is a tangible object, the lesson plans we implement, or the course guides we follow, rather than the process of running the racecourse. This apparently simple concept has been responsible for a profound shift in the understanding of curriculum development for many educators. As postmodern curriculum development emerges in the 1990s, the Reconceptualization of the 1970s will remain an important historical phenomenon that informs schooling praxis. Understanding curriculum, from the perspective of the Reconceptualization, must take precedence over traditional curriculum development and program planning. William Schubert (1986) summarizes this position clearly:

> One of the most recent positions to emerge on the curriculum horizon is to emphasize the verb form of curriculum, namely, *currere.* Instead of taking its interpretation from the race course etymology of curriculum, *currere* refers to the running of the race and emphasizes the individual's own capacity to reconceptualize his or her autobiography. The individual seeks meaning amid the swirl of present events, moves historically into his or her own past to recover and reconstitute origins, and imagines and creates possible directions of his or her own future. Based on the sharing of autobiographical accounts with others who strive for similar understanding, the curriculum becomes a reconceiving of one's perspective on life. It also becomes a

> social process whereby individuals come to greater understanding of themselves, others, and the world through mutual reconceptualization. The curriculum is the interpretation of lived experiences. (p. 33)

Schubert's summary leads us back to Pinar's concept of *currere*, where the method is described in four stages of autobiographical reflection: regressive, progressive, analytical, synthetical. Pinar (1976) writes:

> It is therefore temporal and conceptual in nature, and it aims for the cultivation of a developmental point of view that is transtemporal and transconceptual. From another perspective, the method is the self-conscious conceptualization of the temporal, and from another, it is the viewing of what is conceptualized through time. So it is that we hope to explore the complex relation between the temporal and the conceptual. (p. 51)

The first step is the regressive moment where one returns to the past as it impinges on the present. The present is veiled because the past is manifested in who we are and what we do in the existential now. Pinar proposes that we enter the past, live in it, observe oneself functioning in the past but not succumb to it. Since the focus of the method is educational experience, special attention should be given to schooling, books, teachers, and other pedagogical experiences and artifacts. We regress to the past but always with an eye toward a return to the present and to the next step, the *progressive* moment. The word progressive derives from *pro* meaning "before" and *gradi* meaning "to step, go." Here we look, in Sartre's language, at what is not yet present. We imagine a future, envision possibilities, and discern where our meditative images may appear to be leading us. The next step, the analytical moment, describes the biographic present, exclusive of the past and future but inclusive of responses to both. Pinar (1976) writes: "Bracketing what is, what was, and what can be, one is loosened from it, potentially more free of it, and hence more free to freely choose the present" (p. 60). This bracketing allows one to juxtapose the past, present, and future and evaluate the complexity of their multi-dimensional interrelations. After the analytical moment, a synthetical moment puts the three steps together to help inform the present. Pinar (1976) concludes:

> The Self is available to itself in physical form. The intellect, residing in the physical form, is part of the Self. Thus, the Self is not a concept the intellect has of itself. The intellect is thus an appendage of the Self, a medium, like the body, through which the Self, the world are accessible to themselves. No longer am I completely identified with my mind. My mind is identified as a part of me. (Descartes' "I think, therefore I am" is thus corrected.) Mind in its place, I conceptualize the present situation. I am placed together. Synthesis. (p. 61)

Pinar's method of *currere* challenges educators to begin with the individual experience and then make broader connections. This parallels our discussion of historical analysis in chapter two. Postmodern curriculum development is attentive to both the interconnectedness of all experiences and the importance of the autobiographical perspective. The work of William Pinar has explored these issues for over twenty years, and the recent publication of *Autobiography, Politics and Sexuality: Essay in Curriculum Theory 1972–1992* provides an accessible summary of Pinar's curriculum theory. Pinar (1994) concludes that autobiographical studies are "windows which permit us to see again that which we loved before, and in so doing, see more clearly what and whom we love in the present. The regressive phase of *currere* asks us to speak again in the lost language of cranes, to see again what was outside our windows, and to become married—that is, in unison—with ourselves and with those around us, by renewing our vows to those who are past, exchanging vows with those who are present, and dancing our way until the morning dawns" (p. 267). Reconceptualized curriculum theory understands time and history as proleptic, that is, as the confluence of past, present, and future. In this sense, the Reconceptualization is an integral part of the emerging postmodern curriculum. However, as we will see throughout part two, there are various other postmodern perspectives that inform curriculum in the 1990s.

The importance of the autobiographical process proposed by Pinar and Grumet, as well as other postmodern perspectives such as critical theory, is not accepted by all curriculum theorists. One example is found in a recent book by Peter Hlebowiths (1993) entitled *Radical Curriculum Theory Revisited*, in which the author attempts to resuscitate the Tylerian rationale. I will cite from Hlebowiths' summary critique of the Reconceptualization at length for two reasons: first, he clearly reflects the philosophical position of those who resist postmodern curriculum, and second, he demonstrates the internal contradiction of the traditional linear approach to historical interpretation of curriculum development as a field of study. Hlebowiths (1993) writes:

> In recent years, the curriculum field has been faced with a new radical commentary that has touted itself as contributing to a reconceptualization of the field's basic tenets. Many of the criticisms offered by these radical elements have been inspired by a critical theory of education that seeks to slay all common sense or conventional outlooks. The call for a reconceptualization derives from the belief that curriculum study has historically been associated with an atheoretical management agenda that compresses the school experience into low level group procedures. There is indeed a facet of curriculum thought that could be characterized in such a manner; there is also a distinctive legacy of behavioristic manipulation, generated by this tradition, that continues to prevail in the schools. However, the formal study of curriculum theory and development cannot be reasonably reduced to the laws of efficiency and control that drive business/management strategy. It strains credulity to posit the entire development of the curriculum field in such a manner when the growth of the field paralleled the growth of the progressive movement in education. The voice of the formidable progressive forces, which included individuals such as Dewey, Counts, Rugg, and Bode, was not unheard in or merely incidental to the curriculum field. Unfortunately, when curriculum history is drawn with a straight ideological line, distortion results and central figures in the field undergo an unjustified revision. While Jesse Newlon, for instance, could be said to have brought the idea of curriculum to the field of administration, he

was not, as has been alleged, driven by the desire to put
everything under control of an administratively controlled
directorate. In stark contrast, Newlon actually worked to
alleviate the central managerial demands of the school by
calling for the release of the classroom teacher's
intelligence and creativity and by advocating
experimentation in the fashioning of learning experiences.
(p. 19)

We can see in Hlebowiths, postmodern curriculum theories,
critical theories, and theories associated with the
Reconceptualization agreement on one point: curriculum
philosophers, scholars, and leaders such as John Dewey, Jesse
Newlon, George Counts, Boyd Bode, Harold Rugg, Franklin
Bobbitt, David Snedden, W. W. Charters, G. Stanley Hall,
Charles W. Eliot, and William Heard Kilpatrick are important
figures in the study of the history of the curriculum field. In fact,
all six texts recommended for the study of curriculum history in
chapter two include an analysis of the impact of these important
figures on the history of the curriculum field. However, much
discussion continues to surround the meaning, impact, and
intention of the theories of these and other educators. Neither
Hlebowiths nor critical scholars have an absolute, final
interpretation of these curriculum theories. As mentioned in the
introduction, John Dewey himself sought to clarify
misapplication of his philosophy in *Experience and Education*.

Another debate surrounds the beginning of curriculum
and instruction as a specialized field of study. Should curriculum
as a field of study be dated from 1918 and the publication of
Franklin Bobbitt's *The Curriculum*? Bobbitt argued for the reform
of existing curricula after what were then contemporary
scientific notions of organization and measurement. However,
his book in a sense crystallized theories that had been
developing for many years. The scientific movement in
education was responding to the dominance of faculty
psychology. Charles Eliot was perhaps most visible in
developing a rationale for utilizing faculty psychology in the
curriculum. This rationale was expressed succinctly in two
reports: the Committee of Ten on Secondary School Studies
(1893) and the Committee of Fifteen on Elementary Education

(1895). Should the birth of the field be located with the publication of these statements?

Another possibility is to date the beginning of curriculum as a field of study with the 1923 Denver curriculum revision project and Jesse Newlon discussed above by Hlebowiths. Herbert Kliebard (1986) also describes the Denver project:

> The Denver, Colorado, project was initiated in 1922 with an appropriation of $31,500 from the school board for curriculum revision. Elimination of waste seems to have been one of the main considerations. Superintendent Jesse Newlon's recommendation to the school board . . . pointed out that, in view of the size of the school budget in Denver, if it turned out that as little as "10 percent of teacher's time is spent on non-essential and misplaced materials in courses of study," that would represent an "annual waste to the Denver taxpayers of $315,000." . . . The most lasting legacy of the Denver program was the emphasis given to active teacher participation in curriculum reform. (p. 212)

Was the Denver project initiated by Jesse Newlon designed to eliminate waste, empower teachers, foster creativity and experimentation, or centralize administrative bureaucracy? Debates about the purpose of the Denver project and Newlon's intentions continue today, with some scholars arguing that curriculum development as a field began in Denver.

Another date that is proposed for the beginning of the field is 1828 with the publication of the *Yale Report on Defense of the Classics* which rationalized the classical curriculum with an emphasis on Greek and Latin as school subjects and memorization and recitation as instructional methods. Variations of both faculty psychology and classical curriculum are discernible in the curriculum debates of the 1990s. Pinar et al. (in press) date the beginning of the field with the *Yale Report*.

What can be seen in the preceding discussion of the debates about dating the beginning of curriculum development as a field of study and the meaning of the events surrounding the history of curriculum studies in microcosm is the dilemma of the modern paradigm. Interpretations depend on the context and perspective of the individual author. Does this mean that historical studies are now irrelevant in the postmodern era? Should we simply focus on the present and future? Obviously not! Contemporary curriculum scholars do not ignore historical analysis. Indeed, Pinar's method insists on a regressive step. However, the postmodern curriculum will insist that the meaning of events cannot be separated from their context, just as the knower cannot be separated from the known, and that all interpreting and bracketing of events must be directed toward an autobiographical synthesis.

Despite the critiques from both the left and right, the postmodern curriculum must include some form of autobiographical analysis in order to appropriately address the important questions of curriculum history. The eclectic, ironic, and artistic elements of postmodernism require such a dimension, and the Reconceptualization has provided curriculum studies with the challenge to explore curriculum history and the self from this postmodern perspective.

By the early 1980s, the movement to reconceptualize the curriculum field had lost the cohesive bonds that maintained the coalition during the first years of struggle and enthusiasm. Opposition to the traditional field was no longer a powerful enough force for coalition, as the movement had succeeded in deligitimating the ahistorical, atheoretical field that often existed prior to 1970. With the continued resistance of Marxist scholars to a multiperspectival conception of reconceptualization, with the emergence of autobiographical studies, with the expansion of existential and phenomenological scholarship, with the burgeoning of feminist theory, and the appearance of postmodernism, the original reconceptualist movement can be said to have disappeared. The success of the Reconceptualization brought on its demise (Pinar, 1988a; Pinar et al., in press).

William Pinar describes the condition of the Reconceptualization in the 1990s:

> From the vantage point of the early 1990s, it is clear that the American curriculum field was reconceptualized swiftly and rather completely. Replacing the nearly exclusive preoccupation with curriculum development and design were scholarly efforts to understand curriculum. These efforts can be characterized now by the

framing of their interest to understand curriculum, i.e., understanding curriculum as a political text, as phenomenological text, as autobiographical text, and the other major sectors of scholarship. (Pinar et al., in press, p. 231)

The Reconceptualization has established a challenge for curriculum specialists, classroom teachers, university professors, and educational administrators to reenvision their pedagogical role, and the autobiographical method provides access to the postmodern visions of curriculum development that are emerging in the 1990s.

Typical of the emerging autobiographical studies in the curriculum field in the 1990s is Robert J. Graham's (1991) comprehensive and insightful book *Reading and Writing the Self: Autobiography in Education and the Curriculum*. Graham examines the place and use of autobiography in the curriculum from the perspective of literary theory, Deweyan philosophy, and the Reconceptualization. Graham also cautiously examines both the advantages and pitfalls of the use of autobiography in education throughout the book. Ultimately, though, Graham (1991) concludes: "Although itself not a principle or a theory, autobiography permits access to valid sources of information that facilitate the recovery and inspection of ideas of great relevance to education and to the field of curriculum in particular" (p. 16). Graham contends that while autobiography provides access to important sources for reclaiming hidden or forgotten aspects of the individual's past, these sources have been "prevented from germinating owing to the constraints imposed by timetables and other institutional practices that mitigate against the use [of autobiography]" (p. 13). The book emphasizes the productive use of autobiography by feminist theorists and ethnic minorities for reclaiming collective voices and redeeming a lost sense of historical consciousness. Thus, Graham (1991) concludes his book by contending, "It behooves all of us who are involved in whatever aspect of public education to begin to consider the extent of our own knowledge and attitudes toward autobiography and its potential as well" (p. 156).

Returning to my autobiographical reflections from the beginning of this chapter, I can now understand the influence of the traditional curriculum methodologies, as well as various reform proposals, on my career as a teacher and principal. I can also place my own teacher training program in the context of the historical events that shaped the philosophy of my undergraduate education program.

My first education course as an undergraduate student was entitled Education Psychology at the College of Santa Fe in New Mexico. The ambiance of the city of Santa Fe and the mystique of the Sangre de Christo Mountains created a wonderfully liberating atmosphere for my studies, but this stood in stark contrast to the physical atmosphere of my education class. At the initial meeting for this course thirty students crowded into a traditional classroom with metal desks facing a blackboard. The walls were bare, and florescent fixtures filled the room with light. There were no windows. It was as though the outside world had been shut out. The professor wrote the following statement on the board: "There is no such thing as motivation." The students dutifully copied these words in their notebooks. The professor turned to the class and paused for comments. No one dared to say a word. Finally, I could not resist the urge to speak. Presuming that the professor had written this obviously incorrect statement on the board in order to elicit a reaction, I began to challenge the premise that there was no such thing as motivation. I was quickly chastised. The professor had been a student of Skinnerian behaviorism at the University of Minnesota. This statement became the basis of our semester study of lesson plans, behavioral objectives, as well as the cognitive, psychomotor, and affective domains of learning. To my dismay, even the affective domain was restricted to observable and measurable lessons such as this one example: "The student will demonstrate appreciation of Igor Stravinsky by listening attentively to a recording of *The Rite of Spring* and by identifying this music in the soundtrack of the Walt Disney movie *Fantasia* on a unit test." There was no room for intuition, ambiguity, emotion, intrinsic motivation, complexity, and uncertainty in the curriculum of my undergraduate training.

I remember meeting with the professor to discuss my concerns about behavioral objectives. I did not feel comfortable with the learning theories and objective lesson plans presented in the course, but over the years I continued to receive a steady dose of this approach to teacher training. However, by the time I started my student teaching I had perfected the methods. I was like the kindergarten student in Harry Chapin's song *Colors of the Rainbow* in which the child uses all the colors of the rainbow to paint flowers. The teacher repeatedly scolds the child and insists that flowers are only red and green. After several punishments, the child finally agrees with the teacher and begins to paint flowers as instructed. The next year the child moves to another school, where the new teacher encourages students to use all their crayons to color flowers. The teacher notices that this new student uses only red and green for coloring. The teacher approaches the child, who adamantly insists that flowers are only red and green. Chapin ends his touching ballad with an uplifting refrain about all the colors of the rainbow, implying that in time the teacher was able to gently invite this child to reinvestigate the aesthetic spirit.

Reflecting on my teacher training program is important for me today as I now teach introductory courses to undergraduate students preparing to become teachers. I constantly recall my own experiences as I select textbooks, structure the learning experiences, and evaluate assignments. Additionally, Pinar's autobiographical method has provided the support for moving from the Tylerian rationale to a postmodern pedagogy. One of the tangible changes in my teaching style affected by the Reconceptualization is that I now always structure my classroom in a seminar circle and encourage the students to share their personal perspectives. The students' concerns about their needs and expectations are valued and honored. Additionally, I expose my students to autobiographical methods and assign a journal to be kept during the course. Some students have volunteered to write a journal throughout their undergraduate career and into their first year of classroom teaching. With this project now in its third year, the ten students involved report that the autobiographical journal has become a very important part of their teacher preparation.

Curriculum development in the postmodern era will see the emergence of more journals, portfolios, and autobiographical methodologies. The Reconceptualization in curriculum studies has reminded educators that we can no longer remain ahistorical, detached, impersonal, and "behaviorly objective." In the process of exploring meaning and knowledge, we can no longer separate the context of historical events from the autobiographical experiences of teachers and students in postmodern schooling.

CHAPTER FOUR

Postmodern Schooling, Curriculum, and the Theological Text

Beginning with the Enlightenment and seventeenth-century empiricism, modernity has gradually attempted to remove theology and religion from the canon of respectable fields of study in public schools and secular universities. Postmodernity seeks to restore the prominence of theology and spirituality in the curriculum discourses and practices of the 1990s. However, these postmodern educational proposals are vociferously opposed to proselytization and denominational sectarianism. A postmodern vision of curriculum as theological text is emerging. This chapter explores the implications of this vision for curriculum development in the postmodern era, especially as this vision is central to curriculum as a field of study. I must acknowledge, however, that this chapter makes no excuse for advocating such a position. This chapter investigates the emerging theological dimension of the reconceptualized curriculum field.

There is a growing recognition that the educational community cannot address the hopelessness, poverty, injustice, violence, and ecological devastation that plague the entire global community and contribute to the decay of the social milieu of schools by simply reacting to the symptoms. Traditional curriculum development models that focus exclusively on improving curriculum guides, expanding technology laboratories, upgrading standards, revising textbooks, and perfecting evaluation procedures ignore the ethical, ecological, sociological, and economic crises that threaten society. At the other extreme, theoretical discourses that simply analyze the latest political or philosophical jargon without reference to the schooling context also overlook the malaise, anguish, and fear that grip modern cultures. Curriculum scholar David Purpel (1989) contends that the moral and spiritual crises in society must be at the forefront of curriculum studies, and postmodern schooling must attend to these important issues. I will use the umbrella term *theology* in this chapter in an effort to distinguish postmodern curriculum development related to morality and spirituality from the political and denominational debates about religion in American schools and society.

The emerging constructive postmodern vision of schooling in the contemporary global community includes an eclectic and ecumenical integration of spirituality and theology into the very fabric of education. This vision of the centrality of spirituality and theology for postmodern schooling is still evolving. The proponents of the two predominant views of religion and schooling have reached an impasse in the 1990s. One segment of society promotes the legal separation of church and state in an effort to protect the rights of minority religious views and freedom of religious expression. This perspective, which I will call the modern ideology, has resulted in the gradual removal of religion from the public schools. This process reached a climax with several Supreme Court cases that ruled against state-sponsored prayer and Bible reading in public schools in the early 1960s, and it continues to be debated in the 1990s.

On the opposite side of the debate are members of religious denominations, often with fundamentalist affiliation, who insist that schooling must include specific prayers, Scripture study, and religious formation. They contend that the "secular humanism" of the public schools is a godless religion in itself, and schooling must return to the traditional Judeo-Christian values and practices upon which *they believe* the United States was founded and on which American schools were modeled before the 1960s. Proponents of this perspective, which I will call the premodern ideology, have fought against the separation of religion and government with numerous legal challenges of curricular practices, textbook adoptions, and school funding formulas. The intense debate between those who hold either the modern or premodern ideology has reached a stalemate with both sides ardently opposing the efforts of the other to control the future relationship between religion and schooling in American society. Additionally, some of those frustrated by this debate have opted out of the public school system by choosing parochial, private, or home schooling. Estimates range from 10 to 13 percent of the school age population that participate in these educational alternatives. This is the current dilemma of religion and schooling in the United States in the 1990s. The effort by some curriculum scholars to uncover a postmodern alternative to this impasse begins with the identification of several major trends concerning religion and education in the postmodern literature of the past decade.

Some scholars promote a postmodern theology that is a new spirituality based on an "imaginative, yet secular, response to nature herself" (Fuller, 1985, p. xiii). Other postmodern writers propose "a shared symbolic order of the kind that a religion provides, but without the religion" (Jencks, 1986, p. 43). Hans Kung (1988) does not share the sacred/secular distinction of Fuller and Jencks, but rather he seeks to "help religion to perform a new critical and liberating function of both the individual and society . . . in a time of transition from modernity to 'postmodernity'" (p. xv). This epochal transition for Kung is a movement toward a new global understanding of various denominations where religion and education, along with art and politics, will be central to understanding the intellectual character of our time. Kung (1988) contends that "the intellectual crisis of our time is decisively *co-determined* by the *religious* crisis, and that without diagnosing and solving the religious crisis, no diagnosis and solution of the intellectual situation of our age can be successful" (p. 6). Religion and education are thus inseparable from this perspective.

Harvey Cox (1984) in *Religion in the Secular City: Toward a Postmodern Theology* shares the view that postmodern education is inextricably linked to religion in the secular society. However, unlike Kung, Cox attributes appeals to "the burgeoning intellectual life of modern times" (p. 177) as the project of modern theology, even from such diverse voices as Friedrich Schleiermacher, Karl Barth, Jacques Maritain, and Paul Tillich. "These disparate modern theologians were all preoccupied with one underlying question—how to make the Christian message credible to what they understood as the modern . . . educated, skeptical . . . mind" (p. 176–177). Thus, for Harvey Cox the challenge of postmodern theologians and educators is not to adapt religion to the modern world but rather to forge a conversation with those marginalized by modernity. Theological dialogue with the despised, the poor, and the culturally dominated sectors of society in order to give credence to global religious pluralism and popular piety is the foundation of Cox's postmodern proposal. Through such a dialogue we come to realize that the marginalized evangelize the mainstream powerbrokers in society. The poor ground the elites in the present and reveal the mystery of spiritual transformation.

Harvey Cox's proposal flows out of the tradition of "problem-posing" pedagogy established in Latin America by the Brazilian educator Paulo Freire (1970), who viewed the problems of education as inseparable from political, social, and economic problems. Peasants were encouraged to examine critically their life situations and take the initiative to transform social structures that denied them meaningful civic participation. Freire's (1971) manuscript "Conscientizing as a Way of Liberating" is considered one of the important philosophical foundations of liberation theology. Liberation theology has utilized Freire's pedagogy to establish *communautes de base* (base communities) that unite religious reflection with social action as a form of praxis that can inspire lasting change in the Latin American community. Theology and education are truly inseparable in this curriculum development model.

Moving in a very different direction than Paulo Freire, Harvey Cox, and Hans Kung, theologian Mark Taylor (1984) proposes a "postmodern a/theology" as a rebuttal to humanist atheists who fail to realize that the "Death of God is at the same time the death of the self" (p. 20). Taylor's solution is the deconstruction of modern philosophical movements that reject transcendence. David Ray Griffin (1988b) challenges Mark Taylor's theology, and by extrapolation Jencks and Fuller's spirituality, on the basis that his postmodern theology is eliminative; that is, Taylor eliminates worldviews of God, self, truth, and purpose in the spirit of the deconstructionism of French philosopher Jacques Derrida. Griffin proposes instead a revisionary theological postmodernism with a reenchantment of the cosmos and a better intuition of its "Holy Center" (p. 52). While acknowledging the contributions of many postmodern scholars, Griffin's constructive and revisionary postmodern theology informs much of the discussion of religion in postmodern schooling in the 1990s.

Despite the postmodern theological proposals reviewed above, modern educational reforms continue to be committed to scientific and technical methodologies with an emphasis on measurable outcomes (see, for example, *America 2000*, 1991). However, postmodern educators recognize that the crises that plague schools in the 1990s will not be resolved by the exclusive use of any of the modern reform proposals thrust upon education in the past century, often by those committed to the continuation of modernity in government, business, industry, and the military (see Kliebard, 1986; Shea et al., 1989; Pinar et al., in press). The contributions of spirituality, theology, and religion are now beginning to be incorporated into new postmodern revisions.

In contrast to the ideology of the current reform proposals for education, other alternatives are being offered that challenge dominant cultural values and practices of modernity such as the emphasis on consumption over sustainable resource use, competition over cooperation, and bureaucracy over authentic human interaction. For example, the Global Alliance for Transforming Education (GATE) in *Education 2000: A Holistic Perspective* (Global Alliance, 1991) contends that these dominant cultural values and practices have been destructive to the health of the ecosystem as well as to optimal human development in education. *Education 2000* states: "[Our] purpose is to proclaim an alternative vision of education, one which is a life affirming and democratic response to the challenges of the 1990s and beyond. We value diversity and encourage a wide variety of methods, applications, and practices" (Global Alliance, 1991, p. 1). Unfortunately, many political leaders and even many religious leaders have hampered the creation of such a revisionary view of postmodern schooling. Some scholars contend that despite the seemingly insurmountable obstacles to this project, a reverent and egalitarian postmodern education will certainly emerge once authentic attention is given to the spiritual and theological issues of the human heart (Moore, 1989).

The incorporation of spirituality, theology, and religious education into postmodern visions of schooling is not universally and uncritically accepted. This is evidenced by the protracted debates over the place of religion in American society in the 1990s. This debate perpetuates the modern notion of religion as a quantifiable event that can be compartmentalized and separated from other life experiences. The suppression of spirituality, theology, and religious education in modern public and private schools can be attributed to the following: the intense theological divisiveness between religious faiths (Marty, 1984); the public display of hypocritical and sometimes illegal behavior by many prominent denominational leaders; the long history of tolerance of racism, sexism, militarism, and colonialism in the churches (Ruether, 1983; Pinar, 1988b); the tradition of separation of church and state (and thus privatization of matters spiritual) in Western societies, especially the United States (Cox, 1984; Whitson, 1991); the apparently irresolvable conflicts over moral issues in the modern technological society (Arons, 1983; Chazan, 1985; Maguire & Fargnoli, 1991); the international politicization of religion with calls for "holy wars" and condemnations of "evil empires" (Wald, 1987; Toffler, 1990); the rise of religious fundamentalism and its impact on education (Provenzo, 1990); transcultural and transnational global evangelization and proselytization by sects and cults, as well as traditional denominations (Glock & Bellah, 1976; Stark & Brainbridge, 1985); scientific empiricism and reductionism that denigrates religion as superstitious and enshrines materialistic atheism in the Newtonian worldview (Cobb, 1988); and the consistent rejection and brutal humiliation of prophetic voices in the churches in both premodern and modern societies (Dewey, 1934a; Bonhoeffer, 1966, 1971). In this milieu there has been a systematic attempt to rid education of all vestiges of religious sensibilities and ensure that "religious intuitions are weeded out from among the intellectually respectable candidates for philosophical articulation" (Rorty, 1982, p. xxxviii), despite the fact that theology was once considered the queen of the sciences with prominent stature in the university curriculum in the premodern Middle Ages.

This litany of factors that have contributed to the decline of theology in the public school curriculum and university programs of study in the modern era has also had a significant impact on religious education in parochial schools. It is not unusual for religion and spirituality to be compartmentalized and institutionalized as simply one among many courses to be studied. Furthermore, there is a conspicuous absence of theology in the educational discourses of avowed secular scholars. This is attributed by some to the fact that religious conflicts are viewed as irresolvable parochial matters, and thus irrelevant to postmodern schooling (Arons, 1983). Postmodern scholars have not yet discovered a way out of the modern dilemma of religion and schooling chronicled above, and thus have often excluded spirituality and theology from their curriculum proposals.

Of course, there are notable exceptions to this macrotrend. David Ray Griffin (1988a) has called for public life to reflect religious values in his postmodern proposals. David Purpel (1989) has challenged teachers to become prophets who orient the educational process toward a vision of ultimate meaning and "infuse education with the sacred" (p. 105). John I. Goodlad (1990) has proposed that the educational community include a vision of morality and values in teacher education programs. Curricularist David G. Smith (1988) has cautioned that education must not simply tell us what we are, but most significantly, what we hope to become. Smith writes that "attention to the eidetic quality of our life together is an attempt to bring into the center of our research conversation everything that we are, as a way of reconciling in the present moment our ends with our beginnings" (p. 435). Philip Phenix (1975) has pointed out the significance for schooling of the "lure of transcendence toward wholeness" (p. 333). William Doll (1993) has written that the postmodern curriculum is imbued with a cosmological character that leads to a personal and spiritual transformation.

Other voices of exception include theologian Gabriel Moran (1981), who has indicated that there is no discernible field that can accurately be called religious education, despite the fact that "religious education is one of the most universal, most urgent, and most practical questions confronting our society today" (p. 9). Denise Larder Carmody (1991) has called for an alliance among feminism, religion, and education because "there will be no optimal alliance unless feminists, people of faith, and educators can agree that religion is the substance of the good life and that feminism and education are privileged ways of expressing religion" (p. 117). Mary Elizabeth Moore, Dwayne Huebner, Donald Oliver, Douglas Sloan, and Nelson Haggerson all have consistently promoted spirituality, process philosophy, and ethics in their educational research. Despite the voices of these and other scholars who share a vision of spirituality and morality for the postmodern era, theology has only recently emerged as an important dimension of the postmodern curriculum field.

Those educators committed to a postmodern vision of schooling understand well the insight of Alfred North Whitehead (1929) in *Aims of Education* when he insisted, "The essence of education is that it be religious" (p. 14). Religious education for Whitehead included duty and reverence: the duty to be involved in human community and global concerns and a profound reverence for the cosmos. Whitehead explains: "And the foundation of reverence is this perception, that the present holds within itself the complete sum of existence, backwards and forwards, that whole amplitude of time which is eternity" (p. 14). Recent scientific discoveries by physicists viewing graphics transmitted from the Hubble telescope reveal images from the very seconds after the Big Bang. Using these images, scientists are beginning to explore the mysteries of creation and eternity. It is fascinating that theoretical physicists in quest of a unified theory are therefore compelled to address theological questions in the face of the new data (Hawking, 1988). The new discoveries have caused astrophysicist George Smoot to exclaim, "If you're religious, it's like looking at God" (cited in Lemonick, 1992, p. 62). Modern science has come full circle since the eighteenth-century rejection of religion as a hindrance to the development of modern scientific progress by Pierre Simon de Laplace and others to a realization that religious questions are at the very heart of science (Griffin, 1988a, 1988b).

Having introduced the landscape that spirituality and theology must traverse in the complex postmodern curriculum dialogue, we are now ready to explore the concept of curriculum as theological text and the struggle of schools to break free from the shackles of modernity. Schooling must resist fundamentalist calls to retreat to premodern religious practices while still preserving ancient religious traditions in the social context of contemporary spirituality and theology. This is a monumental task. And thus, for those who agree with Whitehead that the essence of education is that it must be religious, the lessons from contemporary curriculum discourses offer valuable insights for all those committed to postmodern curriculum development.

Throughout the first part of this chapter the terms *theology, spirituality,* and *religion* have been used interchangeably. However, it is important to note that these words have a unique and evolving etymological history. Volumes have been written over the centuries to explain the precise nuanced meaning of each term. Crusades, inquisitions, witch burnings, and excommunications have all been initiated as a result of theological disagreements involving the interpretation of these words and their codification in sacred books. While religion has traditionally been associated with denominational practices and beliefs, theology is sometimes considered a more systematic and rational study of faith and the holy (i.e., God, transcendence, dogmas, and sacred texts) as related to patterns of meaning that prevail in a historical period or culture (Cox, 1984). Spirituality is associated with the realm of personal faith and supernatural revelation. Following Alfred North Whitehead, religious education in contemporary curriculum discourses is viewed as a process that includes duty, reverence, and personal participation as a form of praxis in exploring cosmology, the mystery of eternity, and transcendence. Postmodern curriculum promotes the exploration of this mystery of eternity and the return of theology to its authentic place as queen of the sciences, not in the premodern sense of an authoritarian monarch to be feared or in the modern sense of an antique barren goddess to be displayed in a museum, but rather as the postmodern benevolent and nurturing Sophia, goddess of eternal wisdom.

T. S. Eliot succinctly critiques the effects of modernity on the churches, society, and schooling in his poem "Choruses from the Rock." He warns that the scientific knowledge and information technology of modernity brings us nearer to death but no nearer to God. Some scholars contend that a postmodern model of curriculum as theological text is our only way out of the stalemate described above. It is also the only way out of this endless cycle of ignorance described by Eliot (1971):

> The endless cycle of idea and action,
> Endless invention, endless experiment,
> Brings knowledge of motion, but not of stillness;
> Knowledge of speech, but not of silence;
> Knowledge of words, and ignorance of the Word.
> All our knowledge brings us nearer to our ignorance,
> All our ignorance brings us nearer to death,
> But nearer to death no nearer to God.
> Where is the Life we have lost in living?
> Where is the wisdom we have lost in knowledge?
> Where is the knowledge we have lost in information?
> The cycles of Heaven in twenty centuries
> Bring us farther from God and nearer to the Dust.
>
> (p. 96)

T. S. Eliot's vision of centuries of knowledge and information technology bringing us farther from God and nearer to destruction serves as a profound metaphor for the challenge of postmodern curriculum development. The desolation of modernity and the impotence of its obsession with information in schooling impel us to reconceptualize school curriculum in order to recover the wisdom that has been lost in information transmission.

In the postmodern reflections on the school curriculum as theological text, the words *curriculum, theology,* and *text* are understood phenomenologically (emphasizing subjective consciousness and its intentional objects in their pure essences) rather than ontologically (emphasizing concrete natural objects studied in the abstract). The understanding of curriculum that is proposed is not restricted to the modern program of studies in the schools of the twentieth century as codified in textbooks, guides, scope and sequences, and behavioral lesson plans.

Rather, the verb form of curriculum, *currere*, which refers to running of the race rather than the race course itself, is primary. This process view of curriculum as *currere*, as we saw in chapter three, emphasizes the individual's own capacity to reconceptualize his or her autobiography, recognize connections with other people, recover and reconstitute the past, imagine and create possibilities for the future, and come to a greater personal and communal awareness. Donald Oliver and Kathleen Gershman (1989) point out that this awareness grounds our knowledge in being, not in methods or techniques. From this postmodern perspective, the curriculum as *currere* is an interpretation of lived experiences rather than a static course of studies to be completed. Likewise, theology is not restricted to the study of objective creeds, codes, and canons. Instead, theology is an autobiographical process, a cosmological dialogue, and a search for personal and universal harmony. This concept of theology is rooted in the tradition of Anselm of Canterbury (twelfth century C.E.) who insisted that theology was *fides quaerens intellectum* (faith seeking understanding) and Jurgen Moltmann (twentieth century C.E.) who situated the believer between the "already" and the "not yet" in an unfolding history with God "ahead" rather than "above." This view of theology avoids a premodern authoritarian confessionalism (e.g., Karl Barth) and a modern subjective decisionism (e.g., Bernard Lonergan). It also responds to the concerns of John Dewey (1934a), who contended that the churches had lost their prophetic voice and were impotent to address the need for social justice.

Finally, the word *text* in the curriculum as understood as theological text is now viewed from a process perspective. Modern schooling has enshrined the written word as a historical artifact to be memorized, comprehended, and regurgitated on a standardized test. In contrast to this dominant view, postmodernity views the text as a phenomenological encounter between word and reader. Reading the text is more closely associated with the Latin *ruminare* (to ruminate and think things over). Like the ruminants (cattle, sheep, and so on) who store their food in a special compartment of their stomachs until they find a place of refuge to digest it at leisure, readers of a text in school store experiences of the world and use them for personal reflection in leisure. Madeleine Grumet (1988a) has explored this process view of reading the text. She writes: "Meaning is something we make out of what we find when we look at texts. It is not the text. [Unfortunately,] the myth of the meaningful text still flourishes in the classroom" (p. 465). The Reconceptualization has challenged educators to wrest meaning from the grips of behavioral knowledge and return it to artistic expression so that students will have something to do with texts in schools. This view of the text brings purpose to the reading process by providing a foundation for personal praxis and intentionality. "It also provides another stage where the possible worlds that the text points to can be identified and experienced as good places for grazing" (Grumet, 1988a, p. 471).

What we see here is a postmodern process view of curriculum as theological text. Each word is reconceptualized by exploring its etymological root in order to reconstitute a fuller meaning. Curriculum, theology, and text are primarily verbs, not merely nouns! They imply movement: running, seeking, and ruminating. Thus, the revisionary postmodern view of religious education is based on phenomenological understandings, and it is identified by the curriculum as theological text.

We can now return to the poem "Choruses from the Rock," where T. S. Eliot laments: "Knowledge of words, and ignorance of the Word. Where is the wisdom we have lost in knowledge?" The curriculum as theological text seeks to uncover the wisdom that has been lost in our preoccupation with discrete parcels of knowledge that are measured on standardized tests in modern schools. The challenge of postmodern schooling is to recover a fuller meaning of wisdom. This journey often begins with an exploration of the importance of Sophia, or wisdom.

Wisdom literature abounds in Hebrew writings, Roman and Orthodox Catholic Deuterocanonical Scriptures, and the Protestant Apocrypha. The books of Wisdom and Ecclesiasticus, for example, teach that "before all other things wisdom was created, [and] shrewd understanding is everlasting" (*Jerusalem Bible*, 1966, p. 902). Wisdom—or Sophia in Hellenistic Judaism and Gnostic mythology—is the power that bridges the gap between divinity and humanity. In Ecclesiasticus (1:4) she is described as "First of all created things" (p. 902). In the Wisdom of Solomon, Sophia is likened to the Deity, and among feminist theologians like Rosemary Radford Ruether (1983b) Sophia is the modern image of Deity abandoned when the masculine imagery of Father was canonized by the churches. Solomon (7:25–28) writes: "Sophia is a breath of the power of God, pure emanation of the glory of the Almighty. . . . Although alone, she can do all, herself unchanging, she makes all things new" (*Jerusalem Bible*, 1966, p. 884).

In Gnostic mysticism wisdom is also divine emanation, sometimes appearing as the bride of the Logos (Christ). In the *Apocryphon of John* (II, 1:5) from the Nag Hammadi documents of Egypt (Robinson, 1977) we read about Sophia. "She became the womb for everything, for she is prior to them all, the Mother-Father, the first man, the Holy Spirit, the thrice-male, the thrice powerful, the thrice-named androgynous one, and the eternal aeon" (p. 101). *The Teachings of Silvanus* (VII, 4:89, 5; 87, 5; 87, 15) (Robinson, 1977) cautions:

> Wisdom summons you in her goodness, come to me all of you . . . that you may receive a gift of understanding which is good and excellent . . . . What else is evil death except ignorance? . . . Do not flee from the education and the teaching, but when you are taught, accept it with joy. . . . Do not lose my teaching, and do not acquire ignorance, lest you lead your people astray. (pp. 348–349)

Curriculum development in the postmodern era also includes attention to the wisdom embedded in Native American spirituality, for it is in the very sacred land of the native people that American education now finds its home. "If we sell you our land, you must keep it apart and sacred as a place where even whites can go to taste the wind," concluded Dwamish Chief Seattle in a speech given in 1854 at an assembly of tribes preparing to sign treaties with whites who had conquered their land. Chief Seattle began his famous oration this way:

> The Great Chief in Washington sends word that he wishes to buy our land. But how can you buy or sell the sky, the warmth of the land? The idea is strange to us. . . . Every part of this earth is sacred to my people. Every shining pine needle, every sandy shore, every mist in the dark

> woods, every clearing and humming insect is holy in the
> memory and experience of my people. The sap which
> courses through the trees carries the memories of the red
> man. . . . We are part of the earth and it is part of us. The
> perfumed flowers are our sisters; the deer, the horse, the
> great eagle, these are our brothers. . . . So we will consider
> your offer to buy our land. But it will not be easy. For this
> land is sacred to us. (cited in Armstrong, 1971, pp. 77–79)

In this speech, which is essential reading in its entirety for all
postmodern thinkers, Chief Seattle also reflects on God and
religion. He contrasts the religion of the White Man's God
written on tablets of stone with the Red Man's Great Spirit. He
says, "Our religion is the traditions of our ancestors—the dreams
of our old men, given them in solemn hours of the night by the
Great Spirit; and the visions of our sachems; and it is written in
the hearts of our people" (cited in Armstrong, 1971, p. 78). These
dreams and visions are never forgotten by the native peoples,
and even their dead never forget the world that gave them being.
For when the last Native American perishes, and the memories
of their tribes have become a myth, Chief Seattle believes that
"these shores will swarm with the invisible dead of my tribe, and
when your children's children think themselves alone in the
field, the store, the shop, upon the highway, or in the silence of
the pathless woods, they will not be alone. . . . They will throng
with the returning hosts that once filled and still love this
beautiful land. The White Man will never be alone" (cited in
Armstrong, 1971, p. 79). The mystery of eternity is clear for Chief
Seattle, and the postmodern curriculum seeks to remember what
is with us and envision the process of becoming.

The wisdom of Chief Seattle is representative of many
global traditions of indigenous people and religious mystics. For
example, Francis of Assisi honored "brother sun and sister
moon" in his oft-repeated cosmological prayer. The intimate
relationship between wisdom, eternity, ecology, and memory is
clearly a dimension of postmodern curriculum development that
scholars seek to recover and nurture.

What has become of the Wisdom described in these
mystical theologies, native voices, and ancient texts? Where in
our educational journey do we encounter Sophia? Where is the
theology of wisdom in our curriculum? Reflecting on these and

other probing questions, contemporary writers are beginning to propose that curriculum must become theological text: a place to encounter Sophia and ruminate on the sacred. Postmodern schooling is seen as a self-immersion into myth, mysticism, cosmology, eternity, and the holy center of life.

In the quest for information and knowledge, the wisdom of the sages of human history has too often been scorned and silenced. Information technology has replaced the encounter with the metaphysical, the eschatological, the soteriological, and the mystical in schooling. Like a disrespectful child or impudent criminal placed in solitary confinement, the theological text has been banished from theoretical discourse and from schools. The warning of postmodern theology that the death of God is also the death of self can also be applied to modern schooling as an admonition that ignorance of curriculum as theological text is educational suicide. Curriculum development in the postmodern era will understand that the theological curriculum is the self in dialogue with eternal communal wisdom. The absence of this dialogue in modern schooling is a nihilism to be resisted.

The words of truth, beauty, sacred, and goodness in the religious myths and ways of enlightenment have been expressed for centuries by indigenous cultures, in philosophical discourses, and by mystery religions in the very breath of their spoken words. This is reflected in the *Tao Te Ching* of Lao Tsu (Needleman, 1989):

> The highest good is like water
> Water gives life to the ten thousand things
>   and does not strive.
> It flows in places rejected and so is like the Tao.
> In dwelling, be close to the land.
> In meditation, go deep into the heart.
> In dealing with others, be gentle and kind.
> In speech, be true.
> In ruling, be just.
> In daily life, be competent.
> In action, be aware of the time and the season.
> No fight: No blame. (p. 10)

The word of life is also expressed in the Hebrew anthropomorphism *Ruach Yahweh* (the breath of God). The Johannine

Christology (1:14) expresses the presence of the deity: "The word was made flesh . . . full of grace and truth" (*Jerusalem Bible* [New Testament], 1966, p. 114). The prophecy in 2 Nephi (chap. 29,2) of the Book of Mormon (1961) explains the role of the word: "I will remember your seed, and that the words of your seed should proceed out of my mouth unto your seed; and my word shall *hiss forth* unto the ends of the earth for a standard unto my people" (p. 100, emphasis added). The theological understanding of breath and word is also found in the centrality of breathing in Zen Buddhism and the awareness of Prana in Yoga. In *The Way of Zen* Alan Watts (1957) writes:

> Because Zen does not involve an ultimate dualism between the controller and the controlled, the mind and the body, the spiritual and the material, there is always a certain "physiological" aspect to its techniques. . . . Great importance is attached to the way of breathing. Not only is breathing one of the two fundamental rhythms of the body; it is also the process in which control and spontaneity, voluntary and involuntary action, find their most obvious identity. Long before the origins of the Zen school, both Indian Yoga and Chinese Taoism practiced "watching the breath" with a view toward letting it (not forcing it) become as slow and silent as possible. . . . Grasping air with the lungs goes hand in hand with grasping at life. (pp. 197–198)

The spoken words about the source of life—this grasping at life—has been evident in the oral tradition of religious communities long before the canon of the written text was promulgated. Sophia and Gaia, Ruach Yahweh and the Christ, El Shadai and Zeus, spirit, wind, and water: these were living and spoken texts long before they became written texts. The religious, spiritual, and mystical experiences of human culture have been textualized in the canons of faith and codes of behavior morality. Tragically, modern religious texts have concretized the hiss, the ruach, and the prana. This process led to an educational approach in premodern societies that enshrined the theological text as the curriculum. Premodern cultures and tribal communities zealously guarded their denominational creeds, canons, and rituals. The young were initiated into the tribal religious practices. The theological text, which was the formal code of religion whether written on scrolls or passed down through oral tradition, was the primary curriculum for schooling and cultural initiation.

Challenges to the official text resulted in schisms, reformations, and excommunications throughout the ages. New theological texts were promulgated as the primary curriculum for the splinter community. This premodern perspective of the theological text as the curriculum provided security and continuity for ancient societies. This same security makes a return to premodern structures appealing in the twentieth century for those who believe that the only way out of the dilemma of modernity is to retreat to a form of schooling that imposes denominational religion and dominant cultural values through the school curriculum. Religious education becomes indoctrination and initiation from this premodern perspective.

Of course, since the eighteenth century the modern world has increasingly ignored this phenomenon and found its security and salvation in scientific positivism and technology rather than traditional religious values. The Enlightenment created a new educational paradigm that understood curriculum as a technological text. This paradigm was as much a proposal to advance society into enlightened thinking as it was a reaction against the authoritarian theology of the Middle Ages. Science replaced religion as the voice of authority on the mysteries of the universe. The ecological, emotional, and sociological dilemmas brought on by the Enlightenment project and the science of modernity require that we not return to another form of premodern authoritarian theology, but rather that we create a revisionary curriculum for the postmodern era that includes theology. The preceding discussion can be summarized in the three modes of analysis in the accompanying matrix.

While not exhaustive, the matrix attempts to delineate some of the major distinctions between premodernity, modernity, and postmodernity in issues related to curriculum, theology, and education. Postmodernity seeks to respond to the worldviews of premodernity and modernity as outlined above. In particular, the concept of predetermined texts as the core cur-

THEOLOGY AS CURRICULUM TEXT	CURRICULUM AS TECHNOLOGICAL TEXT	CURRICULUM AS THEOLOGICAL TEXT
PREMODERN	MODERN	POSTMODERN
DENOMINATIONAL	SECULAR	ECUMENICAL
TRANSCENDENT	ANTHROPOCENTRIC	ANTHROPOMORPHIC
AUTOCRATIC	INDIVIDUALISTIC	COMMUNITARIAN
MYTHOLOGICAL	TECHNOLOGICAL	ECOLOGICAL
DEPENDENT	INDEPENDENT	INTERDEPENDENT
PAST TRADITION	PRESENT EVENT	FUTURE HOPE
METANARRATIVE	CARTESIAN DUALISM	INTEGRATED WHOLE
DOGMATIC	SCIENTIFIC	SPIRITUAL
FUNDAMENTALISM	POSITIVISM	PROCESS PHILOSOPHY
"GOD IS ABOVE"	"GOD IS DEAD"	"GOD IS AHEAD"
FAITH IN THE CANON	FAITH IN HUMANITY	FAITH SEEKING WISDOM
LITERACY/READING AS COMPREHENSION	LITERACY/READING AS DECODING	LITERACY/READING AS RUMINATING
CULTURAL LITERACY	FUNCTIONAL LITERACY	CRITICAL LITERACY
NATURAL LAW	BEHAVIORAL GOALS	CURRERE

riculum has met with intense debate in the educational
community since the publication of E. D. Hirsch's (1987) *Cultural
Literacy* and William Bennett's (1987, 1988) *James Madison School.*
The current debate over reform proposals in education is similar
to the reaction to the dependence on inflexible official texts in
some religious sects. For example, the Gnostic *Testimony of Truth*
(IX 3:29, 6–25) begins with a bitter polemic against the scribes of
the law who have perverted the light of truth. *The Testimony of
Truth* is a homiletic that contends that undefilement belongs to
those of the light:

> I will speak to those who know to hear not with the ears of
> the body but with the ears of the mind. For many have
> sought after the truth and have not been able to find it;

because there has taken hold of them the old leaven of the
Pharisees and the scribes of the Law. (Robinson, 1977, pp.
406–407)

In Christian Scriptures, Jesus also condemns the scribes
and pharisees who have become bound by the written code and
are unable to be self-reflective. He speaks seven woes in
Matthew's Gospel (23:29–34):

Alas for you, scribes and pharisees, you hypocrites! You
who build the sepulchers of the prophets and decorate the
tombs of holy men, saying, "we would never have joined
in shedding the blood of prophets, had we lived in our
fathers' day." So! Your own evidence tells against
you! . . . Serpents, brood of vipers, how can you escape
being condemned to hell? That is why I am sending you
prophets and teachers. (*Jerusalem Bible* [New Testament],
1966, p. 36)

It is significant to note here that prophets and teachers are sent to
challenge the hypocrisy of the pharisees, who, like teachers of
the law in modern schooling, have abandoned a vision of the
spirit infusing education. Teachers in postmodern schools have
the opportunity to be prophets and create a fresh new vision of
curriculum as theological text.

As premodern theological texts concretized their vision,
the path to wisdom and holiness was narrowed. In the *Koran* this
is clearly articulated in the opening words:

In the name of Allah, the Beneficent, the Merciful. All
praise is due to Allah, the Lord of the worlds. . . . Thee do
we serve, and thee do we beseech for help. Keep us on the
right path. The path of those upon whom thou hast
bestowed favors. Not the path of those upon whom thy
wrath is brought down, nor of those who go astray.
(Shakir, 1990, p. 1)

Additionally, in some traditions not one word of the text
may be altered as seen in the Revelation of John (22:18–20) in
Christian Scriptures: "I warn everyone who hears the words of
the prophecy of this book: If anyone adds anything to them, God
will add to him the plagues described in this book. And if
anyone takes away words from this book of prophecy, God will

take away the tree of life in the holy city described in this book" (*Jerusalem Bible* [New Testament], 1966, p. 339). These two examples create an image that condemns to darkness and death those outside the text. The text becomes truth incarnate, and thus the curriculum of initiation for future generations.

Despite the warnings in these texts, we must remember that prophecy begins with revelation, and mysticism is ignited by an encounter with wisdom, beauty, or the holy. The postmodern curriculum as theological text is rooted in such an experience. Paul Ricoeur (1981) locates the birth of the text in the oral tradition and spoken word:

> The difference between the act of reading and the act of dialogue confirms our hypothesis that writing is a realization comparable and parallel to speech, a realization which takes the place of it and, as it were, intercepts it. Hence we could say that what comes to writing is discourse as intention-to-say and that writing is a direct inscription of this intention, even if, historically and psychologically, writing began with the graphic transcription of the signs of speech. This emancipation of writing, which places the latter at the site of speech, is the birth of the text. (p. 147)

The rebirth of theology in contemporary curriculum research is embedded in the spirituality, religious myth, and oral rituals—the *Ruach Ephphatha* (the spoken breath)—of communities and cultures that experience divine revelation, cosmological harmony, and the journey toward wisdom. Exegetes have used the principles of hermeneutics, the process of interpretation, to uncover the layers of religious experience in these theological texts. The hermeneutical process produces what Ricoeur (1981) calls "a double eclipse of the reader and writer" (p. 147). It replaces the relation of dialogue, which directly connects the voice of one to the hearing of another. (We will examine hermeneutics in detail in chapter five.)

Unfortunately, the theological texts have been used by religious fundamentalists, cult leaders, gurus, and other preservers of unexamined truth to further eliminate this dialogue. The theological text has been converted into the rigid curriculum that we have been warned about: a voiceless, breathless prescription for a code of behavior to reach nirvana, perfection, salvation, and eschatological bliss by those who would propose their religion as *the* curriculum in an appeal to premodern worldviews. Joseph Campbell complained about this problem in an interview with Bill Moyers in *The Power of Myth* (1988, pp. 91–121).

The model of the theological text as a religious curriculum must be inverted if it is to be appropriate for the postmodern era. This paradigm has forced our society into a perverse and untenable choice: eliminate religion from the public schools—as if students and teachers could remove their metaphysical souls as one would remove their hat before entering the classroom—or impose a state-sanctioned orthodoxy on the schools—as if religious education could be reduced to a melting pot formula for universal salvation. There is an alternative in postmodern curriculum scholarship. However, the alternative becomes recognizable only once the premodern paradigm of the theological text as curriculum is critiqued for having led the global community into a tragic stalemate characterized by contemporary versions of inquisitions, crusades, witch hunts, and assassination contracts. Iranian Ayatollah Khomeini's call for the murder of Salmon Rushdie (1989), the author of *The Satanic Verses*, is an obvious example. The dogmatism of the model of the theological text as curriculum will lead only to further ideological conflagration.

Likewise, the modern technological approach to curriculum development will continue to avoid the questions of morality, spirituality, and theology as essential elements of schooling because these issues are considered outside the modern scientific parameters of the schools. This stalemate requires that we invert the syllogism and reexplore the theological dialogue. Thus, revisionary postmodern scholars propose a model of curriculum as theological text where the educational enterprise will include the metaphysical dialogue. In this proposal self-reflection, intuition, nonrational discourse, nonlinear teaching methodologies, meditation, and wisdom are all encouraged and nurtured in the curriculum. Only in this context will T. S. Eliot's probing question to modernity, "Where is the Wisdom we have lost in knowledge?" become intelligible.

The seeds of the current debates about religion and education in the United States can be found in the curricular debates in the 1840s between Horace Mann, the first state superintendent of education in Massachusetts, and Orestes Brownson, Catholic publisher of the Boston Quarterly Review. Horace Mann's common schools included a common political creed and a common morality based on nonsectarian religion. Mann (1848) explains his position:

> In this age of the world, it seems to me that no student of history, or observer of mankind, can be hostile to the precepts and the doctrines of the Christian religion, or opposed to any institutions which expound and exemplify them. (p. 102)

The common school movement prevailed in the United States in the 1800s, but the Catholic minority immigrants vehemently opposed Mann and proposed instead publicly funded sectarian schools. Orestes Brownson argued with the minority that nonsectarian Christianity, as put into practice in the common schools, was really nondenominational Protestantism. Brownson (1839) explains: "Education, then, must be religious and . . . political. Neither religion nor politics can be excluded. Indeed, all education that is worth anything is either religious or political and fits us for discharging our duties either as simple human beings or as members of society" (p. 280). Brownson established the argument that the exclusion of religion and politics would make education worthless, but the inclusion would make education offensive to the minority. He continued:

> [Mann's] board assure[s] us Christianity shall be insisted on so far, and only so far, as it is common to all sects. This, if it mean anything, means nothing at all. All who attempt to proceed on the principle here laid down will find their Christianity ending in nothingness. Much may be taught in general, but nothing in particular. No sect will be satisfied; all sects will be dissatisfied. (pp. 280–281)

Despite Brownson's logic and a vocal Catholic protest, Horace Mann's common schools became the norm. The Catholic minority reacted by establishing a parochial school system that expanded dramatically from the 1840s to the 1960s, reaching a peak of over 12,000 schools and 7 million students. However, the Catholic school system has experienced a decline since the 1960s. Some would attribute this phenomenon to the fact that Catholics moved into the mainstream American culture, John F. Kennedy was the first Catholic elected president, the Supreme Court ruled against prayer and Bible readings in the public schools and thus made public schools less threatening to Catholics, and the Vatican Council II opened Catholicism to new relationships with the modern world. It is also interesting to note that Protestants who once condemned Catholics for establishing separatist schools steadily began opening parochial schools from the 1960s to the 1990s. Protestant Christian schools have flourished while Catholic schools have declined. While much has been written about this phenomenon (see, for example, O'Gorman, 1967; Beutow, 1988), our interest here is in the direction of religious schools in the 1990s in relation to postmodern curriculum.

Andrew Greeley's (1992) proposal for the reform of Catholic schools is an example of the frustration of some with the closing of parochial schools. Andrew Greeley's proposal appeals to many reform-weary lay leaders who have struggled to resolve the dilemmas facing parochial schools only to be thwarted by a premodern authoritarian clerical bureaucracy. His proposal also appeals to many reform-weary bishops and pastors who have struggled to provide funding to improve or expand parochial education only to be blackmailed by self-serving lay contributors committed to modern public and private school models. Andrew Greeley's solution is the laicization of Catholic education. Some educational leaders who are frustrated with the status quo will defend this proposal as an opportunity to break with authoritarian structures of the past. Others who value strong pastoral leadership in a premodern spirit will be horrified by the prospect of secularization of the schools.

Laicization of parochial schools has already been implemented in some parts of the United States where consolidation, declining revenues, dwindling enrollments, and the loss of religious teachers in the schools reached a peak a decade ago. The experiment with laicization was viewed by some as a miserable failure. Only time will tell if postmodern structures emerge or if a reactionary return to premodern visions of parochial education evolves. Andrew Greely's proposal offers several insights into the dilemmas of the model of curriculum as theological text for the postmodern era for both parochial schools and public schools.

First, there has been a loss of identity in parochial schools brought on by the ravages of modernity. Having moved out of the cultural ghettos of the 1800s and into mainstream American culture by the 1960s, many religious minorities in contemporary society have become immersed in the ideology of modernity. While the messages of materialistic self-gratification, militaristic competitiveness, rampant overconsumption, and pandering paternalism pervade the media and the marketplace in an orgy of technological splendor, the subtler influences of modernity on the religious psyche have been ignored. The language of popular culture in modern society says as much about the human spirit as it does about material objects: "terminate," "slash and burn," "random acts of senseless violence," "leveraged buyout," "hostile takeover," "nuke," and so forth.

Greeley's assertion that there can be laicization of parochial schools without further secularization assumes that society has somehow transcended these ravages of modernity. However, the problem still exists that there is a numbness that pervades our entire culture. William Faulkner (1950) identified this phenomenon when he wrote in his speech of acceptance upon the award of the Nobel Prize for Literature that the tragedy of modern society is a general and universal physical fear so long sustained that we can even bear it. Walker Percy (1960) has also addressed this issue through his characters, who struggle against the cultural numbness of modern society and seek to emancipate the alienated self. Binx Bolling in Percy's *The Moviegoer* typifies the malaise that has overtaken the spirit of the individual and deadened the desire to search for meaning and wisdom. Binx is, in effect, hypnotized by the ideology of modernity.

Søren Kierkegaard (1849) in *The Sickness unto Death* spoke to this hypnotic state when he wrote that the specific character of despair is the fact that it is unaware of being despair. Postmodern education no longer suppresses the despair. The impact of hopelessness on society, which also permeates the educational milieu in the schools, is integral to postmodern curricular revisions. As long as educators continue to dicker over bureaucratic issues like clericalism versus laicization and centralization versus site-based management, parochial, public, and private schools will all remain moribund.

All educational institutions must address the despair, the malaise, and the fear that has overtaken the human community as the result of oppressive and destructive modern structures. Contemporary curriculum scholars probe the question of what good it will do for any school system to survive if spiritual disintegration and despair continue unabated. Like Percy's Binx Bolling, curriculum development in the postmodern era undertakes the search for something more important; and this search includes the attempt to envision an appropriate theological education for postmodern schooling that will help society to transcend this fear and malaise.

Second, the impact of modernity discourages support for theological self-reflection by deemphasizing, for example, autobiography, ethnography, phenomenology, spirituality, mystical traditions, ecumenism, and narrative research. This is coupled with zealous preference for theological foundations through emphasis on, for example, systematics, textual criticism, canonicity, and formal catechesis. This preference actually emerges from cultural and individual isolationism. Modernity has encouraged the isolation of the individual, frozen in quantifiable time and space, unable to establish personal relationships, unable to remember past experiences, and incapable of affecting the future course of global events. A modern intelligentsia that disparages self-understanding is no better than premodern fundamentalists who denigrate rigorous intellectual investigation. A constructive postmodern curriculum, however, integrates both theology and self-reflection. While the intelligentsia and the fundamentalists battle for religious superiority like the scribes and pharisees described above, society wallows in cultural malaise. In commenting on the unresolvable conflict between individual conscience and state-sanctioned orthodoxy, Stephen Arons calls for the complete separation of school and state. Arons (1983) writes:

Without a complete separation of school and state, the governing process of American schooling has been increasingly undermined by unresolvable value conflict, and individual freedom of belief, expression, and political participation have been hobbled. Schooling has become a major means of transmitting culture. When government imposes the content of schooling it becomes the same deadening agent of repression from which the framers of the Constitution sought to free themselves. (p. 189)

Critics characterize Arons' position as an adventure in monopolis because the realm of freedom is confined to a private sector threatened by a monopolistic, totalizing public sphere. Both Stephen Arons and Andrew Greeley are theoretically blinded by a crude social Darwinism that promotes individual freedom in lieu of a genuine sociopolitical theory or a postmodern educational theology. Arons' critics refuse to concede the public educational struggle for emancipatory education to a premodern denominational religious culture (Whitson, 1988a). Likewise, postmodern scholars refuse to concede the theological curriculum struggle for spiritually emancipatory education to those entrenched in modernity and dependent upon oppressive cultural structures. They also refuse to concede the debate to premodern reactionaries who ignore ecumenical developments. Stephen Arons and Andrew Greeley remind us of the untenable alternative facing educators today: a premodern, insensitive autocracy (which they abhor) or a modern, ineffective bureaucracy (which they unconsciously perpetuate). A postmodern curriculum development theory rooted in theological self-reflection is the only viable alternative to this stalemate.

The postmodern schooling debate in the 1990s is moving away from bureaucratic solutions and shifting to a new vision rooted in spiritual liberation. Reorganizing responsibility and authority does not address the theological issue of how to confront cultural malaise, despair, and fear in modern American society. In order to appropriately address these important issues, a reconceptualization of religious education that includes a synthesis of community models of education is emerging. For some parochial schools this would reflect the best features of community-based models like *To Teach as Jesus Did* (NCCB,

1972). For public schools this would reflect the empowerment models found in programs like the Dade County Florida Public Schools (Dreyfuss et al., 1992) or the Windham Southeast District in Vermont (James et al., 1992). Postmodern schooling will reject the negative features of bureaucratic reform structures of any school system and promote the spirit of postmodernism found in emerging models of education globally. The goal is to move the parochial school debate beyond the structural issues such as vouchers, laicization, and funding and move the public school debate beyond the legal issues related to separation of church and state and site-based management. The postmodern vision for curriculum and schooling includes, but is not limited to, the following three elements.

First, community cooperation rather than corporate competition will characterize the postmodern school. The corporate business model that lay boards impose on public, parochial, and private schools will perpetuate the destructive competitive atmosphere that exists in our contemporary American society. This is certainly true of lay boards in public education, where bureaucratic gridlock has reached a peak in the 1990s. The postmodern school is a place where relations between people are viewed primarily in cooperative terms and not in coercive business terms. Peter Sola (1989) contends that the growing alliance between business and education is embedded in the free enterprise philosophy of corporate capitalist institutions. He contends that during the era of local control of schools in the early 1800s, school boards reflected the community. However, since the mid-1800s there has been a radical change in the social composition of school boards. Sola (1989) writes:

> By the end of the progressive era, school boards consisted mainly of business persons and professionals and seldom of teachers, blue collar workers, or women. If . . . school boards represent largely business and professional classes, and if the school administrative staff largely keeps their collective eye on "the bottom line," who is ensuring that schools are performing their primary tasks? (p. 78)

Postmodern curriculum research challenges the structures of modernity that are reflected in the composition and ideology of school boards.

Additionally, postmodern curriculum research also promotes other important elements of schooling, including the search for wisdom through theological experiences, the creation of cooperative and ecologically sustainable learning environments, and the commitment to reverent, democratic, and just community models of schooling. Schooling should not serve the interests of economic competition and corporate greed. The postmodern educational community is moving beyond this modern phenomenon identified by Sola (1989) when he writes: "The business of America is developing educational policy for business. The business of American education has really become inseparable from American business" (p. 81).

The Reconceptualization in curriculum theory challenges educators to no longer view the world as being at the service of the competitive, mechanistic, and materialistic self-interests of business and individuals. Schools are viewed as dynamic communities committed to discovery learning, theological inquiry, autobiographical analysis, ecological sustainability, justice, compassion, and ecumenism. Of course, this is demonstrated not simply by promulgating a district mission statement that reflects these values but rather by enhancing the quality of cooperative relationships embedded in the local community.

Second, a holistic process perspective rather than reductionism will permeate the postmodern curriculum and the theological milieu. Theologians such as Karl Rahner, Carl Peter, and Jurgen Moltmann have established a foundation for a renewed understanding of the future. This theology, called proleptic eschatology because the future is viewed as that which brings to completion what has already been set in motion, replaces the modern concept of time that denies the future and promotes immediate self-gratification. It also replaces the fundamentalist's futuristic view, in which salvation is disconnected from the present and experienced only after death. These are the two predominant visions of the future that the American public brings to schools from popular culture, but neither informs postmodern curriculum development models.

Curriculum development in the postmodern era understands that the past and the future are integral to a self-reflective spirituality. As we discussed in chapter two, history is not taught as a series of events on a linear timeline to be memorized. Rather, history is an unfolding story in which each student is an active participant in shaping the meaning of events and in constructing the future course of global communities. This anticipatory view of history, which many scholars contend is urgently needed to justly address global crises, is accessible through postmodern theology. This concept will be explored further in chapter thirteen.

Third, postmodern schooling provides a multilayered, interdisciplinary curriculum that integrates spirituality and theology into every dimension of the educational process. In the 1990s it is no longer assumed by curriculum scholars that the best way to study a problem, especially with an eye toward coming up with a solution, is to do so in terms of one of the traditional disciplines, subdisciplines, or courses. A new understanding of knowledge in conjunction with a vision of interdependence, spirituality, and wisdom rather than the values of the modern engineer, scientist, and economist is emerging. The curriculum as a theological text provides expanded opportunities for students and teachers to explore alternative solutions to the ecological, health, and economic problems of the world today. The traditional behavioral-technical curriculum of the public school system, which many private school boards and administrators are so apt to imitate, is seen as outmoded and inappropriate for all school systems. It is thus considered foolhardy to emulate this model in the development of postmodern curriculum. Many religious schools, for example, are evolving into clones of public and private institutions that happen to teach a few religion courses. Likewise, many public schools and universities smugly believe that the addition of a course in the Bible as literature, a degree program in comparative religion, or a moment of silence at graduation ceremonies will fully address the theological question in the curriculum. These views are severely problematic. A vision of a new model that integrates spirituality and theology throughout the school curriculum and community is the alternative that is now being proposed to address the crises of the postmodern world.

Because the very nature of postmodern schooling is eclectic, ecumenical, and inclusive, the first and most important lesson to be derived from this chapter on theology and education is that postmodern schooling will *not* simply add a new course in theology to the curriculum in order to pacify religious interest groups. Rather, the nature of schooling will change to reflect postmodern values. Although there is not a monolithic master plan for including religious education in postmodern schools, the discussion of curriculum as theological text has presented insights into the evolving milieu proposed for postmodern schooling in the 1990s, which is understood as reverent, reflective, inclusive, cooperative, just, holistic, and caring.

Creating a reflective environment in schools is not dependent upon Supreme Court decisions. It flows out of school architecture, school schedules, teacher attitudes, and classroom environments that encourage flexibility, critical literacy, ethics, autobiography, ecumenism, global interdependence, ecological sustainability, narrative inquiry, and other postmodern values. Beginning in the earliest years of schooling and continuing throughout the educational process, students should be given time and space during the day, within academic organizations, and throughout academic experiences to question, reflect, investigate, meditate, and ponder. Leisurely and thought provoking visits to museums, nature trails, and local historical sights will be integral to the curriculum. Reflective dialogue with grandparents, younger students, multicultural professionals, community activists, politicians, and religious leaders will be regular occurrences. Active community involvement in environmental projects, health and social services, and ethnic preservation will become a priority. The borders between the school and the community in the postmodern curriculum will be dissolved, and thus, the *quality* of reverent relationships will replace the *quantity* of correct answers on tests as the focus of education. Curriculum theorists contend that in this environment prayer does not need to be mandated or prohibited, for it will flow from within the individual's experiences of life. This is one postmodern response to the dilemma of prayer and religion in the curriculum. In *Exiles from Eden: Religion and the Academic Vocation in America*, Mark R. Schwehn writes that achieving community at the end of modernity and the beginning of postmodernity means connecting to virtues and experiences that have traditionally been thought to be spiritual. In a review of this book, Yvonna Lincoln (1994), following Schwehn, points out that these spiritual values are equally essential to "the process of genuine learning (and therefore meaningful teaching). Those virtues—faith, humility (piety), charity, self-denial, and friendship—tend to be both social virtues and those that sustain genuine communities" (p. 36). Schwehn argues that education must be attentive to these virtues or all attempts at internal reformation will prove ultimately useless.

Creating a cooperative learning environment in schools is not dependent upon classroom lesson plans. Cooperation will evolve only after a dramatic change takes place in the concept of schooling itself. Empowering teachers to cooperate in the development of an interdisciplinary curriculum that is not limited to compartmentalized blocks of time is one important first step. Encouraging student cooperation in the development of seminar-style classes where circles and centers replace rows of desks is another step. Laboratories, interviews, multisensory projects, seminars, workshops, playshops, and field experiences involving groups of students, teachers, and other community members will become the norm rather than the exception. Socratic dialogue that seeks understanding, respect, and synthesis rather than predetermined answers will be the hallmark of the postmodern theological curriculum.

Creating stimulating learning environments is not dependent on the latest technology. Teachers do not need to be actors, barkers, magicians, or technicians to interest young people in education. Teachers and parents are encouraged to become mentors and guides who will inspire students to seek wisdom and understanding as part of a community of learners. In postmodern schooling teachers, administrators, and parents will recognize that they are not experts with all the answers but fellow travelers on the lifelong journey of learning. T. S. Eliot (1971) answered his question "Where is the wisdom we have lost in knowledge?" in his poem "Little Gidding":

We shall not cease from exploration
And the end of all our exploring
Will be to arrive where we started
And know the place for the first time.
Through the unknown, remembered gate
When the last of earth left to discover
Is that which was the beginning;
At the source of the longest river
The voice of the hidden waterfall
And the children in the apple-tree
Not known, because not looked for
But heard, half-heard, in the stillness
Between two waves of the sea.
Quick now, here, now, always —
A condition of complete simplicity
(Costing not less than everything)
And all shall be well and
All manner of thing shall be well
When the tongues of flame are in-folded
Into the crowned knot of fire
And the fire and the rose are one.

(p. 145)

If the theological curriculum is the active process of seeking, running, and ruminating, then the evolution of postmodern schooling will provide the milieu where spirituality, mystery, intuition, poetry, ethics, and religious sensibilities can flourish. Contemporary scholars conclude that the time of the usefulness of the modern bureaucratic model of curriculum development has ended. Public, private, parochial, apprenticeship, and home schooling are all challenged to transcend this model by contemporary curriculum scholars. It is time to return to that place where we started and know the place for the very first time as we envision curriculum development in the postmodern era.

This now brings us to the end of part one. We have explored postmodern curriculum development as a field of study with particular emphasis on the meaning of postmodernism, historical analysis, the Reconceptualization, and theology. Of course, there are many other ways of framing curriculum development in the postmodern era, and part two will introduce the scholarship of various postmodern curriculum discourses that are emerging in the 1990s. The chapters in part two will each provide a short introduction to these postmodern curriculum discourses in order to acquaint students and curriculum specialists with the scope of the postmodern curriculum. However, it must be remembered that the eclectic, aesthetic, ironic, playful, linguistic, social, theological, and political dimensions of postmodernism will necessitate that the short vignettes in part two serve as an introductory guide to postmodern curriculum and not a definitive normative outline. The theological process challenges educators to explore postmodern curriculum in a way that gives possibility to the living word, in all its mystery, ambiguity, and complexity. The theological curriculum leads us directly into this exploration, sometimes called hermeneutics, which begins our focus on contemporary curriculum development paradigms in the next chapter.

PART TWO

Contemporary Curriculum Development Paradigms

CHAPTER FIVE

The Hermeneutic Circle and Postmodern Community

Curriculum development in the postmodern era includes an approach to understanding the meaning of texts, language, relationships, historical artifacts, and schooling called hermeneutics. Many scholars, for example Roy J. Howard (1982), describe hermeneutics as the art of interpretation. Several forms of interpretive inquiry in educational research explore such understanding: phenomenology, critical theory, semiotics, poststructuralism, heuristics, autobiography, aesthetics, and ethnography. Edmund C. Short (1991) has edited an excellent collection of essays that explore these forms of curriculum inquiry. Without denying the uniqueness and importance of each of these approaches to understanding postmodern curriculum development, this chapter will introduce interpretive inquiry from the perspective of hermeneutics. Later chapters will return to the other forms of curriculum inquiry.

David Jardine (1992) writes: "The returning of life to its original difficulty is a returning of the possibility of the living Word. It is a return to the essential generativity of human life, a sense of life in which there is always something left to say, with all the difficulty, risk, and ambiguity that such generativity entails. Hermeneutic inquiry is thus concerned with the ambiguous nature of life itself" (p. 119). Postmodern curriculum inquiry is also concerned with the ambiguous and ironic dimensions of education: an unexpected question triggers an exciting and provocative tangent; the changing moods and emotions of individuals create a unique and often perplexing life-world in classrooms; the same methodology is not always successful with every group of students; atmospheric changes in the weather alter the atmosphere of the school. Teachers cannot predict the ambiguous and ironic nature of life itself, especially in the classroom, and postmodern understandings of hermeneutics as an investigation into the ambiguous nature of being and knowledge now inform and enrich contemporary curriculum paradigms. Thus, along with David G. Smith (1991), I will argue that all discourses about postmodernism are interpretive and hermeneutic endeavors. Two important scholars, Hans-Georg Gadamer and Jacques Derrida (1989), have debated this point in the book *Dialogue and Deconstructionism*, and some of their concerns will be part of our discussion in this chapter.

Before addressing postmodern hermeneutics, this chapter will begin with an overview of the historical understandings of hermeneutics and the contemporary philosophical discourses on hermeneutics. This overview will seem complex and esoteric to those unfamiliar with hermeneutics. Additionally, the meaning of knowledge and interpretation itself is disputed by various scholars, making the discourse about hermeneutics appear contradictory at times. However, this introduction is necessary in order to make the proposals for understanding postmodern curriculum development as a "hermeneutic circle" later in this chapter more comprehensible.

Hermeneutics has a history of serious scholarship in biblical interpretation and nineteenth-century philosophical attempts to deal with the problem of how we understand the complex actions of human beings. Contemporary hermeneutics, as derived from the phenomenological philosophers Martin Heidegger and Edmund Husserl, acknowledges that discourse is an essential constituent element of textual understanding. Understanding sets free what is hidden from view by layers of tradition, prejudice, and even conscious evasion. While these prejudices must be acknowledged as a starting point for hermeneutic inquiry for Hans-Georg Gadamer, hermeneutic interpretation, for Heidegger, was moving toward understanding as emancipation from tradition, prejudice, and evasion.

Hermeneutics, in its broadest formulation, is the theory of interpreting oral traditions, verbal communications, and aesthetic products. Aristotle used hermeneutics in the title of one of his works (*Peri Hermenia*), and there was a school of interpretation in ancient Alexandria. In early Christian communities hermeneutics referred to the criteria for textual interpretation in order to establish normative religious and legal community practices. The Greek *Hermeneuenin* (to interpret) referred to Hermes, the winged messenger of the Greek gods, who explained the decisions of the gods to other gods and to mortal humans. Hermes conveyed messages of both clarity and ambiguity. Hilly Bernard (1994) explains:

> Perhaps this [clarity and ambiguity] was a deliberate contrivance on the part of the heavenly rulers, an act attempting a representation of the complexity of language, in order to keep their subordinates in a state of humble submission. The hermeneutic tradition confronts the issue of complexity, ambiguity, interpretation, intentionality, and meaning, and asserts the inescapable subjective in human inquiry. As such, it serves as a rejection of the scientific philosophy and its premise of an objective reality "out there" to be discovered using a prescribed methodology. This mono-methodological approach of science stresses causal relationships, while the quest of the hermeneuticist is the development of theories of understanding through the interpretation of language. (p. 10)

Bernard's concise summary of hermeneutic inquiry is consistent with the approach to postmodern interpretation in many contemporary curriculum discourses.

Hermes, in addition to explaining and interpreting the messages of the gods, was also a trickster. Postmodernists revel in the irony that the official messenger of the gods was also a cunning deceiver! This reminds us that layers of meaning, prejudice, and intention surround all curricular artifacts, thus necessitating a hermeneutical study to expose not only the irony of deception but also the implications of historical analysis. Historical, textual, artistic, and autobiographical interpretation in the postmodern era all acknowledge this double-edged dimension of clarity and ambiguity in hermeneutics. However, unlike modern empiricists who demand unbiased certainty and scientific proof, postmodern scholars celebrate the irony of interpretation by recognizing that ambiguity is integral to the human condition and the natural world. Postmodern hermeneutics affirms the primacy of subjective understanding over objective knowledge and conceives of understanding as an ontological (study of being) problem rather than an epistemological (study of knowledge) problem. Therefore, Hermes the messenger and deceiver becomes the model par excellence of interpretation in the postmodern era.

Hermeneutic inquiry was almost exclusively empirical prior to the nineteenth century. As a science of interpretation, traditional hermeneutics was originally concerned with understanding religious texts, canonical scriptures, and non-canonical writings within their own historical, cultural, and social milieu. The difficulty of such interpretive tasks is immense, postmodernists would contend impossible, because the worldview of contemporary societies cannot replicate ancient cosomologies and subjectivities in which the original text was produced. Prior to this postmodern understanding, hermeneutics represented a concern for the process of defining the meaning of the text, especially normative religious texts, and the development of the criteria for authoritative text interpretation.

Early Greek and Jewish thinkers were concerned with appropriate interpretation of the Torah, the prophets, and the wisdom literature of the Hebrew Scriptures. The allegorical method was employed to understand linguistic and grammatical components of scriptural texts to appropriate this meaning within the wider spiritual framework of the time. Werner Jeanrond (1988) explains: "Philo of Alexandria united the Jewish and Greek hermeneutical traditions and developed the thesis that an interpretation should disclose the text's spiritual sense on the basis of an explanation of the text's literal sense" (p. 462). This concept of hermeneutics expanded with the influence of Christian interpreters who sought to confirm their belief in salvation in Jesus Christ. Hebrew Scriptures were interpreted in the light of the Christian faith in Jesus, arguing that the promises to Israel were fulfilled. The Christian hermeneut, Origen, emphasized the need for text interpretation in both the historical-grammatical (literal) sense and the spiritual sense so as to provide access and understanding for every interpreter of sacred writings. Following Origen, Augustine developed his philosophy of language, where the "sign" points to the "thing," a concept that is understood differently by postmodern semioticians.

Semiotics, the study of the meaning of language and the relationship between signs, symbols, and historical representation, critiques hidden assumptions, uncovers excluded meanings, and deconstructs linguistic interpretations. Both texts and contexts, agents and objects of meaning, social structures and forces, and their complex interrelationships together constitute the irreducible object of semiotic analysis. Robert Hodge and Gunter Kress (1988) explain:

> The term "semiotics" is relatively new for many people, and a number of conceptual difficulties continue to attach to its use. Semiotics has been defined as "the science of the life of signs in society" (Saussure 1974). So defined it has a scope which is breathtaking in its simplicity and in its comprehensiveness. . . . Semiotics offers the promise of a systematic, comprehensive and coherent study of communications phenomena as a whole, not just instances of it. . . . "Mainstream semiotics" emphasizes structures and codes, at the expense of functions of social uses of semiotic systems. . . . It stresses system and product, rather than speakers and writers or other participants in semiotic activity as connected and inter*acting* in a variety of ways in concrete social contexts. It [traditional semiotics] attributes power to meaning, instead of meaning to power. It dissolves boundaries within the field of semiotics, but tacitly accepts an impenetrable wall cutting off semiosis from society, and semiotics from social and political thought. Many . . . have rejected semiotics because of such objections. (pp. 1–2)

Hodge and Kress do not reject semiotics but offer an approach to interpretation that addresses the problem of social meaning as well as ways that meaning is constituted. Bowers and Flinders (1990) call this critical semiotics, "where attention is given to cultural conventions or codes, that in turn, generate the signs that serve as the basic unit of communication" (p. 22). Bowers and Flinders draw on a number of areas of inquiry concerned with different aspects of the culture-language-thought connection that are related to the judgments that teachers face as they attempt to direct and orchestrate communication in the classroom. Bowers and Flinders (1990) conclude: "In one sense, these processes, which constitute the symbolic medium of the classroom that teachers and students must continually interpret and give meaning to, are interrelated" (p. 23).

In this sense, semiotics, like hermeneutics, is concerned with interpretation of texts, contexts, or artifacts. It provides the possibility of analysis of contemporary social problems and the possibility of explaining the processes and structures through which meaning is constituted. This emerging understanding of critical semiotics challenges Augustine's literal meaning of signs. In postmodern semiotics the "sign" may point to nothing or it may point to many "things" simultaneously, and in every case the culture-language-thought interrelationship must be interpreted. Additionally, the meaning of power and the processes through which meaning is constructed are becoming the focus of semiotic as well as hermeneutic analysis in the postmodern era. Let us now return to our investigation of the development of hermeneutics.

Like Augustine, Thomas Aquinas, author of the *Summa Theologiae*, emphasized the literal sense of language. Aquinas became the definitive authority on textual interpretation, and since the thirteenth century, Aquinas was presumed to support the literal interpretation as the accurate bearer of truth. Jeanrond (1988), echoing centuries of Thomistic theology, writes:

> According to Aquinas, appropriate interpretation is the task of dogmatic theology while exegesis concentrates on the purely philological task of preparing the text for theological understanding. Since the Council of Trent (1545–1563), the ultimate decision on the criteria and the validity of results of biblical interpretation remained the prerogative of the teaching office (Magisterium) of the Roman Catholic Church. (p. 463)

A major controversy concerning the status of Thomistic hermeneutics has occurred in the 1990s. Matthew Fox, a Dominican priest (until his removal in 1993), as was Aquinas, published in 1992 a new interpretation of the works of Thomas Aquinas entitled *Sheer Joy: Conversations with Thomas Aquinas on Creation Spirituality*. Fox had already been silenced for one year by the Vatican prior to the publication of this book, primarily as the result of an ongoing debate over the doctrinal purity of Fox's "creation spirituality" and "original blessings." In his work Fox emphasizes a cosmological vision of creation with the ontological goodness of human beings, rather than their sinfulness, as primary. Charles Jencks (1992) comments:

> The lesson Fox draws from many such recent discoveries is that the universe is a fairly benign place, with a countless set of "gifts." These show Christians have had some priorities wrong: they should acknowledge not just original sin, which has been bearing down and repressing consciousness for sixteen centuries, but "original blessing." Although there are indeed accidents, suffering, real evil and constant warfare (creativity can be as much negative as positive) we can clarify from our existence here the answer to a perennially important question. It is one that Einstein posed: is the universe a fundamentally good place, should we be optimistic? The answer, of course, hangs in the balance and depends on how we treat the earth and ourselves, as well as the other endangered species. (p. 36)

In developing his postmodern vision, Fox (1992) relies heavily on the hermeneutic interpretation of Hebrew and Christian scriptures. And now, with the publication of *Sheer Joy*, Fox has produced a hermeneutical narrative study that reevaluates, and possibly replaces, seven centuries of Christian hermeneutics in the Thomistic tradition.

Fox begins by claiming that Thomas Aquinas was not a Thomist. Fox (1992) asserts: "I descholasticize Aquinas by interviewing him. I . . . ask him our questions and allow him access to our pressing issues in spirituality. This is important because the questions that preoccupied his thirteenth-century contemporaries are of course not always the issues that concern us" (p. 2). Fox explains that his interview method is designed to uncover the "person behind the analytic mind" so as to interpret the meaning of philosophical categories such as "evil" or "morality" for contemporary society. Fox offers new interpretations of Aquinas' biblical commentaries to move beyond the scholastic methodology that typified Aquinas' other works. Fox (1992) writes: "Following the inner logic of the biblical text, he [Aquinas] is free to make connections, let his creative genius work, and allow his heart as well as his head to speak. Here his passion often comes tumbling out—especially when he is speaking of his favorite love, wisdom" (p. 3). This historical perspective of the dual role of hermeneutic interpretation as both analytic and intuitive confounds scholastic theologians, and by way of extrapolation it also confounds those committed to modern curriculum development methods and materials. The irony of the double-coded discourse of multiple understandings challenges the binary logic of modernity and the absolute metanarratives of the Enlightenment project. Postmodern curriculum recognizes this dual role of hermeneutics and accepts the irony of apparent contradictions in interpretation, as we saw in our discussion of Hermes.

Fox is working to move beyond the modern era's fix on hermeneutical interpretation as mechanistic and literalistic. "Enlightenment prejudices have often been employed in interpreting Aquinas over the centuries" (Fox, 1992, p. 7). Fox terms his creation spirituality "postmodern" (p. 7) in the constructive rather than deconstructive sense, and he employs hermeneutics to recover premodern wisdom embedded in the Biblical treatises written by Thomas Aquinas in the thirteenth century in order to bring those insights to a contemporary, postmodern cosmology. Fox concludes that some Thomists, while frequently rejecting much of Descartes and modern philosophy in argumentation, in fact have often succumbed to rationalist tendencies in vigorous attempts to prove Aquinas was scientific and respectably rational. This has often limited them to the scholastic texts of Aquinas and the linear thinking of scholasticism. "I believe Aquinas deserves—and we today require from Aquinas—a nonlinear celebration of his amazingly mystical **and** intellectual thought" (Fox, 1992, p. 12). As students of curriculum, we can see in Matthew Fox's interpretation of Aquinas' biblical commentaries a hermeneutical process that seeks to reevaluate scholastic theology. This is the hermeneutics of a double-edged sword that offers fresh insights for some but anxiety for others. Regardless of the ways that the work of Matthew Fox will be judged by scholars in years to come, he has "raised the ante" in the debate over hermeneutical interpretation. For students of curriculum, Fox's work offers suggestive parallels to issues of text interpretation and in particular underlines the religious origins and present uses of hermeneutics. The theological debates over the meaning of hermeneutics will illuminate the contemporary discussions of hermeneutics in philosophical and educational scholarship.

While the literalistic practice of biblical interpretation in the Thomistic scholastic tradition continued to dominate through the Protestant Reformation, the emphasis on the scriptures during the Reformation promoted reading and understanding biblical texts by individual believers rather than papal officials. Thus, the Protestant Reformation had the effect of deemphasizing the interpretation of Scripture by the Roman Magisterium. Following the Enlightenment, hermeneutics was reevaluated by Friedrich Schleiermacher (1768–1834), who rejected all formal, extratextual authorities as illegitimate imposition on individual acts of understanding. Schleiermacher's work discredited special theological or legal hermeneutics. Schleiermacher explained, "Rather, **every** written text must be understood both in terms of its individual sense (psychological understanding) and in terms of the linguistic procedures through which this sense is achieved (grammatical understanding). Hermeneutics is now understood as the art of understanding the sense of the text. Allegorical interpretation is ruled out, the text must be allowed to speak for itself" (quoted in Jeanrond, 1988, p. 463). Schleiermacher's work paved the way for contemporary developments in hermeneutical understanding.

Paul Ricoeur (1981) has contended that a movement of deregionalization began with the attempt to extract a general problem from the activity of interpretation that is each time engaged in different texts, and "the discernment of this central and unitary problematic is the achievement of Schleiermacher" (p. 45). Before Schleiermacher a philology (historical linguistic study) of classical texts and a literalistic exegesis (critical analysis) of sacred texts predominated. After Schleiermacher, it became clear that the hermeneutical process required that the individual interpreter must discern the operations that are common to these two traditional branches of hermeneutics, philology and exegesis. The possibility of the value of the individual subjective interpreter began to gain ascendancy in philosophical hermeneutics.

Awareness of historical conditions came to dominate hermeneutical understanding during the nineteenth century. Interpreters were now understood to move within a hermeneutical circle that required the specification of historical conditions in textual interpretation. Hans-Georg Gadamer (1975) calls attention to preunderstandings that underpinned interpretation. Gadamer terms the condition and the perspectives of interpreters their "horizons" and the act of understanding the sense of a text "the fusion of horizons." Through this fusion of horizons the interpreter enters the tradition of the text, and thus shares in the text's particular representation of truth. Gadamer (1976) writes about relationships in the hermeneutic circle that transcend the "technical sign-systems" of the modern age:

> Each [person] is at first a kind of linguistic circle, and these linguistic circles come in contact with each other, merging more and more. Language occurs once again, in vocabulary and grammar as always, and never without the inner infinity of the dialogue that is in process between every speaker and his [or her] partner. That is the fundamental dimension of hermeneutics. (p. 17)

Gadamer concludes by stating that genuine speaking, which has something to say and therefore is not based on prearranged signals but rather seeks words that reach the other human person, is the universal human task. This is the hermeneutic circle that educators must enter in the postmodern era.

Although Gadamer's hermeneutics has been criticized by some for his refusal to allow for methodological controls of the act of interpretation, many education scholars in the 1990s rely on Gadamer to support their critique of narrow instrumental views of schooling. Truth, they contend, cannot be collapsed into methods, the mainstay of the traditional approach to modern curriculum development, especially in "methods" courses in colleges of education. Rather, we must approach texts with our preunderstandings, suspend our prejudices, and engage in dialogue. David Blacker (1993), for example, argues that Gadamer's effort involves a reconstruction of the humanist sense of education as *Bildung*, which emphasizes what is done *to* individuals rather than what individual persons actually *do*. Blacker (1993) writes:

> To make the notion of *Bildung* more concrete, then, Gadamer recasts it as a dialogue between interpreter and tradition in which the latter is experienced as a Thou. This point must be stressed: he is not saying that individuals like teachers and students in every case ought to engage in an intersubjective give-and-take. . . . Accordingly, sharing in this historically-constituted conversation does not mean that I experience tradition as the opinion of some person or other, but that I am able to enter into it as into a game made up of myself and other persons but not reducible to any one of us. In this edifying tradition-forming, revising and conversing dialogue taking place in language— Hegelian Spirit conversing with itself—arises *Bildung*, which I see as the normative dimension of philosophical hermeneutics. (p. 7)

Traditional theological hermeneutics, as we have seen above, will insist on a normative methodology. However, this normative methodology is not Blacker's conversing dialogue. The traditional normative methodology is determined by an external authority. In contrast, postmodern philosophical hermeneutics will validate text interpretation that arises from the dialogue of individuals working within the context of a community circle where the other, whether human person, tradition, or artifact, is experienced as a "Thou" and not an "it." For Gadamer, the hermeneutic circle is used to facilitate understanding and open up "possibilities," while the traditional technical approach to hermeneutics is seen as dehumanizing. This is the same deadening effect of technical authoritarian approaches to curriculum development that have emerged from the application of the Tylerian rationale in schools.

Paul Ricoeur (1981) takes a different approach in his important work *Hermeneutics and the Human Sciences*, where he argues that the first understanding of the sense of the text must be validated through some explanatory procedures to ensure the sense of the text. Ricoeur contends that the movement from a structuralist science to a structuralist philosophy is bound to fail. John Thompson, translator of Ricoeur, explains that structuralism, insofar as it precludes the possibility of self-reflection, can never establish itself as a philosophy:

> An order posited as unconscious can never, to my mind, be more than a stage abstractly separated from an understanding of the self by itself; order in itself is thought located outside itself. A genuinely reflective philosophy must nevertheless be receptive to the structuralist method, specifying its validity as an abstract and objective moment in the understanding of self and being. This imperative forms one of the principal guidelines for Ricoeur's recent work on the theory of language and interpretation. (cited in Ricoeur, 1981, p. 10)

Ricoeur's interest evolved, in part, from his initial efforts to formulate a concrete ontology infused with the themes of freedom, finitude, and hope at the Sorbonne as a graduate student with Gabriel Marcel in the 1930s. However, Ricoeur became intent on discovering a more rigorous and systematic method than he found in Marcel. The phenomenology of Edmund Husserl provided this method, and in turn led to the development of a reflective philosophy disclosing authentic subjectivity for understanding human existence. At the same time, Ricoeur was convinced that necessity and freedom were integral aspects of that existence. Finally, he turned to the problem of language, and here he engaged hermeneutics. Ricoeur (1981) explains:

> I propose to organize this problematic [the historicity] of human experience and communication in and through distance around five themes: (1) the realization of language as a discourse; (2) the realization of discourse as a structured work; (3) the relation of speaking to writing in discourse and in the works of discourse; (4) the work of discourse as the projection of a world; (5) discourse and the work of discourse as the mediation of self-understanding. Taken together, these features constitute the criteria of textuality. (p. 132)

Ricoeur thus moves the hermeneutical process beyond theological understanding to a more general level of human understanding. Ricoeur's work has influenced a number of contemporary curriculum scholars, including William Reynolds. In *Reading Curriculum Theory: The Development of a New Hermeneutic*, Reynolds (1989) presents an analysis of conservative and critical traditions in curriculum theory, employing the method developed by Ricoeur for reading literary texts. In keeping with the Ricoeurian project, the Reynolds' study is also a documentary of the growth of self-understanding emerging from a fusion of horizons with the texts.

Ricoeur's theory of hermeneutical understanding was judged as politically naive by contemporary German philosopher Jurgen Habermas (1970). Habermas insisted that "only a critical and self-critical attitude toward interpretation could reveal possible systematic distortions in human communication and their impact on our interpretive activity" (quoted in Jeanrond, 1988, p. 463). Thus, in its contemporary form, hermeneutics is faced with three interrelated concerns: understanding, explanation, and critical assessment. The last implies that a community of interpreters must work to unmask ideological distortions, limited "objective" interpretations, and analysis of the meaning of the text. This community of interpreters opens hermeneutics to the postmodern discussion. Interpretation in postmodern philosophy must include a relational dimension that is mutually critical.

These developments in hermeneutics in the nineteenth and twentieth centuries from Schleiermacher and Dilthey to Heidegger and Husserl, to Gadamer and Ricoeur, and most recently to Habermas have confronted traditional scholars with a difficult dilemma: either engage philosophers in debates over the nature of hermeneutics in a mutually critical correlation or remain committed to a formalist, extratextual hermeneutics as provided by direct divine inspiration and/or ecclesiastical and bureaucratic authority. Some propose dialogue with philosophers to make use of the philosophical developments in hermeneutics to enhance textual interpretation, and thus identify and correct possible ideological distortions in understanding, especially if the process includes a wide spectrum of contributors to the development of a renewal in education.

Just as theology and philosophy are being challenged to enter the "hermeneutic circle" and be open to new understandings, so, too, the curriculum field faces similar challenges. There remain curriculum specialists at work today who would seek to return to the security of a traditional authority, the curricular magisterium that has provided legitimation for the modern paradigm of curriculum development in the spirit of the Tylerian rationale. However, hermeneutics has also influenced those who seek to understand curriculum phenomenologically, as well as others who seek political and autobiographical understanding. Originally confined to scriptural interpretation, hermeneutics now engages all those involved in the project of understanding and critical assessment. This tradition is discussed in a recent book on curriculum inquiry entitled *Informing Education Policy and Practice Through Interpretive Inquiry* by Nelson Haggerson and Andrea Bowman (1992). In this text the authors seek to recover mythopoetic, cosmological, and narrative dimensions of theological hermeneutics while engaging the philosophical hermeneutics of Ricoeur, Gadamer, and Heidegger. Haggerson and Bowman's scholarship demonstrates the importance of qualitative and interpretive research, and it appears that in the 1990s there will be an intensification of interest in hermeneutics in the curriculum field.

Haggerson and Bowman bring to contemporary curriculum debates what Hans Kung, David Tracy, and other contemporary theologians have brought to theology, a mutually critical correlation between hermeneutics as understanding, explanation through multiple qualitative paradigms, and critical assessment from the multiple viewpoints of theology, philosophy, and the human sciences. The affirmation of these multiple viewpoints is the essence of the hermeneutic circle for curriculum development in the postmodern era. From this perspective knowledge combines the infinite with the finite; knowledge is provisional, contextual, and temporal. There is no terminal point of knowing, only continual movement through the hermeneutic circle.

Haggerson and Bowman (1992) use the metaphor of a running stream from four perspectives to explain the multiple viewpoints of hermeneutic inquiry. In their first perspective, called the "rational/theoretical" paradigm, the researcher is on the edge of the stream assuming the role of the objective observer who makes generalizations and predictions about the flow of the water. This parallels traditional social science experimental research. Second, in the "mythological/practical" paradigm the researcher gets in a boat, experiences the stream, and becomes a participant observer. Here the researcher is interested in the mutual impact of the stream and the researcher on each other. Haggerson and Bowman (1992) write: "She doesn't want to predict what the stream will do or be in the long run, but how it will respond to her probing at the present and how she will respond to it. That is the 'mythological' aspect of the paradigm" (p. 12). They see ethnography, oral history, and phenomenological research as representative here. The third paradigm is called the "evolutionary/transformational" because the researcher becomes the stream as a total participant. This parallels Gestalt therapy, dream analysis, and autobiographical methods of inquiry. Bowman (1992) comments, "I came to understand this phenomenon when I started to write a personal journal. As I wrote, I was able to get in touch with myself, as well as with my teaching practice. The more I reflected through my writing, the more my teaching and knowledge of myself evolved or was transformed. I realized I was the stream. My practice had been informed in a very subtle way, actually through my intuitions" (p. 13). In this paradigm there is only a very subtle difference between therapy, teaching, and inquiring. These first three stages prepare the researcher for the fourth paradigm, which leads to hermeneutics. The researcher actually crosses the stream to the other bank bringing all the previous experiences along. Haggerson and Bowman (1992) explain:

> Having had all of those other experiences, the researcher now climbs out of the stream on the other side and dries off. When she looks back at the stream she is confident of the forces that direct the stream and she takes on the responsibility of helping all concerned with the stream become aware of the forces so they can be emancipated

> from those that are detrimental to human well-being. In
> other words, she demystifies the stream. Furthermore, the
> researcher takes appropriate action to help remove the
> coercive forces as well as to reveal them. . . . The stream, of
> course, can be the curriculum, the school, the
> administration, or the teachers' organization, all of which
> have manifest and hidden agendas. (p. 14)

This fourth paradigm is called the "normative/critical" because
through critical analysis the researchers attempt to identify all
the manifest and hidden factors and emancipate themselves and
others from them. The forces are the norms by which society
functions, and the critical research informs both educational
policy and practice in relation to these norms, rules, myths, and
traditions. Critical analysis and action research are the examples
of methodologies of this paradigm.

In the metaphor of the stream, Haggerson and Bowman
provide one concrete example of the way that curriculum
theorists work to explore interpretive inquiry. This, they claim, is
the basis of a postmodern hermeneutics in curriculum studies.
No longer will objective, experimental projects that attempt to
verify hypotheses for the purpose of articulating generalizations,
predictions, and causal probabilities dominate educational
research. Other research paradigms will also be legitimated and
encouraged. As a result, understanding, awareness, emancipation, demystification, and transformation will all become
possible, thus forming the basis of hermeneutic interpretation in
curriculum studies.

In this postmodern milieu, curriculum development will
focus on the community of interpreters working together in
mutually corrective and mutually collaborative efforts. The
entire curricular experience is now open to reflection because
everything requires recursive interpretation. Without this
postmodern perspective, Hermes the trickster would continue to
have the opportunity to deceive educators. Postmodern
curriculum development will no longer turn to bureaucratic
authorities to dictate the official methodologies of instruction
and the official interpretation of texts. Educators will not be seen
as passive receptors of a "teacher proof curriculum" who simply
implement standardized goals and objectives. Rather, a

postmodern community of interpreters and teachers will enter the hermeneutic circle and engage each other in the process of understanding the text, the lived experience, and the self in relation to the other. This will support the three fundamental elements of inquiry that comprise the hermeneutic circle at work in all human understanding as originally defined by Schleiermacher (1978): the inherent creativity of interpretation, the pivotal role of language in human understanding, and the interplay of part and whole in the process of interpretation. Thus, hermeneutic inquiry is a creative act and not just a technical function. Curriculum development in the postmodern era supports efforts to include this community circle of creative interpretation that respects the interplay of individuals and the groups to which they belong into the fabric of the schooling experience. By doing so, postmodern curriculum incorporates the position of James B. Macdonald (1988), who insisted, "The fundamental human quest is the search for meaning and the basic human capacity for this search is experienced in the hermeneutic process, the process of interpretation of the text (whether artifact, natural world, or human action). This is the search (or research) for greater understanding that motivates and satisfies us" (p. 105).

As a final caveat, curriculum scholars must be cautioned that hermeneutic inquiry has the potential of infuriating and inciting those committed to traditional authoritative and bureaucratic structures. David G. Smith (1991) has written an eloquent and accessible summary of hermeneutic inquiry in which he offers the following insights into Hermes and the hermeneutic tradition as a warning for postmodern curriculum studies:

> Hermes, as well as being the deliverer of messages between the gods and from gods to mortals on earth, was known for a number of other qualities as well, such as eternal youthfulness, friendliness, prophetic power, and fertility. In a sense, all of these features are at work in the hermeneutic endeavor to this day, as the practice of interpretation attempts to show what is at work in different disciplines and, in the service of human generativity and good faith, is engaged in the mediation of meaning. There is one further aspect of Hermes that may

be worth noting, namely, his imprudence. . . . Students of
hermeneutics should be mindful that their interpretations
could lead them into trouble with "authorities." (p. 187)

Postmodern hermeneutics can be dangerous, for it uncovers,
interprets, clarifies, deconstructs, and challenges all fields of
study, including curriculum development models and methods
that have been enshrined in the sacred canon of curriculum texts
for decades. Postmodern hermeneutics is troubling to the
traditional curriculum magisterium in the 1990s but refreshing
and empowering to curriculum theorists who employ it in their
interpretive inquiry. As we explore the discourses on race,
gender, ethnicity, philosophy, ecology, politics, aesthetics,
autobiography, and science in the coming chapters, the
hermeneutic circle will continue to inform our discussion of
curriculum development in the postmodern era.

CHAPTER SIX

Race, Gender, and Ethnicity in a Multicultural Milieu

The scholarship on race and ethnicity in postmodern curriculum studies is more than a review of the legal issues related to segregation, integration, and affirmative action in schools, debates about the validity of assessment for minority students, the development of programs to reduce ethnic tension on school campuses, or the inclusion of multicultural literary selections in language arts classrooms. While these topics are important, racial issues in the postmodern curriculum emphasize investigations of the self and conceptions of the self in relation to the other. Toni Morrison (1989) has written that "the trauma of racism is, for the racist and the victim, the severe fragmentation of the self" (p. 16). She includes this additional caveat that reflects the thinking of many postmodern curriculum theorists as well: "We are not, in fact, 'other'" (p. 9). James Baldwin (1971) expands on Morrison's position:

> If . . . one managed to change the curriculum in all the schools so that [African Americans] learned more about themselves and their real contributions to this culture, you would be liberating not only [African Americans], you'd be liberating white people who know nothing about their own history. And the reason is that if you are compelled to lie about one aspect of anybody's history, you must lie about it all. If you have to lie about my real role here, if you have to pretend that I hoed all that cotton just because I loved you, then you have done something to yourself. You are mad. (p. 8)

African-American authors and poets, particularly Toni Morrison, Langston Hughes, James Baldwin, Maya Angelou,

Alice Walker, and Ernest Gaines, as well as Latin American authors and other ethnic writers, have become moral voices in the wasteland of modernity where race has been reduced to a social problem in need of a quick-fix solution or a token ethnic event for "cultural awareness week" or "Black History Month." Ronald Wilhelm (1994) discusses some of the problems associated with the latter:

> When historian Carter G. Woodson initiated Negro History Week celebrations in 1926, he . . . sought to establish the legitimacy of [African American] presence in past and present U.S. society as well as to strengthen contemporary African-American culture and values. . . . Almost 70 years later, the official curriculum of many U.S. public schools sanctions only selected elements of African-American history and culture. Fragmentary evidence suggests a discrepancy between the rhetoric of official school district policy and the actual classroom practices regarding Black History Month. (p. 217)

Maya Angelou, along with other poets and spokespersons for ethnic and gender issues, has often commented that it is preferable to integrate African-American, Asian-American, Native American, and Latin American history openly and comprehensively throughout the curriculum rather than limiting black history or women's history to a single month. However, until such time as multicultural studies are widely accepted and incorporated into the curriculum, ethnic celebrations such as "Black History Month" will remain necessary in the schools. Others are not as conciliatory. Khallid Muhammad (1994), outspoken follower of Nation of Islam leader Louis Farrakhan and controversial for his racist and anti-Semitic rhetoric, denounces the concept of Black History Month:

> For black history celebrations, white people give us one month out of the year—the shortest one they could find—to celebrate our greatness, our glory, our honor and to celebrate our infinite history. With 12 months out of the year we must study their moment in time. We can no longer accept a Black History Day, a Black History Week, or a Black History Month, knowing that we are father and mother of all who walk on this earth. (p. 1)

It is clear from these varied voices that racial, multicultural, gendered, and ethnic issues will remain at the forefront of heated campus debates and curricular investigations in the postmodern era.

Ernest Gaines' most recent novel, *A Lesson Before Dying*, is perhaps typical of the literary works that can inform our understanding of curriculum in the postmodern era and support efforts to move beyond the discrepancies reported by Wilhelm. Gaines' text is particularly appropriate for students of curriculum because the protagonist, Grant Wiggins, is a teacher struggling to understand his career and the meaning of education in a racist society. In the excerpt below Wiggins is speaking to Jefferson, a young black man who has been falsely accused of murder and is awaiting execution. In his trial, Jefferson had been called a hog. Jefferson, it was argued by his court-appointed defense attorney, was not responsible for his actions because he was less than human and not intelligent. Wiggins, who had left home to earn a college degree, has returned to teach at a black plantation school. He has been coerced by an aunt to meet with Jefferson daily in the final thirty days before the execution and to teach Jefferson to read and thereby appreciate his own self worth.

I use this novel as a reading in many of my graduate curriculum courses not only because it passionately conveys important contemporary curricular themes, but also because it demonstrates that postmodern curriculum development must include aesthetic, autobiographical, political, and literary dimensions. Additionally, the excerpts from Jefferson's journal in chapter twenty-nine are a powerful indictment of modern approaches to language that have dominated English classes and suppressed the important autobiographical dimension of the writing process. Jefferson's journal also provides support for the whole language philosophy that is emerging in many curriculum programs in the 1990s. Gaines' novel is perhaps the clearest literary example of this postmodern understanding of the interrelationship of race, culture, and teaching in curriculum studies. Gaines' (1993) character Grant Wiggins begins:

> "Jefferson," I said. We had started walking. "Do you know
> what a hero is, Jefferson? A hero is someone who does

something for other people. He does something that other
men don't and can't do. He is different from other men.
He is above other men. No matter who those other men
are, the hero, no matter who he is, is above them." I
lowered my voice again until we had passed the table. I
could never be a hero. I teach, but I don't like teaching. I
teach because it is the only thing that an educated black
man can do in the South today. I don't like it; I hate it. I
don't even like living here. I want to run away. I want to
live for myself and for my woman and for nobody else.
(p. 191)

Gaines introduces the dilemma facing Grant Wiggins as a
teacher. Wiggins is the reluctant emerging hero, trying to
understand himself and the social context of the South that
shapes his life. Soon Wiggins turns his attention to Jefferson and
continues:

The white people out there are saying that you don't have
it—that you're a hog, not a man. But I know they are
wrong. You have the potentials. We all have, no matter
who we are. Those out there are no better than we are,
Jefferson. They are worse. That's why they are always
looking for a scapegoat, someone else to blame. I want you
to show them the difference between what they think you
are and what you can be. To them you're nothing but a
nigger—no dignity, no heart, no love for your people. You
can prove them wrong. You can do more than I can ever
do. I have always done what they wanted me to do, teach
reading, writing, and arithmetic. Nothing else—nothing
about dignity, nothing about identity, nothing about
loving and caring. (Gaines, 1993, pp. 191–192)

Postmodern curriculum scholars understand the frustration of
Gaines' protagonist. Race and gender studies ultimately allow
educators to see that dignity, identity, and caring are central to
understanding curriculum. Feminist scholar Nel Noddings
(1984, 1992) is recognized for bringing these issues—particularly
the concept of caring—to the forefront of contemporary
curriculum discourses in her popular books *Caring: A Feminine
Approach to Ethics and Moral Education* and *The Challenge to Care in
Schools: An Alternative Approach to Education*. Noddings (1984)
writes:

> The one-caring, male or female, does not seek security in abstractions cast either as principles or entities. She remains responsible here and now for this cared-for and this situation and for the foreseeable futures projected by herself and the cared-for. . . . Today we are asked to believe that a woman's "lack of experience in the world" keeps them at an inferior stage in moral development. I am suggesting, to the contrary, that a powerful and coherent ethic and, indeed, a different sort of world may be built on the natural caring so familiar to women. (pp. 43, 46)

This natural caring is also seen in Gaines' novel when Wiggins laments the fact that white society never thought that blacks were capable of learning about caring and identity. Just as Noddings rejects the belief that women are inferior because of their perceived lack of experience, Gaines rejects the belief that blacks are inferior because of their perceived lack of common humanity and ability to care. Gaines' (1993) protagonist continues:

> "[They would say] 'Teach those niggers how to print their names and how to figure on their fingers.' And I went along, but hating myself all of the time for doing so. . . . Do you know what a myth is, Jefferson?" I asked him. "A myth is an old lie that people still believe in. White people believe that they are better than anyone else on earth— that's a myth. The last thing they ever want to see is a black man stand, and think, and show that common humanity that is in all of us. It would destroy their myth." (p. 192)

Race, gender, and cultural studies in the postmodern curriculum are about shattering myths, especially those that perpetuate repression of the dignity and identity of the self and those that perpetuate racism, sexism, violence, homophobia, genocide, religious bigotry, political repression, and cultural elitism. In support of the dignity of the individual, as well as an indictment of racism, Gaines concludes this scene with Wiggins imploring Jefferson to stand tall and not crawl to his death like a hog to be butchered. Gaines (1993) writes:

As long as none of us stand, they're safe. . . . I want you to
chip away at that myth by standing. I want you—yes
you—to call them liars. I want you to show them that you
are as much a man—more a man than they can ever be.
That jury? You call them men? That judge? Is he a man?
The governor is no better. They play by the rules their
forefathers created hundreds of years ago. Their
forefathers said that we're only three-fifths human—and
they believe it to this day. . . . When I showed him the
notebook and pencil I brought you, he grinned. Do you
know why? He believes it was just a waste of time and
money. What can a hog do with pencil and paper? (p. 192)

In order to understand postmodern curriculum as a racial,
gendered, and multicultural experience, students of curriculum
must listen carefully to voices such as Grant Wiggins and
Jefferson in Ernest Gaines' novel. Postmodern scholars, like
Wiggins, insist that if we continue to play by rules created by our
ancestors that no longer make sense in the postmodern world
and that repress the dignity and identity of students, then
curriculum will continue to be a meaningless technocratic
endeavor removed from human experience. Additionally tragic
is the fact that not only will schools suffer the debilitating effects
of malaise and hopelessness, but society will continue to
experience the violent reaction of those who have experienced a
loss of dignity and identity. In a controversial book written from
prison entitled *Makes Me Wanna Holler*, Nathan McCall (1993)
reflects on his angry youth and shows why young black men
who feel that they have no options in a society that devalues
them try to gain self-respect by adopting a code of macho
violence. The postmodern curriculum must address issues of
self-identity and dignity, not only to improve education but also
to promote justice and compassion in society.

Following thematically from our discussion of race, the
scholarship on gender in curriculum studies in the postmodern
era is more than an analysis of the role of schoolmarms in the
nineteenth century, the impact of the womans' suffrage and gay
rights movements on schooling, sex-role differentiation in
classrooms, gender bias in textbooks, sex education programs,
and health clinics on campuses. While these issues are very
important and worthy of continued study, gender issues in the

curriculum, like racial issues introduced above, are primarily about ways of knowing, embodiment of social and textual relationships, male and female identity, empowerment, and conceptions of the self. Madeleine Grumet, as we discussed in chapter four, addresses these issues in her book *Bitter Milk: Women and Teaching*. Grumet (1988b) introduces her book as follows:

> In Sri Lanka, young women sometimes experience psychotic responses to adolescence as they struggle with the ambivalence provoked by the separation from families. In *Medusa's Hair* the anthropologist Gananath Obeyesekere tells us that these periods of distress are called "dark night of the soul" experiences. He describes a ritual tonic that the afflicted girls drink to release them from their trouble. It is called bitter milk and is a mixture of milk and crushed margosa leaves, the same bitter portion that mothers apply to their nipples when they wish to wean their babies. Bitter milk, fluid of contradictions: love and rejection, sustenance and abstinence, nurturance and denial. . . . I have written this book to explore these contradictions. . . . I am attempting to understand what teaching means to women. Women constitute the majority of all public school instructional personnel; nevertheless, our experience of this work is hidden. . . . It is hidden from our students, our colleagues, and even from ourselves. Its absence is not a mere oversight. Nor is it that we have been so busy doing it that we haven't taken the time to think about it. There is something about the task itself, the way it wedges itself into our lives, the way we place it somewhere between our work and our labor, our friendships and our families, our ambition and our self-abnegation, that has prohibited our speaking of it. Sometimes it seems to me that it is everything that could possibly matter to us. . . . the fundamental argument of this text is that knowledge evolves in human relationships. (pp. xi–xix)

The conception of the self as student, teacher, parent, or scholar emerges, for Grumet, from the knowledge that evolves, especially for women educators, in "bitter wisdom of this sweet work" (p. xx). Curriculum development in the postmodern era engages women, men, people of color, European Americans,

North American First Nations, gays, lesbians, heterosexuals, and every person of diverse heritage, religion, and life-style in the dialogue about knowledge, relationships, and the self. And with Grumet, this knowledge is seen as evolving within human relationships.

Particular emphasis is given to different ways of knowing and learning by scholars concerned about race and gender issues. Even legal and bureaucratic structures are acknowledging the diversity of ways of learning with recent enforcement of Section 504 laws, bilingual programs, and educational inclusion regulations. Many curriculum scholars have also explored ways of knowing and learning, and a text that articulates this theme especially well is *Women's Ways of Knowing: The Development of Self, Voice, and Mind*. Case studies, narratives, and interviews are described throughout the book, and chapter nine, entitled "Toward an Education for Women," begins with two poignant stories about women who were in their first year of undergraduate studies. The first story is about a woman in an introductory science class:

> The professor marched into the lecture hall, and placed upon his desk a large jar filled with dried beans, and invited the students to guess how many beans the jar contained. After listening to an enthusiastic chorus of wildly inaccurate estimates, the professor smiled a thin, dry smile, revealed the correct answer, and announced, "You have just learned an important lesson about science. Never trust the evidence of your own senses." (Belenky et al., 1986, p. 191)

The authors report that this student's sense of herself as a knower was shaky, and it was based on the belief that she could use her own firsthand experience as a source of truth. However, this professor took away her only tool for knowing. The woman dropped the course immediately.

The second story is about a woman in an introductory philosophy course where the professor came into the class carrying a large cardboard cube and asked the class what it was. The students said a cube. The professor then asked the class to describe a cube, and they said that a cube had six equal square sides. Finally, the professor asked how they knew the object had six equal square sides when they could not see all sides of the cube, and then responded:

> We can't look at all six sides of a cube at once, can we? So we can't exactly *see* a cube. And yet, you're right. You know it's a cube. But you know it not just because you have eyes but because you have intelligence. You invent the sides you cannot see. You use your intelligence to create the 'truth' about cubes. (p. 192)

The student then explained her reaction to this classroom encounter:

> It blew my mind. You'll think I'm nuts, but I ran back to the dorm and I called my boyfriend and I said, "Listen, this is just incredible," and I told him all about it. I'm not sure he could see why I was so excited. I'm not sure I understand it myself. But I really felt, for the first time, like I was really in college, like I was sort of *grown up*. (p. 192)

The authors contend that both stories are about the limitations of firsthand experience as a source of knowledge—either the truth about the jar of beans or the cube:

> The lesson the science professor wanted to teach is that experience is a source of error. Taught in isolation, this lesson diminishes the student, rendering her dumb and dependent. The philosophy teacher's lesson was that although raw experience is insufficient, by reflecting on it the students could arrive at truth. It was a lesson that made the students feel more powerful ("sort of grown up"). (p. 193)

Belenky, Clinchy, Goldberger, and Tarule use these and similar stories to confirm the self as knower and thus empower students, especially women whose intuitive and perceptive sense of the truth has been ignored in schooling, to develop their voice, their mind, and their affirmation of self.

As Belenky, Noddings, and other feminist scholars remind us, the postmodern curriculum is moving beyond inane attempts to cast racial, gendered, and cultural issues simply in terms of tolerance and representation of minorities and historically excluded groups. Cultural literacy programs designed to assimilate all students into a great American melting pot culture are being challenged for their innate biases, which perpetuate explosive structures of dominance and control. Curriculum is about empowerment and liberation. In this sense, racial, gender, and cultural dimensions of the postmodern curriculum are also concerned with the politics of power (Apple, 1982, 1993; Roman and Apple, 1990; Aronowitz, 1992; Giroux, 1992), which we will explore in more detail in chapter nine. Patricia Hill Collins (1990) recognizes that race, gender, and class are interlocking categories that must be reconceptualized and transcended to create new categories of connection. She describes black feminist thought as a process of self-conscious struggle to empower women and men to create a humanist community vision. Curriculum theorists such as Peter McLaren (1993), Louis Castenell and William Pinar (1993), Madeleine Grumet (1988c), and Camron McCarthy (1988, 1990) (among others) have cautioned, however, that these issues, particularly race, must not be subsumed under political scholarship.

Grumet adamantly resists limiting her curriculum scholarship to the domain of gender analysis. She insists that it is also phenomenological, autobiographical, aesthetic, and much more. The tendency to divide curriculum development into various competing discourses vying for ascendancy is counter-productive and the antithesis of postmodern thinking. Grumet (1988c) writes: "Feminist scholars work to bring together domains of experience and understanding that history and culture have kept apart. For what it means to teach and learn is related to what it means to be male or female and to our experience of reproduction and nurturance, domesticity, sexuality, nature, knowledge and politics" (p. 538). Although I share Grumet's sentiment, the arbitrary categorization of the postmodern discourses in this book could be challenged by feminist scholars as a contradiction of Grumet's premise. However, I hope that the fluidity of curriculum discourses is evident throughout the chapters in part two, thus minimizing rigid categorization of individual authors or texts.

Another contemporary feminist curriculum theorist is Janet L. Miller. Miller began to make links between feminist theory and those curricularists who privileged autobiography and the study of the individual's educational experience in the

1970s. Following a feminist critique of patriarchal modes dominant at that time in the curriculum field, Miller argued for an integration of emotion and intellect as well as an examination of the curricular forms that distort and deny women's educational experience. Miller (1992) writes that equity is not enough. Feminist theory requires that one change the very character of educational institutions, the academic disciplines, and the curricular representations of academe. In her early work, Miller (1980, 1987) excavated the unconscious ways she and other female teachers internalized patriarchal assumptions about who they were as women and teachers, and she established a linkage between women curriculum theorists and philosophers of education such as Maxine Greene.

Following from the example of Janet Miller's feminist autobiographical scholarship, the diversity of race, gender, culture, and ethnicity in the schools in the 1990s is seen by postmodern scholars as an opportunity for all students to learn from each other not only about differences but also about the self. Camron McCarthy (1988, 1990) utilizes the concept of *nonsynchrony* in curriculum development to highlight this point, arguing that the strength of the curriculum comes from its inclusiveness and diversity rather than from its uniformity and cultural homogeneity. McCarthy and Apple (1988) write: "The issues of culture and identity must be seriously incorporated into a nonsynchronous approach to racial domination in schooling" (p. 276). McCarthy (1993) identifies three approaches for dealing with racial inequality in schooling:

> Proponents of cultural understanding advocate sensitivity and appreciation of cultural differences—a model for racial harmony. Cultural competence proponents insist on the preservation of minority ethnic identity and language and "the building of bridges" between minority and mainstream culture. Finally, models of cultural emancipation go somewhat further than the previous two approaches in suggesting that a reformist multicultural curriculum can boost the school success and economic futures of minority youth. (p. 242)

While McCarthy investigates race from the perspective of the curriculum, philosopher Cornel West (1990) perhaps best summarizes the postmodern questions of race and society when he writes: "Black cultural workers must constitute and sustain discursive formations and institutional networks that deconstruct earlier Black strategies for identity formation, demystify power relations that incorporate class, patriarchal, and homophobic biases, and construct more multivalent and multidimensional responses that articulate the complexity and diversity of Black practices in the modern and postmodern world" (p. 105). West and McCarthy represent those scholars who are leading the discussion of race in the postmodern era to another level of understanding that includes identity, complexity, and diversity.

Curriculum development programs in the past have tended to ignore issues of race, gender, and ethnicity because curriculum was seen as something that reflected an objectively knowable structure that existed "out there" independent of race and gender and simply waiting to be discovered and memorized by students. Anthony Whitson challenges this assumption with his concept of "heteroglossia" in the curriculum, the inclusion of multifaceted and conflicting voices. Whitson (1988b) explains:

> . . . Partial discourses [that deny the political reality of diverse policies and practices in the curriculum] operate by representing education as a monological process, [thus] denying the educational importance of the principle Bakhtin refers to as "heteroglossia": the principal of dialogical otherness intrinsic in all social language use, including effective pedagogical communication. One implication of heteroglossia is that a political struggle among social dialects and voices is to be found at the heart of any single utterance, animating the contextualized meaning of that utterance, and supporting the linguistic competence that speakers must command in order to participate in social life. From this perspective, it is absolutely essential that the public school curriculum *must* include the mutually discordant voices and accents of diverse race, class, and gender elements of our society. (p. 281)

Whitson (1991) also seeks to break free from the reproduction of the status quo to a more open and free society in which students learn to navigate through more than one discourse in an effort to communicate and make decisions. Whitson argues that students must investigate confrontational ideas outside their prior knowledge and experience—especially in the realm of race and gender—in order to develop social competence. Through this confrontation, students alter conceptions of the self and society. Whitson advocates entering "otherness" to establish authentic dialogue and new understanding. Whitson takes the cultural literacy debates of the 1990s beyond the mainstream inculcation models represented by E. D. Hirsch, Jr. (1987).

The postmodern aversion to master narratives, cultural literacy programs, disembodied learning, homogenized curriculum guides, and disconnected objective goals are evident in the curriculum discourses surrounding race, gender, and ethnicity in the 1990s. Additionally, multicultural issues have often been ignored in modern schooling practices because they are controversial and contentious. Any serious examination of race, gender, and ethnicity causes bureaucrats and technocrats to be fearful of what turmoil might erupt if these issues are addressed openly. There is a pervasive distrust of the capacity of individuals to engage in dialogue in a democratic milieu for the purpose of achieving greater understanding. Therefore, schooling has reflected the societal preference of suppressing what seems to be either irrelevant or controversial in the curriculum. Curriculum development in the postmodern era is exposing the disastrous consequences on the human psyche of this modern notion of curriculum as racially, gender and culturally neutral, and it is bringing these discourses to the forefront of conscious reflection in scholarship and schooling in the 1990s.

In chapter five we introduced the concept of postmodern hermeneutics as a community circle of interpretation and understanding for the purpose of affirming a meaningful lived experience. In this chapter, we now see that curriculum scholarship insists that the hermeneutic circle is impossible outside the context of race, gender, culture, and ethnicity. The opposition to multicultural voices in modern society is pervasive. This has led some to conclude that radical separatist movements are the only viable alternative. Others continue to work within existing structures to expose the bankruptcy of modern hierarchical bureaucracies that have traditionally excluded women, gays, lesbians, Hispanics and Latinos, Native Americans, Asians, people of color, hearing impaired, physically challenged, religious sects, or any number of other individuals excluded from the dominant power positions in American society. Peter Maas Taubman (1993b), following Michel Foucault, suggests three strategic possibilities for bringing about the transformation of the dominant sexual grid. These include a detotalization and deconstruction of sexuality, a temporary reclaiming of the fixtures of "women," "lesbian," and "homosexual" for political purposes, and a radical nominalism that views sexual categories as abstract concepts with no objective reference or universal meaning. Taubman's work initiated poststructural investigations of gender issues in curriculum studies.

No matter what method of critique or investigation is selected by gender-focused and multicultural scholars, one thing is abundantly clear in their writing: the postmodern curriculum will no longer ignore race and gender and no longer accept minimal gratuitous tolerance and tokenism as a solution. The deconstruction of traditional master narratives related to race, gender, and ethnicity and the emergence of autobiographical, phenomenological, and poststructural analyses are integral to postmodern curriculum scholarship. Chapter seven will explore the philosophical foundations for such a move.

Multicultural debates recognize that people look at the world through different lenses. Our metaphysics, coupled with the social milieu in which we live, influences the creation of our worldview and our sense of self. We are also influenced by cultural norms and social constructions of others, both consciously and unconsciously. The story of a recent cross-country move by friends who were relocating to Louisiana from Arizona provides an example of this social construction. The couple asked me to secure a rental house for them prior to their summer arrival. A house on my street was available, so I made the deposit and necessary arrangements. The family arrived in Louisiana exhausted, U-Haul trailer in tow. I gave them a tour of their new house, and then we began to unload the trailer. The couple noted the extreme difference in climate between the dry desert landscape of Arizona and the tropical humidity and lush vegetation of south Louisiana. Particularly, they noted that the yard was in need of immediate attention. Not having a lawn mower and lawn care equipment, my friend (who is white) walked to the house next door where a bare-chested black man, sweating profusely, was cutting the grass. Before I could make introductions, my friend asked the gentleman how much he charged for cutting the grass. The man mowing the lawn smiled and said, "Nothing, I live here."

Prior to their arrival in Louisiana, I had failed to mention to my friends the ethnic composition of the neighborhood. Not having had much contact with African Americans in his previous Arizona community, my friend unconsciously projected a culturally conditioned bias in this new context and assumed that this black man must be a hired laborer. My friend is a teacher who openly professes a strong commitment to social justice and religious values. However, even his personal commitment to egalitarian values was not sufficient to help him deconstruct and understand the social context of his new neighborhood and recognize his sedimented perceptors. This scenario is repeated in classrooms and other social institutions all the time, and it demonstrates the urgency of addressing the complexity of race and gender issues in curriculum studies, especially from the perspective of the social construction of reality and the politics of identity formation. There is an abundance of literature emerging in this sector of the curriculum field.

If the curriculum ignores sedimented perceptors, identity formation, and social construction and suppresses individual visions and dreams in the content and context of education, and if individuals are constantly required to conform to someone else's worldview, then either dreams will be repressed, hope will be suppressed, people will incorporate the other's vision of themselves into their own self-understanding, and/or they will lash out in anger against those systems that exclude their voice. The latter is occurring in the 1990s as splinter groups vie for dominance and control. Riotous gangs, manipulative cults, separatist organizations, fascist political movements, conservative retrenchment, fundamentalism, subversive violent activism, and reactionary ideology all share one thing in common: fear and anger. The postmodern curriculum attempts to deconstruct modern society in order to expose the futility of this fear and anger. It is important to note that postmodern deconstructionism is not intent on destruction but rather the exposition of the internal contradictions of the metanarratives that have led to racial and gender bias and the accompanying global conflagration and degradation that have threatened to annihilate humanity.

The absurdities of modernity, especially in the twentieth century, are regularly incorporated into the curriculum scholarship of the postmodern era, not in order to perpetuate paralysis and hatred but to constantly remind us of the consequences of racism, sexism, and cultural elitism: Auschwitz, My Lai, Salem, Sarajevo, Rwanda, Little Rock, Hiroshima, Birmingham, Los Angeles, and so on. Racial and gender studies are not intent on further reducing human persons into the shell of the "minimal self," a term popularized by Christopher Lasch (1984). Lasch exposes the bankruptcy of modernity and the effect of devastation of modern concepts of the self on the human psyche. Rather, race and gender studies are the vehicles for exposing the impotence of traditional curriculum development in the face of the tragedies of contemporary global society. No serious curriculum scholar in the postmodern era can ignore these issues despite efforts by many to do so.

Of course, before scholars explore the issues surrounding race, gender, and ethnicity in curriculum scholarship, it is important to note that there is not consensus on the approach that should be taken to address these issues in postmodern schooling. For example, Canadian philosopher H. Ed Thompson, III (1993) has written that he is a feminist by virtue of the fact that he supports feminine values in educational scholarship and androgynous relationships for both men and women. The feminine is not limited by genitalia, but rather androgyny is an integral dimension of the human person. Others will disagree, arguing that the feminine, while incorporating a diversity of values and perspectives available to both men and women, can be fully experienced and understood only by women. Some feminist separatists demand such gender stratification.

An analogy that I often use for my graduate students may be instructive. The analogy centers on the idea of *black* and *white* from two different perspectives: physics and pigment. In physics, black is the absence of all light and the absence of all color, as in the void of total darkness. On the other hand, white light is the fullness of the entire spectrum of color, as in the refraction of white light entering a prism to form a rainbow. In pigment, black and white take on the opposite values. Black is the fullness of all colors mixed together, while white is the absence of all color. Thus, depending on the context, black and white may represent similar or opposite perspectives. Especially it is important to note that black and white are dependent on the other for their very definition and existence.

I use this analogy to suggest that objectifying and condemning persons based on color is not only immoral but also illogical. The objectification of *blackness* or *redness* or *yellowness* or *whiteness,* and by extrapolation *masculinity* and *femininity,* all result from socially constructed norms. There are numerous historical examples of the absurdity of our socially constructed racial and gender values. In the state of Louisiana a birth certificate was required to list a child as *negro* if the child had as little as one thirty-second non-Caucasian, African ancestry. This practice was not challenged until the 1970s (Diamond & Cottrol, 1983). Another law—called *commorientes*—that was not repealed until 1985 established inheritance procedures that assumed that if both a husband and wife were killed in an accident simultaneously, the female would have expired first and the stronger male would have survived longer. Inheritance disputes were settled based on this assumption. Another example involving race was widely reported in March of 1994, when a high school principal in Alabama threatened to cancel the prom when he heard that a black student and a white student planned to attend the dance as a couple. The principal's ban on interracial dating caused an avalanche of both protest and support. Pertinent here is the comment of one student who asked, "Who am I to date since I am biracial with a white mother and a black father?" The principal, she reported, chastised her parents for making a mistake, noting that she was evidence of the damaging result of tolerance of interracial dating. The principal has a history of controversial positions, and this case continues to draw national attention. There is also some opposition to interracial dating from African-American leaders as well. Khallid Muhammad (1994) warns black men: "You want to wear your X hat, but you want to have a white girl on your arm. . . . Now don't get me wrong. A white girl is alright for a white boy, but I'm talking about rebuilding the black family" (p. 2). Racial purity has proponents among extremists and bigots in all ethnic groups.

Historically, European Americans and African Americans are two sides of the same cultural coin, two interrelated narratives in the American story, two interrelated elements of the American identity. Projected as "other" and repressed, African-Americans' presence in the American self has been explored by Frantz Fanon (1967, 1970). Like James Baldwin (1971) and others, Fanon understood that *white* is a fabrication made possible by the construction of the concept *black*. For Fanon, there can be no *black* without *white* and vice versa. One cannot understand the identity of one without the other. The sequestered suburban white student is thus uninformed without understanding that he or she is also—in the historical, cultural, and psychological sense—African American. Because *white* does not exist apart from *black* the two coexist and intermingle, and the repression of this knowledge deforms us all. All Americans can be understood as racialized beings; knowledge of who we have been, who we are, and who we will become. In this sense, the postmodern curriculum—our construction and reconstruction of this knowledge for conversation with the young—is a racial experience (Castenell & Pinar, 1993). Put another way, "neglecting the experiences of African-American [and other] people in our curriculum is not only detrimental to African-American children, it is also a great source of the miseducation of other children who continue to be poorly prepared for a multicultural world" (Boateng, 1990, p. 77).

An examination of the ways that cultures deal with contradiction is illustrative. In Western philosophy there is a history of difficulty with oppositional aspects of reality: male and female, body and soul, thinking and feeling, light and dark, good and evil, machine and living organism, black and white. Oliver and Gershman (1989) contend that we employ two intellectual and practical techniques for dealing with these contradictions. The first is domination and/or destruction. We attempt to control or eliminate the oppositional pole of the bifurcation. The second strategy is dialectic. We attempt to transform both poles of a contradictory set of metaphors into a higher level of understanding. Thesis and antithesis are debated until a higher level of synthesis emerges as the departure point of a further dialectic seeking the perfect society or ultimate truth. Eastern philosophies, especially as seen in the yin and the yang, offer another alternative, where opposites are seen as complementary sets within a single entity. Oliver and Gershman (1989) explain: "There is maleness within femaleness and vice versa; males and females also comprise an organic unity; in essence all being is both mystical unity (or 'in' a unity) as well as differentiated form" (p. 148). Unfortunately, the result is that those who view the world as a multiplicity of antagonistic and dangerous dualisms and opposites see domination, destruction, and endless dialectic as the only solution. Postmodern curriculum studies view the world as complementary and organic, and thus the destructive nature of modernity must be overcome.

The examples presented above demonstrate that socially constructed norms and values must be deconstructed, a practice integral to postmodern philosophy. Southern literature, especially in the novels of William Faulkner, reminds us that the blood of many races—especially Native American, Black, and White—courses through the veins of all southerners. While the mixed bloodlines of the South may be denied and repressed in order to support the myth of an elite aristocracy and perpetuate unequal power relations and economic slavery, the presence of the "other" in the bloodlines of southerners is indisputable. (For a detailed review of this concept as well as the philosophy of curriculum as "place," see Kincheloe & Pinar [1991] and Kincheloe, Pinar, & Slattery [in press] in the journal *Curriculum Inquiry*.)

Another similar analogy is used by Carl Sagan, who has often written that there are a finite number of hydrogen and oxygen atoms in our ecosphere. These same atoms have formed and reformed water molecules throughout history. Since the human body is primarily composed of water molecules, all of which are continuously recycled to create new rivers, oceans, plants, animals, and human beings, we are literally created from the same atoms of "the other." While this analogy may be helpful, postmodernists caution that race must not be reduced to biological or genetic analysis. Hitler's racial science with cranial measurement is an obvious example of the abuses that can result from hereditarian ideologies. There continue to be debates about race and heredity in educational literature. Ornstein and Levine (1993, p. 380) present a concise summary of this research.

An additional example from a poststructural perspective will expand on this concept. (Poststructuralism as a postmodern philosophy is introduced here and will be discussed in more detail in the next chapter.) The assumption of modern rationalism is often that *black* or *white* refer to antecedent biological or genetic conditions and express essential qualities. They derive meaning from an invariant transhistorical system that is glued together by the binary opposition of black and white (Pinar et al., in press). Postmodernists reject the transhistorical assumptions of black and white, and poststructuralists expand the critique to argue that the meaning of *black* or *white* is discursively created. Poststructuralism seeks understanding of how "blackness" or other racialized categories are constructed in particular discourses and how those discourses are selected, organized, and inscribed in a particular society.

William Pinar et al. (in press) explain the poststructural reaction to these appeals to unities, totalities, origins, and metanarratives as a discursive strategy used to legitimate and disguise the exercise of power:

> At its most general level, poststructuralism attacks not only essentialism, universalism, transcendentalism, and humanism, but the very idea of a Western logos as well. It mounts this attack at the level of discourse where it works to reveal and resist the oppression of specific discursive practices, such as discourses on sexuality and race. Dispersion and multiplicity replace unity and totality. Or, to put the matter another way, the assumed truth of constructions is deconstructed. One does not ask, for instance, what is the Good, the True, the Beautiful, or, what is "woman," the "self," or what is "homosexual"?

> Instead, one investigates the various discourses which create each of these by articulating them as somehow essential and universal truths. We can see emerging in this attack an "enemy" whose identity becomes explicit [in] the work of deconstruction, associated with the name Jacques Derrida. That "enemy" is Western thought itself, and the primacy given to "reason" as a way of grasping reality and truth. (p. 370)

Pinar succinctly explains the poststructural objections to reason, totality, and metanarratives. He continues by showing how Derrida would challenge the privileged position of reason itself. Poststructuralism, then, attempts to map discursively how the idea of truth as a grasp on things must necessarily have a nonmetaphorical sense and how the "nonmetaphorical" and the "other" are constructed by the intersection of discursive and non-discursive practices. Ultimately, postmodern curriculum discourses, particularly those rooted in poststructuralism, seek to deconstruct modern constructions of race, gender, and ethnicity based on Enlightenment notions of reason and to expose the ways that this construction perpetuates unjust power relations.

I have found over the years that these poststructural insights, as well as the analogies presented above, infuriate many students. These analogies shatter the stereotype of the self as genetically pure, biologically unadulterated, culturally unified, and totally separated from the "other," especially the racially, sexually, gender, or culturally different and dangerous other. In my analogies, however, I also present the position of other postmodern scholars, especially David Ray Griffin, that although we all share in a common humanity with common molecular heritage, the uniqueness of the individual cannot be minimized. Constructive postmodernism, as we saw in chapter one, recognizes that the strength of the whole is derived from a respect for the contribution of each individual, a contribution that is preserved only if the entire edifice of life is understood as an integrated and interdependent whole. In this sense, curriculum development in the postmodern era from both the poststructural and constructive perspectives insists that racism, patriarchal structures, sexism, and cultural elitism must be exposed and challenged. Additionally, it is recognized that

Cartesian dualisms and the denial of the interconnectedness of experiences actually undermine personal and global survival.

In summary, curriculum development in the postmodern era respects and celebrates the uniqueness of each individual person, text, event, culture, and educative moment, but all within the context of an interdependent cosmological view. All occasions are important and dynamic parts of the fabric of the whole. By ignoring race, gender, and ethnicity as integral to education, modern curriculum development models have actually contributed to the frustration, anger, and violence that threaten to destroy civilization. The analogies and poststructural insights above should help to reinforce the critical importance of racial, gendered, and cultural curriculum discourses in the postmodern era.

Students of curriculum development must explore education from these perspectives in order to understand the complexities of postmodern curriculum. Some prominent authors and texts that should be included in a review of gender and cultural studies, in addition to those already cited in this chapter, are Patti Lather (1989, 1991, 1994), Jo Anne Pagano (1990), Patricia Hill Collins (1990), Linda Christian-Smith (1987), Nel Noddings (1984, 1989, 1992), Elizabeth Ellsworth (1989), Leslie Roman and Linda Christian-Smith (1987), Leslie Roman and Michael Apple (1990), James T. Sears (1990, 1992), William Pinar (1994), and Jesse Goodman (1987, 1992). On issues related to race and culture, Peter McLaren and Michael Dantley (1990), Keith Osajima (1992), Barry Troyna and Richard Hatcher (1992), Lois Weis (1983, 1988), Camron McCarthy and Michael Apple (1988), and Susan Edgerton (1993) provide additional scholarly insights. There is a growing body of curriculum research emerging from scholars sensitive to the postmodern understandings of race, gender, and ethnicity in the 1990s as introduced in this chapter. Race and gender will continue to be central to efforts to understand curriculum development.

The effort to include multiculturalism in the curriculum has often been understood as a postmodernist project. In this regard, Bridges (1991) writes, "What troubles us [conservatives] about multiculturalism is its inevitable association with the agenda of postmodernism" (p. 3). For Bridges postmodernism represents a threat to cultural values and norms enshrined in the modernist canon. Bridges discusses the rhetorical tradition in Western thought that there are at least two sides to every question, and that any question is best understood by one who can argue both sides with equal effectiveness. The goal then of inquiry, understood rhetorically, is not objective truth but reasonable belief, the state of being persuaded. This led in the seventeenth century to an embrace of the logic of Cartesian dualism, giving rise to the natural sciences. Bridges writes that the Enlightenment project started a rejection of rhetorical conceptions of reason and knowledge. Thus, it should not be surprising that multiculturalism has created controversy, especially among radical conservatives who see their task as defense of the Enlightenment project of reason and order or rhetorical conceptions of knowledge.

The emerging curricular concerns about gender equity, human sexuality education, racial and ethnic bias in hiring practices and classroom instruction, sexual orientation, minority representation, multicultural literature, cultural and civic literacy, and a litany of other volatile issues remind us of the importance of integrating race, gender, and ethnicity into the fabric of our understanding of curriculum development. As this chapter has reminded us, all these issues must ultimately focus on the autobiographical expression of the self-in-relation and the cultural context of the postmodern society.

CHAPTER SEVEN

Postmodern Philosophies in Curriculum Studies

All educators at one time or another in their preservice training or graduate degree program have studied philosophy of education. Many teachers dread taking these philosophy courses, often for good reasons. In some cases, philosophy of education is presented as a sacred depository of uncontestable ideas and relics of the golden ages of human thinking. These timeless truths and values may be understood as latent in student's minds waiting to be brought to consciousness, as idealists believe. On the other hand, truth may be uncovered by studying objects in the natural world using the scientific method, as realists believe. However, in both cases, since perennial truths and values are beyond reproach, they often become inert ideas or scientific facts to be memorized rather than tentative contextualized discourses to be evaluated from a postmodern perspective. Additionally, the individual thinkers and writers who articulate perennial philosophies are either enshrined as icons of humanity or castigated as subversive villains intent on destroying the truth, depending on the prejudice of the professor.

Philosophy of education is all too often presented in a way that is inaccessible to students. The specialized language and unintelligible jargon of many philosophical discourses are dense and obtuse. Some professors of philosophy of education are dense and obtuse as well, lacking passion, praxis—reflection and action beyond verbalism and activism (Freire, 1970)—wisdom, and *phronesis*—a personal practical knowledge that engenders social competence. Their pedagogical styles and methodologies are contrived and impersonal. As a result, education students

145

often feel that philosophy is removed from their lived experience and their classroom practice.

School districts often promulgate philosophy and mission statements that many teachers, parents, students, and school personnel find irrelevant or inadequate. Committees are sometimes formed to revise the philosophy of the university or school district, only to discover that their real concerns and problems are never clearly articulated and seldom addressed in practice. As a result, many educational philosophies collect dust until it is time to bring them off the shelf, almost like a religious ritual, to be presented for accreditation or evaluation. Somehow the philosophy statement magically justifies the existence and value of the curriculum and instruction programs in the institution. Many disturbing practices are justified in the name of philosophy and ideology, and we need only explore the education system in Hitler's Germany, Stalin's Russia, and Mao's China to find some obvious examples (Pinar et al., in press, chap. 14). However, philosophy and ideology have also supported abuses in American education: segregation and tracking (Oakes, 1985; McNeil, 1986; Weis, 1988; Page, 1991); racism (Stannard, 1992; Castenell and Pinar, 1993); corporate manipulation (Shea et al., 1989; Spring, 1990); gender research bias (Gilligan, 1982); patriarchal structures (Lerner, 1986; Grumet, 1988b; Pagano, 1990); savage economic inequalities and injustices (Daly and Cobb, 1989; Kozol, 1991) religious proselytization (Provenzo, 1990); social control (Franklin, 1986, 1988); and political conflict of interest and indoctrination (Apple, 1979; Giroux and McLaren, 1989; Apple and Christian-Smith, 1991; Wexler, 1992; Spring, 1993). Philosophy of education obviously cannot be a neutral bystander in the schooling debates and cultural controversies of contemporary American society.

The research cited above has created an atmosphere where the field of philosophy of education is being forced to consider new understandings of itself in the postmodern era. While philosophy of education has enjoyed periods of respect and notoriety, particularly during the time of John Dewey in the early twentieth century (Schubert, 1986), the field has been marked by controversy and a concern for leadership in recent decades (Maxcy, 1991, 1993). Part of the responsibility for the turmoil in the field of philosophy of education clearly rests on the shoulders of professors in the 1950s and 1960s, a time when the field sought legitimacy by aligning itself with departments of philosophy rather than education. In the 1950s there was a move to create separate departments of philosophy of education, history of education, and sociology of education. Professors with degrees in the "parent" disciplines of philosophy, history, and sociology were preferred to lead these programs in many universities. John Dewey and Boyd Bode, both of whom received degrees in philosophy rather than education, were models for those who sought legitimacy for the ascendancy of pure philosophy in philosophy of education studies.

John Dewey (1859–1952) was both philosopher and educator. His synthesis of Darwinian evolutionary theory, the scientific method, democracy, and the philosophy of pragmatism was the basis of his work as an educational reformer. Dewey viewed education as a process of experience and social activity, and the school was intimately related to this process in the society it served. Dewey actually taught philosophy at several universities after receiving his doctoral degree in philosophy from Johns Hopkins University in 1884. However, it was his work as the director of the University of Chicago Laboratory School from 1896 to 1904 and his leadership of the combined departments of philosophy, psychology, and pedagogy there that integrated his philosophical and educational interests. Dewey's pragmatic educational philosophy became the basis of learning activities at the laboratory school. By the time of his death in 1952 other philosophers of education considered Dewey's movement from philosophy to education to be the preferred model for all university departments of philosophy of education.

By the early 1960s, some philosophers of education argued against the notion of analytic philosophy as the primary discipline that directs the field. Philip G. Smith (1965) in *Philosophy of Education* argued that the issues and problems in the educational field are unique, thus making it problematic to do analytic philosophy "on top of" education. Reading the journal of the Philosophy of Education Society, *Educational Theory*, and the yearbooks of the National Society of the Study of Education reveals a constant tension over this issue for the past thirty years. Whereas one editor may emphasize analytic philosophy and alienate scholars closely aligned with pedagogical practice, a new editor may emphasize the application of pragmatism in schooling and offend analytic philosophers. However, this trend to promote philosophy *or* education was not universal. For example, the rise of a foundations of education program at the University of Illinois in the 1950s underlines the growing interest in an eclectic approach to anthropology, history, sociology, and philosophy within the field of education.

Once the theoretical split between philosophy and education occurred in many universities, it created much tension and suspicion within both departments. Philosophers of education often were not accepted in either philosophy or education departments, and when some professors attempted to shift allegiances back to education departments in the 1980s the division was too intense for easy reconciliation. Spencer Maxcy (1993) in *Postmodern School Leadership* chronicles these contemporary crises, especially in educational administration, and concludes that philosophy, education, and leadership cannot be separated in postmodern schooling. Maxcy recognizes that the central issue for philosophy of education in the 1990s is how to conduct research and theoretical investigations that will be viable from the perspective of the social sciences and humanities, while remaining firmly rooted in the particular concerns for postmodern leadership in schools. Maxcy acknowledges that the contentious battles over the meaning of philosophy of education in the past thirty years have had a profound impact on the field, especially as reflected in its inability to engender leadership in education. A postmodern philosophy of education must move beyond the modern bifurcation of philosophy and education to an eclectic integration that incorporates and celebrates both if dynamic and respected leadership is to emerge.

In recent years I have attended the conferences of the PES (Philosophy of Education Society), LPES (Louisiana Philosophy of Education Society, of which I am the president-elect for 1994), APA (American Philosophical Association), APPE (Association for Process Philosophy of Education), and the summer institute of APPE at the University of the South. I presented formal papers at some of these conferences and attended many sessions with other professors of philosophy of education. Theoretical tension and methodological debates in the field still exist. Analytic methodologies, the logic of rationalism, decontextualized discourses, dialectical analysis, and/or the mainstream social science emphasis of empiricism still dominate the scholarship of many philosophers. Richard Rorty (1979) in *Philosophy and the Mirror of Nature* exposes philosophy's difficulty in shifting from this analytic mode. Along with Rorty, Stephen Toulmin (1982) recognizes multiple ways of knowing and has rejected the aspiration to achieve *episteme*—true and certain knowledge. Belief, says Toulmin, is about as close as we can ever get.

In this milieu, and as a result of the reconceptualization of curriculum studies in the 1970s, the field of curriculum theory rather than the field of philosophy of education has often taken the lead in promoting the postmodern philosophical discourses that integrate education and philosophy. Curriculum theorists deconstruct and often reject the search for *episteme* and the dominant methodologies of empiricism, the Hegelian dialectic, rationalism, and analytic philosophy. They generally draw eclectically and combinationally from one or more of the following theoretical approaches in their pedagogy and research: phenomenology, autobiography, existentialism, pragmatism, aesthetics, theology, deconstructionism, poststructuralism, feminism, hermeneutics, chaos theory, and critical theory (Pinar, 1988). Thus, fundamental differences have emerged between some educational philosophers and curriculum theorists, and philosophy of education in the 1990s remains a field in search of a soul.

One of the primary reasons for the ostracization of philosophers of education by philosophy departments at some universities is that education professors are generally shunned and ignored on college campuses. The following comments by philosopher Bruce Wilshire (1990) of Rutgers University in his provocative book *The Moral Collapse of the University: Professionalism, Purity, and Alienation* will help to illustrate this situation:

> Educators in universities seldom talk about education.
> Administrators talk about administrative problems,

professors talk about problems in their special fields of study, and those who do talk about education, professors in education departments, are generally despised and shunned. Besides, even if one does listen to this latter group, one usually hears education talked about as if it were just another special field of study, not as something that vitally concerns us all just because we are human. (p. 21)

Wilshire's indictment of education professors should be taken as a challenge rather than an insult. Many curriculum theorists have accepted this challenge to move the field of education beyond the rigid parochialism and instrumentalism Wilshire condemns. They also address another problem identified by Elliot Eisner who contends that philosophy is often regarded as an academic distraction in programs preparing researchers in the social sciences. Eisner (1991) writes: "Philosophy is nagging, it cajoles students into asking questions about basic assumptions, it generates doubts and uncertainties, and, it is said, it keeps people from getting their work done" (p. 4). Eisner proposes that the central concepts in the social sciences are themselves philosophical in nature: validity, truth, fact, theory, objectivity, structure. Curriculum theory incorporates the scholarship of many disciplines, especially contemporary philosophies, in order to address Wilshire's and Eisner's concerns and to revive the vital issues of the meaning of human life, knowledge, schooling, justice, democracy, compassion, and ecology in the postmodern era.

Philosophy of education in the first half of the twentieth century was an important and independent genre in the study of the foundations of education. However, as its importance began to diminish by the 1960s, departments of philosophy of education were consolidated or dismantled. Philosophy of education was subsumed under departments of educational leadership, administration, or policy studies in many universities. This association has been, as we have seen above, an uneasy alliance. Especially insulting to some is the fact that philosophy of education has become either an elective (opposite history of education) or a short unit of study in foundations courses in most undergraduate and many graduate degree programs. Since the Reconceptualization of curriculum studies in the 1970s, the field of curriculum theory has begun to incorporate philosophical discourses into the very fabric of the study of curriculum and instruction. It may be that curriculum theorists will provide the leadership that will help to return philosophy of education to prominence in the postmodern field of education.

The renewal of philosophical understandings of curriculum studies might offer the best hope for finally transcending the drudgery and disconnectedness of the curriculum methods courses that continue to be driven by objective lesson planning. Too many preservice programs continue to focus exclusively on systematic planning and objective codification; the concerns of postmodern society militate against the continuance of trivial pursuit in education. Yet this is what classroom practice has been reduced to in the modern age. Postmodern philosophical understandings insist that we must deconstruct and/or transcend modernity because it has reached the apex of absurdity in schooling practices that prioritize rote memorization, reward mastery of trivial facts, and proclaim the winners of *Wheel of Fortune* or *Jeopardy* as the most intelligent.

This postmodern vision proposes that curriculum development courses that have traditionally been taught as methods for practical application or systematic implementation of the Tylerian model in the schools must be replaced by courses that emphasize curriculum theory. This is exemplified by the explosion of recent theoretical positions, including what William Pinar and Madeleine Grumet (1976) call *"currere,"* Nicholas Burbules (1993a) calls "dialogue in teaching," Cleo Cherryholmes (1988b) and Nicholas Burbules (1993) call "critical pragmatism," Spencer Maxcy (1993) calls "postmodern leadership," Donald Schon (1983, 1991) calls "reflection-in-action," Nel Noddings (1984, 1992) calls "caring," Paulo Freire (1970, 1985) calls "praxis," William Stanley (1992) calls "curriculum for utopia," Donald Oliver and Kathleen Gershman (1989) call "ontological knowing," Joe Kincheloe and William Pinar (1991) call "social psychoanalysis of place," Maxine Greene (1978) calls "wide awakenness," Paulo Freire and Donaldo

Macedo (1987) call "critical literacy," Jurgen Habermas (1970) calls "emancipatory knowledge," Hans-Georg Gadamer (1976) calls "fusion of horizons," William Doll (1993) calls "a transformative vision," Hannah Arendt (1958) calls "emancipatory interests," James Anthony Whitson (1991) calls *"phronesis,"* Henry Giroux (1992) calls "border pedagogy," Peter McLaren (1989) calls "empowerment," William Schubert and William Ayers (1992) call "teacher lore," and many other approaches to incorporating philosophical dialogue into pedagogy that parallel the themes of qualitative humanistic inquiry. Courses such as curriculum development, elementary and secondary curriculum, supervision of instruction, and curriculum evaluation are now exploring the meaning and context of education from these various philosophical and theoretical perspectives. Curriculum development in the postmodern era emphasizes discourses that promote understanding of the cultural, historical, political, ecological, aesthetic, theological, and autobiographical impact of the curriculum on the human condition, social structures, and the ecosphere rather than the planning, design, implementation, and evaluation of context-free and value-neutral schooling events and trivial information.

The growth of curriculum theory as a field of study in the past decade has presented a formidable challenge to philosophers of education: either engage curriculum theorists in philosophical dialogue or retreat into the security of a moribund field. (The field of curriculum development itself has been called moribund in the past. Before the Reconceptualization, Joseph Schwab [1970] identified the field's "flight from the practical." Six years later Dwayne Huebner [1976] declared the field dead because of a lack of focus and unity. By the end of the 1970s William Pinar [1978] declared the field "arrested" and suggested that Jurgen Habermas' notion of emancipatory knowledge might stimulate movement.) While there will always be a few philosophy of education courses offered in departments of educational foundations and leadership, curriculum theorists and philosophers of education are joining together to move the philosophic dialogue beyond the moribund and arrested field of the past to a new vision of curriculum development in the postmodern era. In some cases the fields naturally merge because philosophers of education teach curriculum theory courses and/or curriculum theorists teach philosophy of education courses in foundations departments. There is even a slowly emerging cooperation between philosophy departments and education departments at a few universities. These encouraging practices indicate that a postmodern perspective, albeit controversial, is beginning to blur the distinctions between curriculum theory and philosophy of education.

In fairness to the traditional field of philosophy of education, it is also important to note that the emerging field of curriculum theory, as pointed out in the introduction to this book, has many hostile and competitive factions at odds with one another: political theorists, feminists, neo-Marxists, phenomenologists, multiculturalists, reconceptualists, poststructuralists, deconstructionists, and constructive postmodernists. Critics are sometimes justified in their caution about engaging curriculum theorists in scholarly dialogue in such a climate. Additionally, curriculum theorists remain in conflict with traditionalists, perennialists, essentialists, and conservatives who have dominated much of the school reform proposals during the Reagan and Bush presidencies in the 1980s. The contentious nature of these debates also raises concerns for those seeking to incorporate curriculum theory into their curriculum development programs. However, despite efforts to silence curriculum theorists using ad hominem labels such as "politically correct" or "feminazi," there is no hope of eliminating the postmodern philosophical discourses that are integral to curriculum development in the postmodern era. The second wave is underway. Additionally, there are many curriculum theorists and philosophers of education who are beginning to bridge these ideological gaps reported above in their scholarship. Maxine Greene, Spencer Maxcy, Jim Garrison, Nicholas Burbules, William Stanley, Anthony Whitson, William Doll, Jackie Blount, Wen-Song Hwu, John St. Julien, Jo Anne Pagano, James Henderson, Robert Graham, Nel Noddings, and Madeleine Grumet are perhaps representative of this trend.

This introduction to the climate of philosophy of education is important because it will help to locate the discussion of postmodern curriculum development in the context of the contemporary field. Philosophic understanding is a central dimension of contemporary curriculum discourses, and exploring this milieu and its ever changing nature is essential for those navigating the waters of the curriculum field in these postmodern turbulent times. Curriculum development courses in the 1990s that do not include these philosophic understandings of education as the foundation of their investigations deny students access to contemporary educational studies. It is irresponsible to ignore the philosophical dimension of postmodern curriculum studies in the 1990s.

I observe four rather distinct perspectives in conflict over the philosophical agenda of curriculum development: essentialists who are committed to the perennial truths of Platonic idealism or scientific realism as it is applied to the school curriculum (for example, Chester Finn, Diane Ravich, William Bennett, E. D. Hirsch, Jr., Allan Bloom, and Mortimer Adler); traditionalists, typically associated with educational foundations departments, who are committed to synoptic reviews and dispassionate analyses of philosophy of education as a field of study (for example, Peter Hlebowiths, Howard Ozmon, Daniel Tanner, Laurel Tanner, and Samuel Craver); curriculum theorists, typically associated with departments of curriculum and instruction, who utilize phenomenology, feminism, poststructuralism, deconstructionism, neo-Marxism, or neopragmatism to support revisionist understandings of the post-Tylerian curriculum (for example, Madeleine Grumet, Shirley Steinberg, Henry Giroux, Kathleen Kesson, Cleo Cherryholmes, Nel Noddings, Joe Kincheloe, Anthony Whitson, Jonathan Kozol, Jo Anne Pagano, Max van Manen, Norm Overly, Craig Kridel, James Sears, Norm Bernier, William Schubert, Jacques Daignault, Cameron McCarthy, Peter McLaren, Janet Miller, David Jardine, William Stanley, Noel Gough, William Reynolds, Michael Apple, Patti Lather, Tom Barone, Jim Henderson, Sue Books, Jeanie Brady, Dan Marshall, Ed Short, and many others cited throughout this book); and finally, those philosophers and theorists who have been able to contemplate the parochial philosophical debates, weigh the arguments, and articulate a broader vision of an emerging postmodern curriculum (for example, Maxine Greene, Ted Aoki, Chet Bowers, David Purpel, David Ray Griffin, William Pinar, Donald Oliver, Paul Klohr, James B. Macdonald, and William Doll). Although listing names of authors is problematic because of omissions and possible misrepresentations, it is nonetheless important for those unfamiliar with curriculum literature to begin associating some names with these discourses. It appears that the last two groups of scholars listed above are representative of those who are leading the movement toward a postmodern philosophical curriculum development paradigm in the 1990s.

Some of the philosophical discourses that are essential for beginning students of curriculum theory to investigate include existentialism, phenomenology, poststructuralism (and deconstructionism), critical theory (as well as neo-Marxism, social reconstructionism, and liberation theology), hermeneutics (and semiotics), pragmatism (as well as critical pragmatism and neopragmatism), process philosophy (as well as constructive postmodernism and process theology), chaos theory (as well as complexity and the new physics), feminism (and ecofeminism), and multiculturalism. Additionally, it is important for curriculum theorists to investigate the foundations of contemporary theories in *revisionist* understandings of traditional philosophies including Plato and idealism, Aristotle and realism, Eastern mysticism and Western theology, and developmental theories. Obviously, this list is overwhelming for those beginning the journey to understand contemporary curriculum discourses and postmodern curriculum development. However, it is important to remember that education is a lifelong journey, and complete knowledge of all philosophies is impossible—postmodernists would even suggest an oxymoron since philosophical discourse is never complete! This overview should serve as a guide or introduction for the journey to understand curriculum theory. The challenge is to begin the process of uncovering the layers of possibilities that exist in the study of curriculum theory that will inform and enrich our understanding of education and our experience of schooling in the postmodern era.

Two of the philosophies that are most challenging to understand, but also widely influential in curriculum studies, are poststructuralism and deconstructionism. Understanding curriculum theory from the poststructural and deconstructed perspective involves enlarging our modes of cognition (Pinar & Reynolds, 1992), engaging in methods of critique and analysis (Cherryholmes, 1988b), and analyzing contemporary culture and history (Jameson, 1991) in order to challenge and subvert the central values, organizing metaphors, and discursive strategies of modernism. In this sense, poststructuralism and deconstructionism share a common purpose with postmodernism: exposing the contradictions and fallacies embedded within the themes of Western thought and Enlightenment rationality. However, the purpose is not destruction. Jacques Derrida, who, along with Paul deMan and Geoffrey Hartman, is most often associated with deconstructionism, explains: "I was quite explicit about the fact that nothing of what I said had a destructive meaning. Here and there I have used the word deconstruction, which has nothing to do with destruction. . . . It is simply a question of being alert to the implications, to the historical sedimentation of the language we use—and that is not destruction" (1972, p. 271).

What is this "historical sedimentation" that Derrida deconstructs? First, it is the dualism of Cartesian philosophy (following from seventeenth-century French philosopher René Descartes) with its separation of ego from the external world and its consequent emphasis on control and manipulation which anticipated the bureaucratic and technological society of the twentieth century. Second, it is Enlightenment philosophy and rational humanitarianism that anticipated the French Revolution and the rise of the political ideologies of the nineteenth century: liberalism, socialism, and radicalism. Allan Megill (1985) concludes: "It is clear, I think, that modern intellectual history, has up to now been mainly defined by the thought of the Enlightenment" (p. 340). Megill predicts that despite the importance of the Enlightenment in defining the terms of contemporary discourse, social problems, and institutions, it will not continue much longer. This is evident because of the decline of the old Kantian, Cartesian, and Hegelian certainties, as well as the malaise and dysfunction within politics and institutions— including schooling—which are products of Enlightenment moral, social, and political theory. Megill explains: "Following Rorty, I have characterized Nietzsche, Heidegger, Foucault, and

Derrida as 'reactive' thinkers. Clearly, it is against the Enlightenment project, and against the elaboration and modification of that project in Romanticism and historicism, that these thinkers react" (p. 340).

I agree that poststructuralism and deconstructionism are reactions to modern philosophies that are rooted in Enlightenment notions that have given rise to liberalism, socialism, and radicalism. Many scholars argue that analytic Enlightenment philosophies have pushed society to the limits of absurdity in the twentieth century: in the economic realm, laissez-faire liberalism has led to unrestrained materialistic capitalism and ecologically destructive consumerism; in the political realm, militant and tyrannical communism has led to oppressive centralized authority and debilitating community malaise; and in the social realm, fascist dictatorships have engendered bigotry, genocide, and violence. Scholars like Allan Megill emphasize that Derrida, Foucault, and other deconstructive and poststructural thinkers challenge the basic assumptions of these economic, political, and social theories in order to support postmodern philosophical perspectives that will expose the contradictions embedded within Enlightenment rationality and hopefully overcome the detrimental and debilitating effects of structuralism and modernity.

Although poststructuralism, deconstructionism, and postmodernism are often used interchangeably to describe the critique of modernity described above (Sarup, 1989), there are important distinctions. Poststructuralism refers to those theoretical movements emerging in France that had grown out of and then opposed structuralism (Descombes, 1980). It is a response to those theories that purport to discover invariant structures in society, the human psyche, history, consciousness, and culture. Poststructuralism is thus an assault on structuralism as well as an outgrowth of it. It includes an attack on humanism, as well as existentialism and phenomenology. While structuralism has many definitions, Cleo Cherryholmes (1988b) presents a general overview of structuralism as an analysis and philosophical orientation that privileges structures, systems, or sets of relations over the specific phenomena that emerge in, are constituted by, and derive their identity from those structures and sets of relations.

Structuralism has sought to identify the systems that create meaning; poststructuralism has sought to dismantle the system in order to expose the variable and contingent nature of systems. Deborah Britzman writes about poststructural views of identity in which the notion of a unitary, cohesive self is deconstructed. Britzman (1992) challenges the idea that individuals have an authentic core or essence that has been repressed by society:

> Rather than appeal to a timeless and transcendent human nature, poststructural thought traces "the constitution of the subject within a historical framework" (Foucault, 1980, p. 117). There is concern with how subjectivities become configured as an effect of history and how they are then produced. . . . In poststructural analysis, meaning is never fixed or stable. Nor is reality, in any sense, understood as objectively "out there" or simply apprehended through language. Instead, meaning becomes the site of departure, a place where reality is constructed, truth is produced, and power is effected. Poststructuralist approaches are concerned with the inherited and constructed meanings that position our understanding of social life. (p. 25)

William Pinar et al. (in press) support this concept of the self and subjectivity in poststructuralism and offer this analysis of structuralist views of subjectivity:

> In general, however, structuralists attempt to stop the hemorrhaging of subjectivity in to the world. Not only would reality and meaning be found in and established by invariant structures, but the subject itself, and human consciousness generally, would be construed as products of invariant structures. What distinguishes the structuralist move . . . is not only the more technical definition of structure, but more importantly, the turn to language as the medium through which structures will reveal themselves. Language becomes for structuralism the field of investigation. (p. 363)

This turn to language is credited to the linguistic theory of Ferdinand de Saussure, who had a broad influence on structuralism. He argued that language should be studied not in terms of its history but in terms of its extant structures, that languages are systems of signs that consist of signifier and signified, that meaning is generated not by correspondence between words and things (signifier and signified) but by the sign's and signifier's relationships and differences from other signs and signifiers, and finally that relationships are dualisms or binary opposites (such as light/dark, male/female) that constitute foundational structures that help determine difference or meaning. Saussure also distinguished between *langue* (language and the collectivity of signs) and *parole* (speech and the empirical reality of the embodiment of language). Saussure (1959) explains:

> The signifier, though to all appearance freely chosen with respect to the idea that it represents, is fixed, not free with respect to the linguistic community that uses it. The masses have no voice in the matter, and the signifier chosen by language could be replaced by no other. The fact, which seems to embody a contradiction, might be called colloquially "the stacked deck." (p. 71)

As a result of the influence of Saussure's linguistic theory, language became a field of study, semiotic structures and systems of signs became gateways to meaning, and traditional ways of articulating knowledge, history, and culture were exploded to reveal deep structures that called into question the taken for granted distinctions between dualisms such as fact and fiction, rational and irrational, or myth and reason.

The attack on the subjective, on humanism, and on the Enlightenment project were utilized by the more radical structuralists and became the basis for the emergence of poststructuralism. The more conservative elements of structuralism, such as linguistic idealism, ahistoricism, and language analysis, were attacked. If, as structuralism maintained, underlying structures constitute reality and meaning, then what is the relationship between the human mind and these systems of meaning? The structuralist answer is that the human mind itself is structured in a way that corresponds to the structures "out there." This is where poststructuralists such as Michel Foucault, Jacques Lacan, Gilles Deleuze, and Julia Kristeva accused structuralism of neo-Kantianism and only a partial break with humanism, for it reproduced the humanist notion of an unchanging human nature. Foucault (1972) argued that structuralism's attempt to "establish a system of homogeneous relations: a network of causality that makes it possible to derive each of them, relations of analogy that show how they symbolize one another, or how they all express one and the same central [structure]" (pp. 9–10) did not take into account the social and political construction of such systems. The attack also included a critique of structuralism's blindness to its own involvement in the articulation of systems using language. This brings us back to Rorty's claim at the beginning of this chapter that traditional philosophy of education is unable to see its own complicity in the analytic paralysis that exists in contemporary philosophy of education scholarship.

As we examine the language critique of poststructuralists, particularly Foucault, it is important to read their work not literally but ironically. In this sense poststructuralism shares with postmodernism a sense of the irony but perhaps with a more playful intent. Therefore, poststructuralists are not so much guides as opponents. Poststructuralism is not a system but opposition to the structure of understanding as a unified system. Megill (1985) explains:

> We ought to view their writings, as we view the work of the artist, as existing in a state of tension with the given. Foucault, for example, is clearly the double of conventional historians, who challenge, and who ought to be challenged by, his work. . . . Derrida's deconstruction— his brilliant self-parody—helps bring to light the latent absurdity residing on both sides of this opposition, and thus helps us to see the limitations of each. In short, we ought to approach aestheticism in a spirit of sympathetic skepticism. (p. 345)

This "sympathetic skepticism" and ironic "latent absurdity" described by Megill are an integral part of postmodern visions, especially as expressed in poststructuralism and deconstructionism.

This very brief introduction to poststructural and deconstructive perspectives on postmodernism demonstrates their complexity. Simple definitions are impossible—even a contradiction of the premise of deconstructionism because every linguistic explanation must be exposed for its internal contradictions. In this sense, deconstructionism is not a method but a critique. Additionally, some would argue for a greater distinction between poststructuralism, deconstructionism, and postmodernism than I have introduced here. However, for those beginning the investigation of contemporary curriculum development discourses, the unifying themes of social, linguistic, and aesthetic critique of modernity and Enlightenment notions of reason, totality, knowledge, and institutions weave a common thread through poststructuralism, deconstructionism, and postmodernism.

While this chapter has attempted to make the contemporary discussions of philosophies in curriculum theory accessible to readers in a brief introductory overview, the attempt to do this is risky. For to simplify complex ideas such as poststructuralism and deconstructionism that continue to evolve over the lifetime of many writers and to summarize multiperspectival philosophies whose meanings are constantly debated by scholars is impossible. Therefore, readers are urged to explore these philosophies in much greater detail in primary texts, critical reviews, and secondary analyses. In doing so, it will be clear that philosophy is not an exact science but rather an ongoing exploration by those who are truly passionate about *wisdom, sophia, currere, praxis,* and *phronesis.*

Having already introduced hermeneutics, theology, feminism, multiculturalism, poststructuralism, and deconstructionism, and in order to provide one concrete example of the application of postmodern philosophies in the schooling context of the 1990s, I will conclude this chapter by exploring one specific application of philosophy in contemporary schooling: the debate over whole language and integrated language arts that is at the forefront of much discussion in American schools in the 1990s.

Whole language or integrated language arts instruction is not a new philosophy of curriculum and instruction, for it has been the basis of a successful approach to literacy and reading instruction in New Zealand and other countries for decades. Lois Bridges Bird (1993) explains: "Whole language as a dynamic, evolving grassroots movement among American educators is not much more than a decade old, but as a learner-centered educational philosophy that stems from such progressive educators as [John Amos] Comenius, [Johann Heinrich] Pestalozzi, [John] Dewey, [William Heard] Kilpatrick, Lucy Sprague Mitchell, Caroline Pratt, and George S. Counts, . . . it spans both continents and centuries" (p. 129). Bird contends that unlike these progressive antecedents, whole language today has a broader research base that includes sociology, developmental psychology, anthropology, and the like. Thus, whole language affirms the philosophies of progressive educators of the eighteenth and nineteenth centuries as to how human beings learn. Whole language is seen as not only a theory of language, learning, and teaching but also a philosophy of curriculum and community embedded in a sociopolitical context. "Following the lead of John Dewey, Whole Language teachers believe that school *is* life and as such should not be conducted as a sterile preparation for living in the real world someday" (Bird, 1993, p. 140). This theme can be found throughout the writings of John Dewey from his publication of *My Pedagogic Creed* in 1897 to *Experience and Education* in 1938. Dewey himself argued, "The ideal of using the present simply to get ready for the future contradicts itself. . . . Wholly independent of desire or intent, every experience lives on in further experiences. Hence the central problem of an education based on experience is to select the kind of present experiences that live fruitfully and creatively in subsequent experience" (pp. 49, 27).

There have been many conservative political and religious reactions to progressive education, Deweyan philosophy, and currently to the whole language approach to education and experience. The growth in popularity of the whole language philosophy in the United States has enraged some segments of the population. The following recent letter to the editor in my local newspaper is perhaps typical:

> As a current parent and former teacher I am seething at your "new age" teaching style. Our education system is failing miserably. Students are not graduating with the basic skills of reading, writing, math, geography, and history. This time spent teaching about dark mountains,

writing in diaries (journals) and studying family values would be better spent learning to read a newspaper, studying current events, and using math to figure out how much we're being taxed for all this wasted time. The shame of it all is that God and the Ten Commandments are not allowed in the school . . . so whose values and morals are you teaching my child? Are you grading my child on his political correctness or is he just allowed to feel good about himself? In closing, you teachers have overstepped the boundary between school rights and parent's rights. I will teach my child *my* values and *my* morals and you stick to the basics. (Newland, 1993, p. E-5)

This letter exemplifies the contentious reaction of the general public, parents, and even some teachers to curriculum development philosophies and modes of understanding that attempt to move beyond the traditional Tylerian rationale. This parent's cry for basic education, fundamentalist religious values, and parental rights reflects the attitudes of many. Curriculum theorists must be aware of the backlash against postmodern philosophies and make every effort to articulate their understanding of curriculum development clearly so as to reduce unnecessary conflict. Whole language, for example, has been misunderstood as a "program" of instruction, when it is actually a philosophical approach to language instruction that heightens creativity and interest in reading. Whole language is not about "new age" religion or sectarian values in education; it is about language, reading, thematic learning, appreciation, and understanding. Ken Goodman (1986) in *What's Whole in Whole Language?* writes:

Careful observation is helping us to understand better what makes language easy or hard to learn. Many school traditions seem to have actually hindered language development. In our zeal to make it easy, we've made it hard. How? Primarily by breaking whole (natural) language up into bite-size, but abstract little pieces. It seemed so logical to think that little children could best learn simple little things. We took apart the language and turned it into words, syllables, and isolated sounds. Unfortunately, we also postponed its natural purpose—the communication of meaning—and turned it into a set of abstractions, unrelated to the needs and experiences of the children we sought to help. (p. 7)

In "Writing Childrens' Books in a Language Arts Curriculum" (Slattery and Slattery, 1993) I have said that television and video games have not destroyed the natural interest of children in reading, rather, the way reading is taught in schools has conditioned children for passive visual entertainment. This echoes the claim of Madeleine Grumet (1988b), who offers insights into the condition of reading instruction and an alternative approach to children's reading experience in schools.

The emphasis on test scores, comprehension of isolated trivial information, decoding skills, and fragmented phonics skills in American schools over the past fifty years is so pervasive that national reports and curriculum reform proposals assume that increasing the measurable outcomes in the "basic" subjects of reading, writing, and mathematics will ameliorate the social and economic ills of the American culture. In whole language classrooms the emphasis is not on drill and practice for tests but on thinking about literature, analyzing ideas, articulating meanings, and evaluating opinions. Rather than using basal readers and isolated words and skills, whole language programs integrate language arts and reading throughout the curriculum with an emphasis on literature, familiar situations, autobiographical experiences, shared inquiry, and probing questions.

Critics have successfully forced some school boards to ban whole language approaches to instruction based on fears that integrated language arts programs are not academically rigorous, and thus student test scores will decline. As a result, the reading curriculum remains driven by competition, linear progress, empiricism, and statistical measurement. Concern for the quality and enjoyment of reading has become secondary to the paranoia about quantifiable grades and comprehension test scores.

What happens to young children in this educational environment? They learn to become passive receptors of discrete parcels of information instead of independent and critical thinkers. Reading becomes a disembodied experience where an "expert adult" and a depersonalized and mechanistic basal textbook inject information into an empty human receptacle, the brain, in the spirit of John Locke's *tabula rasa*. In this environment the conditioning of students to be passive receptors of video imagery and entertainment begins. In the culture of modernity, where life is often timed by the pace of television and punctuated by commercials, and where the audience sits passively waiting to be entertained or instructed, learning, creativity, thinking, and understanding are impossible. Donald Oliver and Kathleen Gershman (1989) conclude that in this modern environment integrated thematic education, whole language instruction, process teaching, and postmodern curriculum are "obviously both inappropriate and futile" (p. 164). In other words, postmodern curriculum development will not emerge in the schools and William Pinar's "second wave" of Reconceptualization will not break as long as the structures of modernity continue to dominate the schooling environment.

The postmodern vision of reading instruction is rooted in another understanding of education from the Latin words *educere*, "to draw or lead forth," and *ruminare*, "to think things over." Reading is a phenomenological and bodily activity that comes from deep within the human person. It is a mystical experience of the passions of the human spirit. Authentic reading instruction allows students to explore the nooks and crannies of their psyche and look forward to the journey within. Like the ruminants (animals that leisurely graze in the fields and chew their cud), students should also ruminate and masticate books and stories. They must leisurely graze in quiet corners, on active playgrounds, and in open fields and then return to the formal places of schooling to create their own books, write their own stories, and explore their own imaginative life histories. It is here that they are also exposed to real literature rather than contrived stories that are designed to parcel out phonics skills aligned to a scope and sequence chart.

Many teachers have begun to make the transition from skill and drill to integrated whole language environments. They have found that this can be done even within the traditional schooling context by allocating more time for autobiographical reflection and the creation of personal books and classroom libraries. An example will be illustrative. Following a traumatic miscarriage during a pregnancy in 1989, and trying to communicate the experience with our three young children who were looking forward to the birth of a sibling, my wife, Cheryl Friberg Slattery (1989), wrote a book about the miscarriage entitled *My Mommy was Pregnant, But then she Miscarried*. The book was written from the perspective of our six-year-old daughter, who was having a particularly difficult time integrating this experience into her life, and it was illustrated by the children's grandmother. This book not only became a source of comfort in our own family, but it has also been shared with many other children in the neighborhood and at school who have had to face similar crises in their families. In fact, the school counselor keeps a copy of the manuscript in her office. Our family autobiography has become an embodied and living text in our community. Additionally, when students hear the story in a personal context they become animated participants in the reading rather than passive receptors of an alienated text. As we saw earlier in the work of Madeleine Grumet, reading has now become an embodied phenomenological experience.

Reading activities such as this celebrate what phenomenologists call "the presence of an absence," the ruminating pasture where students individually create that which has never been. This, then, is the emerging context of reading instruction in postmodern schools: no longer passive imposition but rather active creation. Children's books have the opportunity to be the catalyst for drawing forth the natural interest of children in reading and reversing decades of overreliance on quantifiable comprehension and phonics texts in the school curriculum. Oliver and Gershman (1989), for example, emphasize the process orientation of this approach to reading instruction as they address teaching and learning:

> All relationships are internal: no one stands outside and "runs" something. The implications of this vision for education are, first, that it is misguided to see an educational setting sharply separated into teacher, students, knowledge, curriculum, materials of instruction, and so forth. Seeing teaching as a set of different components driven predictably toward a controlled

objective derives directly from the modern machine metaphor. In the modern cosmology, the *student* is a substantial being who can be caused (motivated) to learn *subject matter* by being provided with an adequate *curriculum* managed by the *teacher*. The student is the product to be developed, manufactured by machines (lessons) once they are provided with the raw materials (the curriculum). . . . Process curriculum [and whole language instruction] on the other hand begins by assuming that teacher, student, curriculum, materials are all moving into a novel occasion. We do not begin from the special position of nothing (before the class begins) to "make something happen." . . . The major thrust of planning for the teacher is to imagine what circumstances might move an occasion from potentiality into concrescence. . . . The teacher is not "transferring" a piece of knowledge or skill to the student; the teacher is seeking to share a common world with the student as the student enters the world of the teacher and *vice versa*. (pp. 161–162)

What we have explored here is an analysis of the whole language philosophy of reading instruction from the perspective of curriculum theory with a particular emphasis on phenomenology and autobiography. This is one among many approaches emerging in the field of curriculum theory that will provide alternative paradigms for understanding curriculum in the postmodern era.

Curriculum theorists utilize contemporary philosophies to expand our understanding of curriculum and instruction, whether it be from phenomenological, poststructural, deconstructive, feminist, process, or critical perspectives. These philosophical perspectives were never a concern in the traditional Tylerian rationale, for the systematic design of goals and objectives superseded the autobiographical, historical, political, theological, ecological, and social context of the learning experience. Contemporary philosophies in curriculum studies remain foreign and irrelevant to many traditionalists in the curriculum field in the 1990s. However, the explosion of their incorporation into the field makes them impossible to ignore any longer. Curriculum development in the postmodern era no longer excludes the essential dimension of philosophical investigations in education, for philosophy provides access to reflective understanding, heightened sensitivity, historical grounding, contextual meaning, and a liberating praxis. In this sense philosophy is not simply a study of perennial truths but rather a vehicle for engendering justice, compassion, self-exploration, empowerment, critical thinking, and, as we will explore in the next chapter, ecological sustainability in a threatened global environment. Quite possibly the emerging discourses shared by curriculum theorists and philosophers of education may signal the beginning of a new respect for education professors in the universities and a return to prominence of philosophical understandings of curriculum in the postmodern era.

CHAPTER EIGHT

Curriculum for Interdependence
and Ecological Sustainability

Jacques-Yves Cousteau is an internationally recognized spokesperson for the Earth and seas. Even in his eighties, the explorer who once reveled in the mystery of marine life and brought the splendor of underwater adventure alive has accepted a new mission. Marlise Simons (1994) reports on Cousteau's campaign against environmental degradation in the 1990s:

> These days, the captain of the Calypso . . . is talking less about nature's beauty and railing more against humans who use dynamite or drift nets to fish, who drain marshes and lagoons, who cut passages through atolls, who change the course of rivers, who wipe out all species, who pollute everywhere. Above all, he has set himself tasks more portentous than his past calls for conservation: he lobbies policy makers to redefine progress, complains of the hypocrisy and cruelty of the free-market system and warns of the self-destructive course taken by humanity. "I'm now fighting for my own species," Cousteau said, "I finally understood that we ourselves are in danger, not only fish." (p. A-6)

Cousteau is intimately familiar with the Earth and seas, and his passionate warning about the self-destructive course of humanity is one among a chorus of voices that have put ecological sustainability at the forefront of policy debates. Among those voices are educators who recognize the dual role of the school curriculum as an opportunity to inform students about the dangers of environmental pollution, unrestrained population growth, destruction of rainforests and wetlands, and

169

depletion of the protective ozone layer and as an opportunity for initiating students into holistic practices that will contribute to a postmodern global consciousness that is essential for ecological sustainability.

Scholars committed to this dual role of the curriculum have sounded an urgent warning to educators in the 1990s: ecological sustainability and holistic models of teaching must be the primary focus of the postmodern curriculum. Mary Evelyn Tucker (1993), for example, has cautioned that "the reality of a global environmental crisis, recently the focus of the Earth Summit in Rio de Janeiro in June of 1992, together with the demise of communism, has suddenly created an urgent agenda in this transitional decade that must be met with novel educational, social, and political programs" (p. 1). Douglas Sloan, professor of history and education at Teachers College, Columbia University, insists that the present crisis includes not only the destruction of the environment and its natural beauty but the virulence of spreading racism and narrow nationalisms, the indiscriminate extension of science and technology into every sphere of life, and the worldwide destruction of cultural richness and sources of meaning. The world is, Sloan (1993) warns, "collapsing under the impact of the homogenizing influences of the modern mindset and its attendant institutions [where] educational systems . . . force children at an ever-earlier age into an adult culture already shot through with futility, greed, and banality" (p. 1). Ecological and holistic visions of curriculum recognize that all these dimensions are interwoven with the others, and all must be grasped together as symptoms of "a deeper crisis of the whole human being" (Sloan, 1993, p. 1).

Along with Jacques Cousteau, Mary Evelyn Tucker, and Douglas Sloan, curriculum theorists understand that human life hangs in the balance. In this chapter we will explore curriculum from a globally interdependent ecological perspective that begins by examining the crisis of survivability of the spirit and the flesh. Postmodern educators understand that destruction of both the ecosphere and the human psyche are forms of violence that are interrelated. Nonviolence will emerge only when the dualisms and scientific bifurcations that have been ingrained in the modern consciousness since the Enlightenment are replaced by a postmodern holistic philosophy. Coretta Scott King (1993) writes about this change in consciousness:

> Nonviolence is not just about one person, one family, or one community, it is a holistic philosophy. All life is interrelated; we are all tied together. Problems that affect people in Beijing, China, also affect people in Harlem, U.S.A., and everywhere else in the world. We must be concerned about others as well as ourselves; we cannot just focus on our own problems. We must study the cultures and languages of the whole world. We need to study the history of people who are different from ourselves, those who are outside our borders as well as those who are inside. Martin [Luther King, Jr.] used to say that we are all tied together in an inescapable network of mutuality. What affects one directly affects all indirectly. (pp. xii–xiii)

Coretta Scott King echoes the postmodern philosophy of curriculum development introduced in this chapter. A holistic perspective is essential for the emergence of compassion, optimal learning environments, nonviolent conflict resolution, just relationships, and ecological sustainability.

We begin this holistic investigation with Fritjof Capra, who, in addition to his technical research in the field of high-energy physics, has written a number of theoretical works on modern science. The methods and theories of modern science, Capra contends in *The Turning Point: Science, Society, and the Rising Culture*, are leading to the self-destruction of humanity. It is only through a vision of a new postmodern reality with a reconciliation of science and the human spirit that a future will be accessible for the global community. Capra (1982) writes:

> We have high inflation and unemployment, we have an energy crisis, a crisis in health care, pollution and other environmental disasters, a rising wave of violence and crime, and so on. The basic thesis of this book is that these are all different facets of one and the same crisis, and that this crisis is essentially a crisis of perception. Like the crisis in physics in the 1920s, it derives from the fact that we are trying to apply the concepts of an outdated world view—the mechanistic world view of Cartesian-Newtonian science—to a reality that can no longer be understood in

terms of these concepts. We live today in a globally interconnected world, in which biological, psychological, social, and environmental phenomena are all interdependent. To describe this world appropriately we need an ecological perspective which the Cartesian worldview does not offer. (pp. 15–16)

Capra succinctly summarizes not only the theme of this chapter but also the postmodern curriculum development paradigm that is being investigated throughout this book.

Modern visions of education as characterized by the Tylerian rationale, behavioral lesson plans, context-free objectives, competitive and external evaluation, dualistic models that separate teacher and student, meaning and context, subjective persons and objective knowledge, body and spirit, learning and environment, and models of linear progress through value-neutral information transmission are no longer acceptable in the postmodern era. In fact, they are at the root of our ecological crisis according to David Orr (1992). David Bohm (1988) warns that "a postmodern science should not separate matter and consciousness and should therefore not separate facts, meaning, and value" (p. 60). Science would then be inseparable from a form of intrinsic morality. This separation is part of the reason for our present desperate situation (Bohm, 1988).

The technical and independent ideology of modernity not only is destructive of the human psyche but also threatens the very survival of the human species. If this sounds alarmist to some, the scholarship of curriculum theorists with an ecological focus does not apologize for this sense of urgency. At the end of Capra's earlier book, *The Tao of Physics*, he tied the conceptual shift of modern physics to these social implications. Capra (1975) warns:

I believe that the world view implied by modern physics is inconsistent with our present society, which does not reflect the harmonious interrelatedness we observe in nature. To achieve such a state of dynamic balance, a radically different social and economic structure will be needed: a cultural revolution in the true sense of the word. The survival of our whole civilization may depend on whether we can bring about such a change. (p. x)

Curriculum theorists have joined in the revolution proposed by Capra and proposed a vision of "sacred interconnections" (David Ray Griffin, 1990), "responsive teaching" (Chet Bowers and David Flinders, 1990), "ecological literacy" (David Orr, 1992), "holistic curriculum" (John P. Miller, 1988), "curriculum as place" (Joe Kincheloe and William Pinar, 1991; Patrick Slattery and Kevin Daigle, 1991), "the sacred circle" (Robert Regnier, 1992), "a post-liberal theory of education" (Chet Bowers, 1987), "insight-imagination" (Douglas Sloan, 1983), "a critical process curriculum" (Kathleen Kesson, 1993), "an inspiring holistic vision" (Ron Miller, 1993), and "the unity of related plurality" (Donald Oliver and Kathleen Gershman, 1989). The vast amount of curriculum scholarship with a holistic and ecological emphasis in the past ten years by these and other widely respected educators is indicative of the centrality of these issues in postmodern curriculum development. How will these ecological and holistic theories of curriculum and instruction be incorporated into postmodern schooling?

The first important change taking place in the postmodern curriculum is in the relationships that exist in classrooms. These changing relationships in turn foster ecological and global sensibilities. For example, in my classrooms, even in lecture halls with fifty students, I learn the names and interests of all students and let them know that their opinions and questions will not only be respected but encouraged. Reflective dialogue, autobiographical journals, nonconfrontational debate, co-operative investigations, and probing questions are the focus of the classroom experience. I begin with the assumption that we all bring important perspectives to the course that need to be explored. I also assume that students, on an intuitive level, are anxious to read, think, write, and engage in the learning experience. While the level of commitment may vary from person to person—and my own intensity may fluctuate depending on personal, family, or university commitments—I have yet to be disappointed by this classroom milieu. In fact, my experience is that when students are trusted and empowered in a holistic environment, the quantity and quality of their scholarly work improve exponentially. Students become far more demanding on themselves, especially when learning and self-discovery replace grades and course credits as the focus of the curriculum.

The traditional modern classroom has not allowed for a holistic and ecological atmosphere, especially because of the power arrangement of rows of desks with a podium and chalkboard in the front of the room. This structure reinforces the role of the teacher as the authority and information dispenser separate from the passive students, who need to be controlled and measured for optimal productivity. Rows of desks in classrooms evolved for two reasons: the need to control and organize larger numbers of students entering schools in the nineteenth century, and the expectation that schools would prepare students for the linear social structures of the modern world. In the early part of the twentieth century the majority of students leaving public schools pursued careers in factories, farming, or the military where assembly lines, planting columns ("a long row to hoe"), and rank and file marching formations not only dictated the physical structure of the workplace but also reflected the ideology of modern society. Students, it was understood, needed to be inculcated into a milieu of social control so that they would be prepared to fall in line, obey commands without thinking, and repeat functions mechanically without hesitation. This was considered to be especially important for the immigrant population, who needed to be immersed in the American melting pot culture in order to ensure cultural cohesion. Social control as a function of schooling was seldom questioned—except by some social reconstructionists and progressive educators.

Barry Franklin (1986, 1988) in *Building the American Community: The School Curriculum and the Search for Social Control* and "Whatever Happened to Social Control: The Muting of Coercive Authority in Curriculum Discourses" explores this issue of social control. Franklin locates social control in the service of the reproduction of cultural structures of the status quo. Mass immigration mobilized sentiment in this country for cultural standardization, a concern that remains in the 1990s and is at the root of conservative educational reform movements. Franklin contends that earlier forms of explicit coercion in schooling (such as the repression of languages, dress, and customs of immigrant children) have been replaced by persuasion, economic enticement, and other "democratic" forms of social control. Franklin argues that social control has not disappeared from curriculum development. Rather, it has been muted and disguised so that its coercive agenda is less detectable. Additionally, social control that once served as inculturation into middle class values and privileges now functions to legitimize and preserve corporate capitalism. Curriculum theorists from a variety of perspectives utilize Barry Franklin's research to contest modern curriculum development models. Those whose research includes an ecological and holistic concern especially see the danger of the deceptive social control that exists in education and society in the 1990s. The challenge to raise our consciousness concerning the ecological, psychological, and spiritual destruction that had resulted from social control in education is becoming ever more difficult, especially since educational institutions are, according to Franklin, complicit in this process. The preservation of the educational bureaucracy depends on the continuation of modernity and social control.

While the development of social control in order to build a cohesive American community continues to have many propo- nents in the 1990s, e' ~~ially among those who believe that schools must repair ' al disintegration that has resulted from rampant indiv{ ι, relativism, and a lack of common values, postmodern phies insist that schooling must tran- scend linear struct ner than return to social and psycho- logical models of (.hat have dominated curriculum devel- opment in the pa onservative reaction of the 1980s reform movements in e n insists on a different agenda: cultural literacy, laissez- .pitalism, traditional values, Western cul- ture, nationalisι .ιd unquestioning patriotism (Shea et al., 1989).

The emerging postmodern holistic and ecological models of curriculum dissolve the artificial boundary between the outside community and the classroom. Postmodern teaching celebrates the interconnectedness of knowledge, learning experiences, international communities, the natural world, and life itself. However, like John Dewey (1938), who warned that not all experiences are necessarily positive educational events, it is also important for teachers to orchestrate holistic learning experiences thoughtfully and carefully. Field trips, guest speakers, nature studies, and visits to museums are encouraged, and not just for the sake of alleviating boredom or for indoctrinating students with a narrow political or cultural perspective. Additionally, if a video presentation, lab project, or field trip is simply used as a reward for good behavior or a filler in a hectic school schedule, the postmodern perspective of the interconnectedness of experiences is lost. Understanding the difference between these two perspectives is essential for appropriate ecological models of education. Dewey (1938) clarifies the distinction:

> Traditional education did not have to face this problem [of utilizing a wide variety of experiences in the curriculum]; it could systematically dodge this responsibility. The school environment of desks, blackboards, a small school year, was supposed to suffice. There was no demand that the teacher should become intimately acquainted with the conditions of the local community, physical, historical, economic, occupations, etc., in order to utilize them as educational resources. A system of education based upon . . . experience must . . . take these things constantly into account. The tax upon the educator is another reason why progressive education is more difficult to carry on than was ever the traditional system. (p. 40)

Dewey's concerns echo the concerns of postmodern educators as well. The classroom environment and interconnectedness of experiences remain a central priority in holistic and ecological curriculum scholarship.

Holistic and ecological models of education have encouraged me to arrange my classrooms in circles in recent years. As simple as this change in architecture may seem, it has been one of the most significant and liberating events in the evolution of my pedagogy over the past twenty years. Manly Hall (1988) discusses the importance of architectural arrangements:

> The Greeks taught that buildings and dwellings profoundly influenced human conduct. The soul receiving into itself the impression of shapes is offended by

deformity and strengthened and inspired by noble proportions. . . . Buildings are thoughts and emotions in stone, concrete, steel, and other materials. All structures have their karmic consequences. . . . All genuine mandalas are intended to picture forth some aspect of universal harmony. The inward experience of the infinite scheme usually results in a refinement of the various expressions of human activity. (p. 167)

Education is one human activity that is profoundly affected by attention to environment and inner experience. Landscape, says David Orr (1992), shapes mindscapes. In seminar circles we can see faces and body language, listen with empathy, and become aware of our interconnectedness. The linear patterns of modernity were designed to eliminate the possibility of human contact, reflection, and thinking. Paul Shepard (1977) explains that the stability of communities is a consequence of the interplay between the psyche and the physical environment: "Terrain structure is the model for the patterns of cognition. . . . Cognition, personality, creativity, and maturity—all are in some way tied to particular gestalts of space" (p. 22). Thus, knowledge of a place, of where you are and where you come from, is intertwined with knowledge of self (Kincheloe and Pinar, 1991). David Orr contends that since it diminishes the potential for maturation and inhabitance, the destruction of places is psychologically ravaging as well. Orr (1992) writes, "If Shepard is right, and I believe that he is, we are paying a high price for the massive rearrangement of the North American landscape of the past fifty years" (p. 130). Hall (1988) also warns about the consequences of modern architecture for the human soul:

Progress, according to **modern** prevailing standards, must be essentially soulless. A building should exist only for utility, art for ingenuity, music for emotional excitation, laws for the advancement of material economic expansion, and recreational activities strictly for sensory enjoyment. As a result of constant association with mediocrity, human conduct is no longer influenced by overtones of beauty and integrity. This has contributed to the disintegration of modern society [and the environment]. . . . When the human being no longer pauses to read what Paracelsus

> called the "living book of nature," he loses contact with
> those basic values which alone can reveal . . . origin and
> destiny. . . . Those seeking genuine mystical enlightenment
> must release a power of soul awareness in themselves and
> allow their own intuition to indicate the direction they
> must travel in their earthly pilgrimage. (p. 167–168,
> emphasis added)

In order to understand the ecological interconnectedness and
holistic curriculum theories of the scholars identified above—
Bowers, Flinders, Orr, Regnier, Ron Miller, John P. Miller,
Tucker, Griffin, Kincheloe, Kesson, Sloan, and Pinar—attention
must be directed to architecture, classroom milieu, the natural
environment, and the inner environment of students and
teachers.

The circle as an important structure for developing
postmodern theories of education is proposed by Robert Regnier
of the University of Saskatchewan. Regnier (1992) proposes a
process pedagogy based on an Aboriginal approach to healing
using the Sacred Circle teachings of Canadian Plains Indians at
Joe Duquette High School in Saskatoon. Healing, as well as
teaching, are seen as integral to the transition toward meaning,
wholeness, connectedness, and balance. Regnier (1992) explains:

> The Sacred Circle is a "traditional symbolic circle" which
> incorporates the spiritual beliefs of many indian tribes of
> North America. . . . It symbolises harmony and the belief
> that life occurs within a series of circular movements that
> govern their relationship with the environment. . . . The
> Sacred Circle drawn into four quadrants differentiates
> physical, emotional, spiritual, and intellectual dimensions
> of personal development. Through this model, students
> are encouraged to view themselves as a whole person who
> can become self determining. This self-determination
> requires envisioning ideals in each area and examining the
> connections within each area. (pp. 1, 13)

Regnier uses the philosophy of Alfred North Whitehead to
demonstrate that human development, learning, teaching, and
curriculum development are all manifestations of process. By
recognizing human growth and learning as genesis and process,
it is possible to construct a pedagogy that reflects the dynamic,

interdependent, and cyclical character of reality. Regnier continues by criticizing Western metaphysics, which abstracts, categorizes, and isolates individuals rather than seeing reality as a unitary continuous process.

An interesting thing happened in one of my classroom seminar circles during a summer session. A woman unexpectedly brought her ten-year-old son to class one day. She was taking three courses and expected that her child would sit quietly and remain attentive in her science lab and physical education activity course. She worried, however, that he might become bored during our history of American education class. She arrived with the boy without time for introductions, and he sat quietly in the room. The next day the woman reported that her son enjoyed his day at the university, and, to her surprise, he particularly enjoyed our education class. He told his mother that it was fun because he spent the entire time listening to everyone discuss ideas in the circle while he tried to figure out which one was the teacher. In postmodern classrooms teachers are guides and mentors who orchestrate self-reflective learning experiences, joining in the sacred circle described by Regnier but not dominating and manipulating in the process.

Donald Oliver and Kathleen Gershman (1989) propose that Eastern thinking will help us to understand the importance of the circle in educational experience. They use the *I Ching* from ancient China (see figure 8.1) to propose that the world, like the classroom, is a unity of related plurality rather than a series of adversarial fragments that compete with one another for domination or privilege.

Mary Aswell Doll (1991) expands on Oliver and Gershman's idea of circles as an image for understanding the local and global interrelationship of postmodern thought in an address entitled "Dancing the Circle":

> Once upon a time the world went to sleep and dreamed that God was the center of the universe. The philosopher Nietzsche woke up, proclaiming the dream a nightmare and God dead. Later, the poet Yeats, agreed, saying, "Things fall apart, the center cannot hold." Both the philosopher and the poet were startled, however, when Heraclitus, dreaming from a deeper dream many centuries

earlier, said, "The center is everywhere," implying "the gods are all around and the goddesses are within." I would like to talk about circles and inner gods and goddesses. The circle's round shape is soft, recursive; it curves back upon itself. It is in constant motion; therefore, it is dynamic, using its own inner energy to spiral movement inward, toward reflection. The circle also spirals outward toward what the new science of chaos calls fractal patterns, which loop and loop again, forming harmonic swirls. The loopings, either inward or outward, are, we could say, geysers for the imagination. (p. 1)

Doll's literary and philosophic reflections on the circle move next to the symbolic circle of the yin and yang of Eastern mysticism, where masculine and feminine principles of dark and light blend together in a permanent dance inside the circle. The masculine principle of reason, logic, and order—the light—is tucked within the feminine principle of intuition, magic, and imagination—the dark. No one principle dominates; the two are enfolded together.

This same principle applies to theories of learning that reject the bifurcation of left brain and right brain in favor of complementary and integrated whole brain philosophies (Caine and Caine, 1991). Additionally, there is an emerging ecological view of cognitive science and situated learning that sees learning processes as including external as well as inside-the-head events (Bereiter and Scardamalia, 1992; St. Julien, 1992, 1994). Lev Vygotsky (1978), for example, writes about externalization—the creation of artifacts and changes in the environment that support and thus become part of cognitive processes. James J. Gibson (1979) in *The Ecological Approach to Visual Perception* contends that our cognitive systems have evolved in such a way that critical elements of the environment and their pragmatic implications are directly perceived without the need for mediating symbolic processes, interpretations, and concepts. Bereiter and Scardamalia (1992) report: "One group of researchers is explicitly concerned with educational implications of what they term 'situated cognition.' [They] are undertaking an ambitious program of research that ranges from studies of learning in work settings to developing an environmentally situated approach to artificial intelligence" (p. 536).

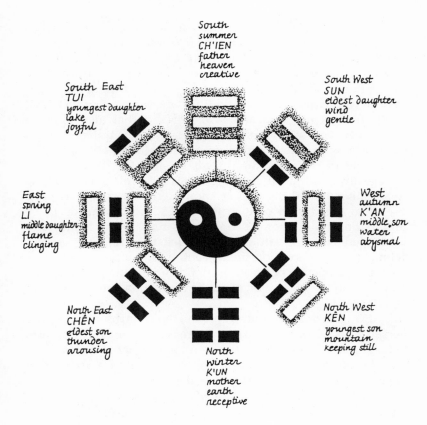

South
summer
CH'IEN
father
heaven
creative

South East
TUI
youngest daughter
lake
joyful

South West
SUN
eldest daughter
wind
gentle

East
spring
LI
middle daughter
flame
clinging

West
autumn
K'AN
middle son
water
abysmal

North East
CHÊN
eldest son
thunder
arousing

North West
KÊN
youngest son
mountain
keeping still

North
winter
K'UN
mother
earth
receptive

Figure 8.1 represents the complementary rather than contradictory nature of diverse elements in the cosmos as presented in the 4000 year old *Book of Changes* or *I Ching* from ancient China. The cosmology represented in the diagram is based on the dynamic unity of the dark (yin—represented by the broken line) and the light (yang—represented by the solid line) principles. We would note the balanced statement of abstractions (the trigrams) in relationship to the grounded concrete aspects of nature (e.g., lakes, mountains) as well as the facts of human community (kin and temperament designations). The world is thus presented as a unity of related plurality, rather than as a series of adversarial fragments which compete with each other for domination or privilege. We are thus not forced to ask, which is superior, the abstract or the concrete? Nature or humans? Earth or heaven? The son or the daughter? Plurality/diversity complements unit.

John St. Julien (1992) explores situated cognition, which he describes as a response to particular projects that are centrally concerned with the contrast between schooling and "real world" experience as they relate to competence. St. Julien develops a conception of the person-thinking (in-the-head-thought) that is at once compatible with the findings of situated cognition that the person is not radically separate and that also offers a principled way to understand how successful transfer might occur across practices and situations. St. Julien (1992) writes: "The field of understanding needs to span the distance from biologically constrained understandings of learning and thinking to socially situated theories of knowledge and cognition to be useful in the design of instruction. The person needs to be understood as neither discontinuous nor unproblematically integrated with the situation in which they find themselves acting" (p. 8). Connectionism, he continues, is a perspective that blurs the distinction between the mind and the brain in the same way that situated cognition blurs the distinction between the self and the world.

St. Julien's scholarship on the confluence of the perspectives of connectionism and situated cognition contributes to the postmodern efforts to transcend bifurcation, Cartesianism, and the modern habit of thinking of the mind as operating logically. He views the way out of this logical mode as a "new analytic" based on networks of relations and interactive representations such as chaos, nonlinear dynamics, and ecology. St. Julien hopes that a material theory of learning may emerge to displace the descriptive theorizing that currently characterizes modern approaches to knowledge acquisition of facts that are separated from the learning context and learner's situation. This modern approach to knowledge acquisition dominates schooling and must be replaced in postmodern education with a new analytic of learning. Such theories are emerging in postmodern and poststructural discussions. St. Julien (1992) comments on this emerging theory: "A solid theory of the material constitution of learning spanning the range from structured external symbols which are materially present in the world to a connectionist approach to the learning of these socially organized categories should prove to be invaluable to our hopes of building a pedagogy that enhances our students' competence" (p. 13). St. Julien echoes the hermeneutic search of James Macdonald as he concludes, "It is this hope that finally, I submit, motivates all of us" (p. 13).

Following from this discussion of situated cognition, connectionism, whole brain learning, and Eastern mysticism, Mary Aswell Doll (1991) offers the following expanded insights:

> This dynamic blending of opposites suggests, to me, what our Western culture needs to hear from Eastern culture. Instead of our Western fascination with moving forward, stepping up, going on—and stepping on—we need to reflect. Progress has polluted our waters both in the environment and in our selves. Progress has endangered our species both in the wilderness and in the wild places of our selves. Chemicals have been abused both against the bugs and against what bugs our selves. We have extended our notion of progress so that we have forgotten our selves, rooted in a collective past. (p. 5)

To be rooted is to be soiled, circled down into nature's roots. However, the words *soil* and *dirt* have taken on a derogatory meaning. Common parlance suggests that soil and dirt no longer nourish our roots, for our roots are planted in shifting sands. Doll reminds us that this is not so with the symbolic circle of the yin and yang—dark and light dance together in continuous improvisation. The circle is a dance.

Susan W. Stinson is a dancer and curriculum theorist. In her essay "Dance as Curriculum, Curriculum as Dance," from the excellent collection of essays on curriculum and the arts entitled *Reflections from the Heart of Educational Inquiry* edited by George Willis and William Schubert (1991), Stinson shares many of the interests of Mary Aswell Doll: sensory experience, metaphors, improvisation. Stinson (1991) writes, "Dance gives me a center, a place to start from: curriculum is the continuing journey" (p. 190). Stinson uses the metaphor of personal knowledge—of knowing something in our bones—that allows us to extend our boundaries and make important connections to the world. Her early dance career was marked by efforts to control and perfect her body, which was an adversary to overcome. She explains: "Control is as much an issue in curriculum as it is in dance: we fear that institutions, as well as bodies, will not work without control" (p. 190). Stinson's curriculum theory, like the other holistic and ecological proposals seen throughout this chapter, provides an alternative to control and manipulation by emphasizing cooperative relationships.

Carl Hammerschlag writes about the dancing circle of Native American spirituality that provides further support for our discussion of curriculum. In his book *The Dancing Healers*, Hammerschlag recalls that as a young medical student from New York he was assigned to the Santa Fe Indian Hospital where he encountered Santiago Rosetta, a Pueblo priest and clan chief. Hammerschlag (1988) writes: "Santiago tried to teach me that if you are going to dance, you have to move. You can't watch the dance; you can't listen to it or look at it. You have to do it to know it. He told me that he could teach me his steps, but I would have to hear my own music" (p. 10).

Hammerschlag was attempting to treat Santiago's illness when they encountered each other. Santiago wanted to see the doctor's healing dance before he would allow him to treat the illness. Hammerschlag recalls in his book that he did a little jig near Santiago's bed but looked in Santiago's eyes and realized that he had missed the point. Santiago was trying to explain that everything is interrelated: body, mind, and spirit. The wholeness suggested by native spirituality and mystical traditions contradicts the modern experience of fragmentation and isolation and exposes the spiritual bankruptcy of contemporary social models rooted in domination, control, and conquest.

Kevin Costner (1990) explores alternatives to this model in his film *Dances With Wolves*, in which he portrays an American cavalryman stationed alone at the farthest outpost on the northern frontier. When the cavalryman encounters a nomadic Sioux tribe early in the film, he epitomizes the modern metaphor: isolated, independent, yet insecure. He attempts to order the environment to maximize control over the unpredictable forces of the frontier, but he is saved from certain death only when he lets go of the security of his fortress and dances before the fire. This lone cavalryman experiences a conversion and transformation as he gradually becomes united in spirit with the Sioux. The soldier learns from the Sioux what

Hammerschlag learned from the Pueblo—the healing dance of native spirituality. The postmodern curriculum, likewise, is a healing dance, a spiral of creation, and a yearning for wisdom embedded in this interrelationship of body, mind, and spirit. Educators must recognize this healing curriculum dance and celebrate the mystical, spiritual, ecological, and holistic dimensions of the school curriculum (Slattery, 1992b). The dancing circle, like the hermeneutic circle discussed in chapter five, depends on interrelationship for learning, healing, and growth to occur.

In a recent paper (Slattery and Daigle, 1991) I have proposed another metaphor using the Mississippi River to expand on the distinction of the linear paradigm of modernity that perpetuates individual isolation and destruction and the circular paradigm of postmodernity that fosters ecological interdependence and rootedness. The Mississippi River is no longer part of natural biological and ecological rhythms but has been converted into a channel to be exploited for economic productivity and commerce. The midwestern United States flooding in 1993 is a warning that even the most sophisticated technology, including massive locks and levees, cannot control the river. I will expand on this metaphor while keeping the modern classroom in mind throughout the reflection.

In the poem "The Negro Speaks of Rivers," Langston Hughes (1973) writes: "I've known rivers: I've known rivers ancient as the world and older than the flow of human blood in human veins. My soul has grown deep like the rivers" (p. 634). The protagonist in Ernest Gaines' (1972) novel *The Autobiography of Miss Jane Pittman* is a former enslaved woman living in the fictional Louisiana city of Bayonne. As she approaches the age of 108, she also reflects on the significance of rivers:

> Before the high water we didn't have school here. The children went to school in the Bottom or at Ned's school up the road. [Huey] Long came in after the high water. The damage from that high water was caused by man, because man wanted to control the rivers, and you cannot control water. The Indians used to worship the rivers till the white people came here and conquered them and tried

> to conquer the rivers, too. . . . And that's when the trouble
> really started. (pp. 147–148)

In the two selections above, Langston Hughes and Ernest Gaines
create images of rivers running deep with ancient powers,
worshiped and respected as a source of life for the soul. The
Mississippi River serves as a metaphor for teachers and students
whose movement through the places of education is often
confined, restricted, and polluted by those who seek to conquer
the mind and spirit. Just like Jane Pittman who lamented the loss
of respect for the river by those who sought to conquer it,
postmodern curriculum rejects modern educational reforms that
limit meandering and self-reflection in our places of education.
Jane Pittman continues in Gaines' (1972) novel:

> I don't know when the first levee was built; but from what
> I heard from the old people the water destroyed the levee
> as soon as it was put there. Now, if the white man had
> taken heed to what the river was trying to say to him then,
> it would have saved a lot of pain later. They tell me he
> said, "This here water got to be confined. . . . We got to get
> the water to running where it's suppose to run. Suppose to
> run in the river, and we got to keep it there." Like you can
> tell a river where to go. (pp. 148–149)

Since the floods of the 1920s, the river has been confined by
levees and spillways. Jane Pittman warns us that these efforts are
futile:

> Now he's [the white man] built his concrete spillways to
> control the water. But one day the water will break down
> his spillways just like it broke through the levee . . . the
> water will never die. That same water the Indians used to
> believe in will run free again. You just wait and see. (p.
> 150)

And in 1993 the Mississippi River did just that!

For millions of years there has been a building up and
tearing down of the land in the Mississippi delta. Geologists
believe that the Mississippi once extended northward to the
southern tip of Illinois. This shallow extension of the Gulf, called
the Mississippi embayment, received the waters and sediment of
the Mississippi, the Ohio, the Red, the Arkansas, and other

tributaries. Over time the sediment filled the embayment and built the Delta. This alluvial soil created the vast wetlands along the Gulf of Mexico that are an immense resource and vital link in the ecological system of the entire Northern Hemisphere (Mancuso, 1991).

As the river meandered unabated, its natural course was not predetermined; rather, the river gradually searched for new directions to the sea. Over thousands of years the river has been free to move and meander to form new lands and destroy others. As the river moved, subsidence occurred, returning some of the land to the sea. New land was formed when spring floods poured fresh water and mud to replace what was lost to subsidence. Floods and erosion, subsidence and deposits, oxbows and deltas: these are the natural elements of the history of the Mississippi River.

Today there has been an attempt to control the process of creation and destruction. The river has been confined in a levee system constructed by a modern corps of engineers. Massive steel locks in Louisiana prevent the river from shifting west to the Atchafalaya River, the old Acadiana home to which it longs to return. Locks and canals have been built to divert the flow of the Mississippi to protect economically productive routes for commerce and industry. And in the process, the irreplaceable mud deposits are lost forever. The environment is in crisis: the marshes are disappearing and the water is polluted. The ecological system is in disarray. The mighty Mississippi no longer meanders and builds new lands, for it has been forced to conform to modern demands. The levees prevent natural flood plains from accepting the waters and rich mud deposits in times of high water. As Jane Pittman warned, the river will eventually overflow and break the levees. A respect for natural process in the environment and in the classroom becomes a mandatory element of curriculum development in the postmodern era. Students and teachers in the postmodern curriculum must be free to meander, flood, shift course, and build a new delta. Modern curriculum engineers must no longer be allowed to build dams that prevent learning and levees that attempt to artificially control thinking and reflection.

Curriculum scholars in the postmodern era have taken the metaphor of ecological and psychological destruction and thoughtfully applied it to the schooling process in many recent books, including *Responsive Teaching: An Ecological Approach to Classroom Patterns of Language, Culture, and Thought* (Bowers and Flinders, 1990); *The Holistic Curriculum* (John P. Miller, 1988); *The Renewal of Meaning in Education: Responses to the Ecological Crisis of Our Time* (Ron Miller, ed., 1993); *Ecological Literacy: Education and the Transition to a Postmodern World* (Orr, 1992); and *Curriculum as Social Psychoanalysis: The Significance of Place* (Kincheloe and Pinar, 1991). David Orr is perhaps representative of those who believe that education must transcend current practices and address ecological sustainability. Orr (1992) writes:

> The modern world arose as a volcanic eruption so suddenly and massively that it buried or transformed all that had preceded it, including landscapes and mindscapes. It is difficult to know how much we have lost, but I believe that for all of the increases in conveniences and speed, we have lost a great deal of the richness and experience of a life that once existed. The losses are not all visible. The most serious have to do with the way we think and what we think about. For all of our gross national product, most live increasingly barren lives in an increasingly impoverished land. . . . Until we confront what modernity has done to us as a people and resolve to do otherwise, we can only put Band-Aids on a terminal problem. (p. 181)

The solution to the ecological and psychological devastation of modernity for Orr and other scholars is the development of a postmodern paradigm. Orr calls it ecological literacy. This will involve recovering older notions of virtue found in antiquity as well as developing a sense that one's self is inseparable from a larger community that is part of a cosmological vision. It will also involve regaining a moral consciousness and historical consciousness that will foster interconnectedness within a larger perspective. "The modern world has destroyed the sense of belonging to a larger order which must be restored as the foundation of a postmodern world" (Orr, 1992, p. 182). Specifically, Orr proposes the reintroduction of moral philosophy throughout the curriculum, community settings on school campuses, and experiences in education that foster virtue. He concludes: "The transition to the kind of postmodern society envisioned in this . . . book cannot be done cheaply. It will cost something, perhaps a great deal. But there is a far higher price waiting to be paid" (p. 183).

To avoid ecological disaster, education must point the way toward "deep cultural changes," according to Chet Bowers. This will not be accomplished through government attempts to engineer social changes or through a politicized system of signs. Bowers (1993) observes: "Nor have modern totalitarian regimes been able to deal with the basic problem of our era: human rights and the ecological crisis. The political process has a dismal record. . . . The development of spiritual languages may have the best potential for helping us avoid the political process moving beyond excessive regulation to the friend-enemy conflicts that now seem to be on the increase" (p. 216). The challenge for educators, according to Bowers, will be to find suitable analogues for songs, stories, dance, and art, either from the histories of the many cultural groups in society or from current cultural artifacts. Ultimately, educators must be receptive to including in the curriculum the contributions of various cultural groups and relate this to living in a sustainable balance within the larger web of life. This receptivity by educators "will require escaping from many of the prejudices that are now the basis of our modern hubris" (p. 216). Bowers, like Orr, recognizes that global change begins with local community efforts and classroom practices by individual educators. Neither Bowers nor Orr proposes a new modern master plan but rather a postmodern receptivity to a vision of education for ecological sustainability. Chet Bowers, like Jacques Cousteau, worries about what we are doing to the physical environment. However, Bowers advances the dialogue by asserting that modern liberalism and Enlightenment rationality have produced an emphasis on individualism and reasoning that prevent ecological sensibilities and cooperative community efforts.

The higher price described by Orr and the modern hubris described by Bowers ultimately refer to the ecological destruction that follows the demise of learning and the collapse of self in the modern world. The meaning of the turmoil in the inner life of the individual is also explored by Joe Kincheloe and William Pinar (1991), who contend that the significance of a person's actions can be understood only in terms of the latent and unconscious content that moves the individual. Thus, postmodern education that is attentive to ecological concerns must begin with attention to the unconscious as well as the physical, emotional, and psychological places of education. Kincheloe and Pinar (1991) write that "successful interpretations that lead to therapy can be formulated only by uncovering the salient unconscious factors" (p. 1). This uncovering of the unconscious occurs in a realm of the place where the individual experiences his or her temporal reality. The subjectivity of place can free persons from the obsession of modernity to objectify and quantify human experience. This subjectivity of place frees us from the pseudo-objectivity of positivism. Along with Henry Giroux, Kincheloe and Pinar propose that a language of hope and possibility can emerge to help transform both schooling and public life. Schools are one of the few places where students can experience a language of community and democratic life, and therefore emancipatory education can emerge from the chaos in the educational milieu (Giroux, 1991). It is thus significant that curriculum scholars promote analyses that explore the external and internal chaos in order to create healing and compassionate environments in classrooms, which in turn will move outward to local communities and ultimately effect global ecological transformations.

We have come full circle in this chapter, so to speak. We have moved from environmental concerns to classroom arrangements, to an ecological metaphor, to psychological investigations. In every case we have seen a concern for interrelationships, deep ecological, holistic models, and natural processes. This understanding of curriculum challenges educators to prioritize global interdependence and ecological sustainability in their postmodern curriculum development paradigms. Chapter nine will explore another approach to postmodern curriculum studies by scholars who take this message seriously, especially as it may inform the political arrangements in postmodern society.

Utopian Visions, Democracy, and the Egalitarian Ideal

In the introduction to the Reconceptualization we saw that feminist theory and political theory gained ascendancy in the curriculum field in the 1980s. One of the leading scholars in the political sector of the field by 1980 was Michael Apple. At that time, Apple was interested in understanding the relationship between education and economic structure and the linkages between knowledge and power. In *Ideology and Curriculum* Apple (1979) summarizes his position: "In essence, the problem has become more and more a *structural* issue for me. I have increasingly sought to ground it [education and economics, knowledge and power] in a set of critical questions that are generated out of a tradition of neo-Marxist argumentation, a tradition which seems to me to offer the most cogent framework for organizing one's thinking and action about education" (p. 1). Apple then outlines an approach to curriculum studies that emphasizes modes of material production, ideological values, class relations, as well as racial, sexual, and politicoeconomic structures of social power and the impact of these issues on the consciousness of people in their historical and socioeconomic situations. Apple (1979) concludes that his curriculum theory "seeks to portray the concrete ways that prevalent (and . . . alienating) structural arrangements—the basic ways institutions, people, and modes of production, distribution, and consumption are organized and controlled—dominate cultural life. This includes such day-to-day practices as schools and the teaching and curricula found within them" (p. 2).

In the postmodern field of the 1990s, feminist and political scholarship are two among many eclectic approaches to curriculum studies. This chapter will introduce recent political scholarship, often called critical theory, that has emerged since the early work of Michael Apple and will explore its implications for curriculum development in the postmodern era. Particularly, the vision of utopia, democracy, and egalitarianism, so integral to the American political and educational psyche, will inform our discussion. Democracy is an ideal that is filled with possibilities but also an ideal that is part of the ongoing struggle for equality, freedom, and human dignity. In a sense, this egalitarian vision reflects the human quest for an educational system that upholds and promotes the highest aspirations, dreams, and values of individual persons, not only in the United States but also throughout the global community.

What should be the focus of the postmodern curriculum if egalitarian ideals, democratic citizenship, and utopian visions are to be integral to education? How can education in the postmodern era transcend the polarization that exists between those who promote equality, justice, and empowerment for all human persons, especially the impoverished and politically repressed, and those who staunchly defend individual liberty because they believe that egalitarianism has led to socialist practices that destroy the rights of the entrepreneur, the genius, or the investor? In short, can we really have both *liberty* and *justice* for all? A postmodernist would answer affirmatively because the two are inextricably bound up in each other.

Following the Renaissance and the rise of the political theories of the Enlightenment, it was widely believed that liberty and justice could be engineered in societies. As we saw in chapter seven, some characterize these movements as liberalism, socialism, and radicalism. Postmodern political perspectives seek to reconceptualize, deconstruct, and/or replace these modern political theories and the resultant devastation that has occurred in the twentieth century because of the materialism, communism, fascism, and individualism that have grown out of them. Postmodernism recognizes that modern political theories have reached a level of absurdity in the 1990s, and even some of the very concepts that have oriented critical educational theories such as emancipation, hegemony, and social transformation have been exposed for problematic applications (Cherryholmes,

1988b; Stanley, 1992). However, postmodernists adamantly uphold the vision of justice, equality, liberation, freedom, and compassion that underline critical theory.

Some critics will question whether political curriculum theorists in the 1990s are simply ultramodernist revolutionaries recycling neo-Marxist ideology; others will contend that critical curriculum theory offers a fresh alternative for education in the postmodern era that will engender social justice. The answer to this debate is not clear, and depending on the individual research being promulgated, both perspectives may have validity at times. Critical theory, while certainly not a unified system of thought, contains some general assumptions: all thought and power relations are inexorably linked; these power relations form oppressive social arrangements; facts and values are inseparable and inscribed by ideology; language is a key element in the formation of subjectivities, and thus critical literacy—the ability to negotiate passages through social systems and structures—is more important than functional literacy—the ability to decode and compute; oppression is based in the reproduction of privileged knowledge codes and practices (Kincheloe and Pinar, 1991).

This chapter will not attempt to categorize various scholars or draw any definitive conclusions about the validity of critical theories. However, the contribution of political scholars to contemporary curriculum discourses is not only enormous but also responsible for focusing attention on the plight of those who are disempowered in society. Samuel Bowles and Herbert Gintis (1976), for example, write about correspondence theories that draw parallels between economic and educational stratification. Schools, they contend, contribute to the cultural reproduction of class relations and economic order that allows for very little social mobility. Beverly Gordon echoes this theory when she writes that the "bootstrap ideology" as part of the American dream has been very difficult for African Americans and other people of color as a group to realize. Gordon (1989) writes:

> What we are witnessing is not simply racism—the picture is far more complex. It is a picture of an evolved culture that combines racism with elitism, an inherited, empirically bounded Spencerian rationale, and capitalism.

> What does this say about fairness, equity, and justice in
> society? . . . Students must know about power and the uses
> of power, that is, political and economic forces. . . .
> Students must develop the will to be active participants in
> the society all of their lives—so that the society, in fact,
> lives up to its democratic ideals. . . . True democracy will
> be achieved only when all citizens have the knowledge
> and the motivation to live up to society's highest values
> and when economic and political opportunities are made
> equally available to all its constituents. (pp. 99–101)

It is abundantly clear that critical theory exercises an
extremely important role in the curriculum field, as we have seen
above in the research of Apple, Bowles, Gintis, and Gordon.
Other political scholars include Philip Wexler (1992); Theodore
Brameld (1956, 1971); William Stanley (1992); Paulo Freire (1970,
1985); Peter McLaren (1989); Jonathan Kozol (1975, 1991); Stanley
Aronowitz (1992); Paul Willis (1977); Dennis Carlson (1992); Lois
Weis (1983, 1988); Joe Kincheloe (1993); and Henry Giroux (1988,
1992, 1993), who is perhaps the most recognized figure in this
sector of the field in the 1990s. Giroux (1988) summarizes the
egalitarian vision of critical theorists:

> We must develop a social vision and commitment to make
> the liberal arts supportive of a democratic public sphere in
> which despair will become unconvincing and hope a
> practice for students and teachers alike, regardless of race,
> class, religion, gender, or age. (p. 261)

Creating a democratic educational vision that provides hope for
all teachers and students is central to critical theory. Some of the
specific questions and concerns that are raised in the process of
developing this vision include the following: How do students
acquire knowledge in schools? Is knowledge reproduced in
schools to support the status quo systems of inequity? How do
students and teachers resist the structures and knowledge that
are conveyed not only in classroom instruction but also in the
lived experience of the school environment? How do schools
shape visions, values, and outlooks on life? Whose interests are
being served by the perpetuation of these outlooks? Do these
visions, values, and outlooks promote equality, justice, and
empowerment, or do they reinforce bigotry, inequality, and

repression? and How can schooling be an instrument to promote social justice?

In the construction of an emancipatory view of education, philosophers and theorists as diverse as John Dewey (1985 [first published in 1916]), George S. Counts (1932), and Hannah Arendt (1958) have contended that schools should challenge the social order. Crises in education and society are reflected in the debate about the role of schools in advancing social issues, democratic themes, and utopian values. Should education, as Dewey (1899) asked, be a function of society or should society be a function of education? In other words, should schools participate in the process of reproducing the knowledge, interests, and values of the dominant society, or should schools advance democracy while promoting an emancipatory approach to knowledge and learning so as to re-create a just and compassionate society? Dewey believed the latter. So did the social reconstructionists of the early twentieth century.

The social reconstructionists were concerned with two major premises. First, society is in need of constant reform and change, and second, such change must involve both structural changes in education and the use of education in reconstructing society. George S. Counts is perhaps one of the most well-known of the social reconstructionists. In his important essay *Dare the Schools Build a New Social Order?* the themes of this movement are clear. Counts (1932) summarizes the feeling of many:

> [Education] . . . must . . . face squarely and courageously every social issue, come to grips with life in all of its stark reality, establish an organic relation with the community, develop a realistic and comprehensive theory of welfare, fashion a compelling and challenging vision of human destiny, and become less frightened than it is today at the bogies of *imposition* and *indoctrination*. (cited in Ozmon and Craver, 1990, p. 189)

Counts points out that the concept of indoctrination in education is horrifying to most citizens, who would reject such imposition. However, schooling is complicit in forms of social control and indoctrination that result in social injustices. What should be done about this? Counts (1932) continues:

> There is the fallacy that the school should be impartial in
> its emphases, that no bias should be given in instruction.
> We have already observed how the individual is
> inevitably molded by the culture into which he is born. In
> the school a similar process operates . . . [and] some
> selection must be made of teachers, curricula, architecture,
> methods of teaching. . . . Teachers, if they increase their
> stock of courage, intelligence, and vision, might become a
> social force of some magnitude. . . . That the teachers
> should deliberately reach for power and then make the
> most of their conquest is my firm conviction. (cited in
> Ozmon and Craver, 1990, p. 190)

Teachers, Counts contends, must accept their role in
reconstructing society because of the problems of the social
situation of the modern era. Counts (1932), reflecting many
sentiments of postmodern political thinkers who will follow him
years later, warns:

> We live in troubled times; we live in an age of profound
> change. In order to match our epoch we would probably
> have to go back to the fall of the ancient
> empires. . . . Consider the present condition of the
> nation. . . . Here is a society that manifests the most
> extraordinary contradictions: a mastery over the forces of
> nature is accompanied by extreme material insecurity; dire
> poverty walks hand in hand with the most extravagant
> living the world has ever known; an abundance of goods
> of all kinds is coupled with privation, misery, and even
> starvation; great captains of industry close factories
> without warning and dismiss the workmen by whose
> labors they have amassed huge fortunes through the
> years; consumption is subordinated to production and a
> philosophy of deliberate waste is widely proclaimed as the
> highest economic wisdom. . . . [We] stand confused and
> irresolute before the future [and] seem to lack the moral
> quality necessary to quicken, discipline, and give
> direction. In a recent paper professor Dewey has, in my
> judgment, diagnosed our troubles: "The schools, like the
> nation, are in need of a central purpose which will create
> new enthusiasm and devotion, and which will unify and
> guide all intellectual plans." (cited in Ozmon and Craver,
> 1990, pp. 191–192)

The search for the central purpose of education, as introduced sixty years ago by George Counts, John Dewey, and social reconstructionists, that will provide new enthusiasm to address the economic and moral decay of modern society remains a concern of critical theories in the postmodern era.

Critical theorists like Henry Giroux (1988) also question "whether schools [should] uncritically serve and reproduce the existing society or challenge the social order in order to develop and advance its democratic imperatives" (p. 243). Giroux, as we noted above, has concluded that the development of a social vision and commitment to make the liberal arts supportive of a democratic public sphere must be a priority in postmodern education. Hope must replace despair as the central practice for students and teachers, regardless of race, class, religion, gender, or age.

In addition to critical theorists like Giroux, liberation theologians also propose the development of a social vision and a commitment to an emancipatory view that would promote hope for all people, especially the poor, regardless of race, class, religion, gender, or age (Gutierrez, 1973). Liberation theologians reevaluate historical realities and advocate changes that are contrary to dominant social trends but that are nevertheless linked to a deep current of desire for liberation of the poor (Kincheloe et al., 1992). Like the postmodern proposals of the 1980s that insist on the elimination of dualisms in favor of integrated wholeness (Jencks, 1986; Griffin, 1988a, 1988b) and the proposals of process philosophy that reject bifurcations of space and time (Whitehead, 1978), liberation movements and political theories seek unity and integration of human life and the social, political, and economic realms. Political scholarship rejects the tendency to separate curriculum from human response in the social order. This gives rise to social action, especially for those excluded and disempowered. This process parallels in many ways John Dewey's concept of ideals and imagination giving rise to social consequences of value (Dewey, 1934a). This understanding of the purpose of curriculum in educational institutions by critical theorists is explained by Giroux (1988):

> All too often [tradition in the liberal arts] translates into an instrumentalism more appropriate to producing disciplinary specialists than to providing forms of moral leadership necessary for advancing the interests of a democratic society. In its most expressive form, this tradition views that the purpose of liberal arts is to initiate students into a unitary [Western] cultural tradition. In this view, excellence is acquiring an already established tradition, not about struggling to create new forms of civic practice and participation. Culture is viewed as an artifact to be taken out of the historical warehouse of dominant tradition and uncritically transmitted to students. (p. 245)

Just as Giroux resists viewing culture as an artifact and the school as an instrument of uncritical transmission of the artifact, so too does the postmodern curriculum resist the concept of knowledge as simply an artifact to be transmitted uncritically by educational institutions. These postmodern theories unite politics and social ethics in such a way that the concept of deferred justice must be challenged.

Critical theory derives from the work of post-Marxist theorists of the Frankfurt school, who study socioeconomic class structures and the ways that school curriculum and curricularists unwittingly perpetuate such structures. These structures, critical theorists argue, enslave subjected classes. Critical theorists contend that these people require a liberating pedagogy. An important early example of critical theory in practice is presented by Paulo Freire in *Pedagogy of the Oppressed*. Freire (1970) demonstrates how the "banking" concept of education is an instrument of oppression:

> Oppression—overwhelming control—is necrophilic; it is nourished by love of death, not life. The banking concept of education [is] an act of depositing in which students are the depositories and the teacher is the depositor. . . . Instead of communicating, the teacher issues communiques and makes deposits which the students patiently receive, memorize, and repeat. [This] serves the interests of oppression and is also necrophilic. Based on a mechanistic, static, naturalistic, spatialized view of consciousness, it transforms students into receiving objects. It attempts to control thinking and action, leads

men to adjust to the world, and inhibits their creative power. (pp. 64–66)

Freire (1970) contends that those committed to empowerment and liberation must reject the banking concept in its entirety and adopt instead a problem-posing concept where people are viewed as conscious beings in relation to the world: "Problem-posing education, responding to the essence of consciousness (intentionality), rejects communiques and embodies communication. Liberating education consists in acts of cognition, not transferals of information" (p. 66). When the illiterate peasants of Freire's Third World classrooms, as well as uncritical students of First World schools, begin to participate in a problem-posing and problem-solving educational experience, they begin to develop a new awareness of self, a new sense of dignity, and ultimately an experience of hope. Freire (1970), speaking for all critical theorists, contends that "no pedagogy that is truly liberating can remain distant from the oppressed by treating them as unfortunates and by presenting for their emulation models from among the oppressors" (cited in Schubert, 1986, p. 313). Paulo Freire is a major figure in political educational discourses, and students of curriculum development should study Freire's works as well as secondary sources such as the important collection of essays by Peter McLaren and Peter Leonard (1993) entitled *Paulo Freire: A Critical Encounter*.

The self-conscious critique is an essential element of critical theory. Giroux characterizes the pedagogical goals of critical theory as a means "to assess the newly emerging forms of capitalism along with the changing forms of domination that accompanied them, to rethink and radically reconstruct the meaning of human emancipation, and [to engage in] self-conscious critique" (pp. 7–8). This critique of the contradictions in culture allows theorists to distinguish what should be from what is. As the conditions of suffering are recognized and articulated, models for change will emerge.

The utopian, democratic, and egalitarian visions of many critical theorists emerge from their own self-conscious critique of their autobiographical schooling experiences. Jonathan Kozol (1967) was inspired to publish his first book, *Death at an Early Age*, as a result of his experiences with disadvantaged African-

American children in Boston's public schools as a beginning
language teacher in his twenties. Kozol relates the story of his
frustration with dilapidated facilities, overcrowded classrooms,
and outdated textbooks. While browsing through a bookstore in
Boston, his eye caught sight of a collection of poems with a
picture of an African-American poet on the cover. He purchased
the book for his class. He not only wanted to show the students
what a new book looked like but also that there were black poets
since none was represented in the school textbooks. Kozol (1967)
explains how he was fired for "curricular deviation" because he
read from Langston Hughes' poem that asked, "What happens
to a dream deferred? Does it shrivel like a raisin in the sun or
does it explode?" Kozol relates how one particularly angry
young woman who had resisted him throughout the course was
enthralled by the poem and asked to borrow the book. She went
home and memorized the poem. The poetry of Langston Hughes
transformed the students and Kozol's classroom, but this poem
also alarmed the school authorities, who were afraid of what
might happen if poor black children were exposed to "radical"
poetry. Since this poem was not included in the curriculum
guide or district syllabus, Kozol was fired. Kozol has gone on to
write many inspiring books about such topics as the lack of
education for the children of the homeless and migrant workers,
the politics of literacy in America, and the savage economic
inequalities of schooling in the United States. Reading the works
of Jonathan Kozol would be a good place to begin the
investigation of educational political commentaries.

Beginning curriculum students might also want to explore
the work of another critical theorist who was originally inspired
by autobiographical experiences, Peter McLaren. McLaren (1989)
has written a comprehensive and accessible introduction to critical pedagogy that includes excerpts from his journal while
teaching at an elementary school in one of Toronto's inner city
suburbs known as the Jane-Finch Corridor. McLaren (1989)
writes in *Life in Schools: An Introduction to Critical Pedagogy in the
Foundations of Education* the following summary:

> In my attempt to understand how schooling "really"
> works, I was soon struck by the range of sociological
> theories that explain how schools can and do disempower,

> deligitimate, and disconfirm the lives of disadvantaged
> children. I discovered as well that schools operate through
> a "hidden curriculum" which incarcerates students in the
> "semiotics of power" and works against the success of
> racial minorities, women, and the poor. Yet I was also
> made aware of how schools could work in emancipatory
> ways to empower students to accomplish, in the words of
> Paulo Freire, "reading the word and reading the world."
> (p. x)

In this book McLaren addressed two important questions. First,
Why is critical pedagogy so important for schooling in the 1990s?
Second is a question that traditional curriculum theory and
mainstream educational theories have avoided, What is the
relationship between what we do in classrooms and our efforts
to build a just society?

McLaren's book provides an excellent outline of the central
elements of critical pedagogy. As we saw above, one of these
elements is the concept of the "hidden curriculum," which refers
to the unintended outcomes of the schooling process. The hidden
curriculum contrasts with the overt curriculum, which is the
official curriculum of the syllabus, lesson plan, or scope and
sequence guide. The null curriculum refers to those elements of
the overt curriculum that are omitted due to time constraints or
prejudice of the teacher. Critical theorists contend that the
hidden curriculum and the null curriculum have a much more
profound impact on students than the overt curriculum. For
example, if a United States history teacher skips the Civil War
and the civil rights movement, a message about the importance
of issues related to racism in American history is indelibly
implanted in the psyche of the students. Also, if the same
American history teacher presents the structure of democracy in
a classroom environment that is repressive and undemocratic,
students learn more about democracy from the classroom
environment than from the course material.

Another important element of critical theory includes the
study of forms of knowledge. Critical theory follows a threefold
distinction regarding forms of knowledge posited by the German
social theorist Jurgen Habermas: technical knowledge, which can
be measured and quantified; practical knowledge, which is
geared toward helping individuals understand social events that

are ongoing and situational; and emancipatory knowledge, which attempts to reconcile and transcend the opposition between technical and practical knowledge. Emancipatory knowledge helps us to understand how social relationships are distorted and manipulated by relations of power and privilege. (See figure 9.1.)

Another important issue that Peter McLaren addresses is the dialectical nature of critical pedagogy, which allows the educational scholar to see the school not simply as an arena of indoctrination or social control or a site for instruction but also as a cultural terrain that promotes student empowerment. This dialectical perspective allows critical theorists to see the school as both a site for domination and liberation, thus incorporating Habermas' notion of emancipatory interests.

TYPE OF SCIENCE OR INQUIRY	Empirical/Analytical	Hermeneutic	Critical
INTEREST SERVED	Technical	Practical	Emancipatory
SOCIAL ORGANIZATION	Work	Interaction	Power
	MODE OF RATIONALITY		
	Posits principles of control and certainty	Emphasizes understanding and communicative interaction	Assumes the necessity of ideological critique and action
	Operates in the interests of law-like propositions that are empirically testable	Sees human beings as active creators of knowledge	Seeks to expose that which is oppressive and dominating
	Assumes knowledge to be value free	Looks for assumptions and meanings beneath texture of everyday life	Requires sensitivity to false consciousness
	Assumes knowledge to be objectified	Views reality as intersubjectively constituted and shared within a historical, political, and social context	Makes distorted conceptions and unjust values problematic
	Values efficiency or parsimony		Examines and explicates value system and concepts of justice upon which inquiry is based
	Accepts unquestioningly, social reality as it is	Focuses sensitively to meaning through language use	

Figure 9.1

Ultimately, critical theory is directed in the interest of emancipation, change, and liberation. William Schubert (1986) summarizes:

> Emancipation refers to freeing one's self to enable growth and development from the taken-for-granted ideology of social conventions, beliefs, and modes of operation. It strives to renew the ideology so that it serves as a basis for reflection and action. This requires modes of social

> organization that emphasize power. It is perceived
> necessary to empower people, whatever their situation in
> institutionalized education, to question the value of such
> forces as the governance structures that direct their
> political life, the systems by which goods and services are
> generated and delivered that govern their economic life,
> the rules and conventions that define their social life, and
> the beliefs and ideals that contribute to their psychological
> life. (p. 318)

In critical theory, as individuals become aware of these political,
economic, social, and psychological dimensions articulated by
Giroux, McLaren, and Schubert, and as students experience a
problem-posing education as proposed by Freire, they will be
stirred by a new hope. People will no longer be willing to be
mere objects responding to changes occurring around them.
Rather they will be more likely to take upon themselves the
struggle to change the structures of society that have until the
present served only to oppress. In order for the experience of
hope to inspire active participation in social change and social
justice, there must be a clear understanding of the meaning and
implications of a liberating ideology, egalitarian ideals, and
utopian visions.

In education, it is teachers, often women, who continue to
empower students despite the institutional burdens that plague
them. Madeleine Grumet (1988b) documents this concept in
Bitter Milk: Women and Teaching as she explores the passage
women teachers make daily between their public and private
worlds, and the contradictions they confront when they bring
their commitments to children into the politics and knowledge
systems of institutional education. Grumet offers a view of
teachers divided by opposing forces. She writes: "The task when
viewed in the structural complexity of our social, political,
economic situation appears herculean" (Grumet, 1988b, p. 29).
However, Grumet offers advice consistent with critical theories.
She challenges women teachers with the following insight:

> Only when we suspend the despair that isolates us from
> our history and our future can our reproductive capacity
> reclaim the promise of our species, not merely to conceive
> but to reconceive another generation. We, the women who
> teach, must claim our reproductive labor as a process of

civilization as well as procreation. The task is daunting.
(Grumet, 1988b, p. 29)

The task is also intimidating; but it is not impossible. Empowering teachers, peasants, students, and laborers to become leaders of emancipatory education and liberating community is the task before curriculum development scholars from the postmodern critical perspective.

What is unique about postmodern critical theory that differentiates it from earlier reconstructionism and neo-Marxism? William Stanley in *Curriculum for Utopia* contends that critical theory of the 1990s presents a more complex and useful critique of educational theory and practice by way of having incorporated the insights of the new sociology, feminism, cultural studies, neopragmatism, and poststructuralism with social reconstructionism, neo-Marxism, and postmodernism. Stanley contends that on occasion reconstructionism has verged on social engineering because the reconstructionists were preoccupied with what they perceived as relativist dangers inherent in pragmatism. Social reconstructionists tended to overemphasize the power of rationality, science, and the possibility of objective knowledge (Stanley, 1992). Stanley continues by arguing that neither despair nor a flight from ethics is appropriate. Stanley (1992) writes:

> The insights of postmodern and poststructural theory have made clear that we can no longer apply totalizing critiques, metanarratives, or any other appeals to objective knowledge or transcendental values. Nevertheless, while radical hermeneutics and poststructuralism have revealed our knowledge to be more contingent and problematic, it does not follow that projects aimed at human betterment are either irrational or impossible. (p. 220)

Stanley listens to the voices and vision of many curriculum theorists from the past as he projects a postmodern understanding of a reconceptualized reconstructionism and proposes a curriculum for utopia. Stanley's vision of curriculum for utopia insists upon the following: competence for practical judgment (*phronesis*); an ongoing critique so that empowerment and social transformation are not rendered impotent and problematic in themselves (Cherryholmes, 1988b); minimal sociocultural conditions must be met in order to enable the realization of human interests; certain forms of domination such as sexism, homophobia, racism, censorship, political oppression, and monological approaches to curriculum distort and limit human interests; and an affirmation that human suffering should inspire compassion for otherness so that "we try to extend our sense of 'we' to people whom we have previously thought of as 'they'" (Rorty, 1989, p. 192). Stanley concludes that this is a "critical pedagogy of neither/nor, oriented by a poststructuralist rejection of false dichotomies, awareness of the unknowable, understanding of the limits of rationality, and an awareness of the dangers posed by both, and the terrorism of closure or monologue" (p. 222).

Along with William Stanley and Madeleine Grumet, I believe that postmodern pedagogy and curriculum development face tremendous barriers due to injustice, inequality, sexism, racism, despair, and other terrors of the modern world that are rampant in our global society. The postmodern utopia offered here is not the perfect world of apocalyptic and idealistic dreams, rather it is a vision of hope, justice, compassion, *phronesis*, community, inclusiveness, and dialogue. This emerging concept of utopia as an ethical vision, as distinct from earlier neo-Marxist critical theories, is apparent in the postmodern literature of many disciplines. If critical scholarship is to move beyond Enlightenment notions of politics and the individual in order to create a postmodern dialogue, this vision of utopia and ethics must be included. Perhaps typical is the conclusion of Libby Falk Jones and Sarah Webster Goodwin (1990) in *Feminism, Utopia, and Narrative* that utopian discourse, as a complex mode of being rather than a naive program, incorporates values that build just, compassionate, and sustainable communities. In this same sense curriculum development in the postmodern era is not a naive program of studies, but rather a complex integration of values that concretize hope in school communities and engender hope for the good of the global community.

As introduced at the beginning of this chapter, the systematic effort to understand curriculum politically began in earnest in the 1970s. The traditional notion that curriculum could be developed, conducted, and evaluated in a politically neutral manner was dismantled. Likewise, the traditional assumption that schools function as avenues of upward social and economic mobility was discredited. The rejection of these ideas by political curriculum theorists has been accompanied by the construction of a political understanding of schooling that includes an analysis of reproduction of status quo values and power arrangements, resistance to dominant structures, ideology as inscribed in cultural and social arrangements, and the predominant influence of these cultural, social, and power arrangements called hegemony. Recent political theory has also incorporated notions of literacy, race, feminism, postmodernism, and poststructuralism into its domain of analysis. For example, Henry Giroux has attempted to revive resistance theory by incorporating poststructuralism and African-American feminism. Others, such as Michael Apple, continue to emphasize neo-Marxist class struggle.

There have been critics of recent political theories in curriculum studies. Philip Wexler, for example, charges that this work is reactionary and that reproduction and resistance theories are simply recycling 1960s activist movements without regard for movements in history and society since that time. Wexler (1992) uses social and historical analysis traceable to the Frankfurt School but also uses poststructuralism as a discursive basis of a social psychology of the schooling experience. Chet Bowers (1987, 1993) has formulated a postliberal theory of curriculum that incorporates communicative competence and ecological models that challenge liberal political theories.

As we have explored in this chapter, there are emerging forms of critical theory that offer the possibility of advancing social, cultural, and ideological arrangements that have an impact on schooling in the 1990s. However, there appears to be conflict as to whether political curriculum theory should remain rooted in Marxism and the Frankfurt school or engage poststructural, racial, ecological, and gendered perspectives in the emerging postmodern curriculum field. The debates over these issues certainly will intensify in the coming years.

CHAPTER TEN

Qualitative Inquiry, Fine Arts, and the Synthetical Moment

There are at least six ways to explore postmodern curriculum development from a qualitative aesthetic perspective: a review of postmodern art and architectural movements and their impact on society and culture, along with their political implications, for example in Charles Jencks' (1986) *What is Post-Modernism?* Dennis Earl Fehr's (1993) *Dogs Playing Cards* or Landon Beyer's (1988) *Art and Society: Toward New Directions in Aesthetic Education*; a study of the interrelationship between postmodern philosophies and art, for example Michel Foucault's (1982) poststructural analysis of René Magritte's painting in *This is Not a Pipe* or Maxine Greene's (1978) phenomenological investigation of education in *Landscapes of Learning*; an analysis of texts that have provided a transition from the dominant quantitative paradigms of evaluation in schooling toward an aesthetic and qualitative understanding of curriculum and instruction, for example in George Willis and William Schubert's (1991) *Reflections from the Heart of Educational Inquiry: Understanding Curriculum and Teaching through the Arts*, Elliot Eisner's (1985) *The Educational Imagination*, or Eisner's (1991) *The Enlightened Eye*; a study of the correspondences between aesthetic experiences and curriculum, for example in John Dewey's (1934b) *Art as Experience* or Ronald Padgham's (1988) "Correspondences: Contemporary Curriculum Theory and Twentieth Century Art"; a review of the phenomenological literature that understands knowledge as a human construction and social life as an enacted, meaning-embedded experience, inseparable from human beliefs, values, and creativity, for example in Ted Aoki's (1988) "Toward a Dialectic Between the Conceptual World and the Lived World" or Max van Manen's (1993) *The Tact of Teaching: The Meaning of Pedagogical Thoughtfulness*; and finally, an exploration of notions of knowledge acquisition and of thinking that are distinct from mainstream social and behavioral science, for example in Thomas Barone's (1993) "Breaking the Mold: The New American Student as Strong Poet" or Denise Palmer Wolf's (1992) "Becoming Knowledge: The Evolution of Art Education Curriculum."

In all six of these approaches to qualitative, aesthetic, and humanistic inquiry in curriculum studies there is an interest in exploring ways of knowing and learning that create what William Pinar and Madeleine Grumet (1976) call "synthetical moments." In the synthesizing moment there is a reconstruction of the self and an experience of solidarity of the intellect, the body, the spirit, and the cosmos, as well as an intrinsic coherence of time, place, and meaning. Michel Serres (1982) writes about a sense of contemporaneousness. Serres uses provoking metaphors and analogies to explain that there is convergence in particular events where many things come together and similar forms provide a passage for making connections on the journey of life. While Serres insists on keeping things separate, his analogies help to make connections through which we experience contemporaneousness. Both Pinar and Serres provide options for rethinking modern obsessions with establishing causal links in space over time. Linear explanations are replaced by concepts of contemporaneousness, convergence, and synthesis. Such meaning-full and awe-full moments are integral to the postmodern curriculum and not peripheral. Herbert Kliebard (1992) warns:

> [Humanism] has come to be associated with a set of subjects, a segment of the school curriculum, believed to have the power to stir the imagination, enhance the appreciation of beauty, and disclose motives that actuate human behavior. . . . The arts—music, painting, sculpture, poetry—[are] the highest forms of expression by which human beings convey their experience and their aspirations. These, it turns out, are the very subjects that have suffered the steepest decline in the American school curriculum during the course of the twentieth century, a decline which, if continued, will at best make artistic

expression and appreciation the province of a handful of
sensitive souls. (p. 3)

The postmodern curriculum takes Kliebard's warning to heart
and prioritizes artistic and aesthetic experiences, especially as
these endeavors will support qualitative research, humanistic
values, synthetical self-understanding, and a sense of
contemporaneousness in the schooling process.

The postmodern curriculum includes the integration of
eclectic, ironic, and kaleidoscopic experiences that affirm the
uniqueness of individual creativity, and contemporaneousness
of time and place, as well as global solidarity. Modern
curriculum development paradigms, with their emphasis on
rational discourse, time on task, lesson implementation, and
objective evaluation, discourage aesthetic experiences while
elevating mathematical computation, scientific methods, and
reading comprehension in the core of the curriculum. Music, fine
arts, drama, dance, poetry, speech, band, painting, and the like
have been relegated to the fringe, often the first casualties of
budget cuts or scheduling conflicts. Postmodern curriculum
prioritizes the dramatic, the artistic, the nonrational, and the
intuitive dimensions of the human person in the learning
process. Rather than cutting art from the heart of the curriculum,
postmodern education encourages aesthetic reflections from the
heart in educational inquiry.

Perhaps John Dewey provides the most cogent analysis of
aesthetics in education in his book *Art as Experience*. Dewey
(1934b) considers the significance of the arts, and concludes, "In
the end, works of art are the only media of complete and
unhindered communication between man and man that can
occur in a world full of gulfs and walls that limit community of
experience" (p. 105). Cleo Cherryholmes (1994) extends Dewey's
position: "I choose to highlight Dewey's emphasis on experience
because it is less restrictive than transactional realism. To
illustrate the possibilities that 'experience' opens up, I extend my
comments to aesthetics. Aesthetics . . . is a central but almost
universally overlooked aspect of research" (p. 16). Cherryholmes
is one of many scholars in the 1990s who recognize the potential
of aesthetics to inform our curriculum research and schooling

practices. Richard Rorty (1982) provides philosophical support for this position:

> The burden of my argument so far has been that if we get rid of notions of "objectivity" and "scientific method" we shall be able to see the social sciences as continuous with literature—as interpreting other people to us, and thus enlarging and deepening our sense of community.... One can emphasize, as Dewey did, the moral importance of the social sciences—their role in widening and deepening our sense of community. Or one can emphasize, as Michel Foucault does, the way in which the social sciences have served as instruments of the "disciplinary society," the connection between knowledge and power rather than between knowledge and human solidarity. (1982, p. 203–204)

In either case, both Dewey and Foucault point the way to a consideration of human solidarity. Following Rorty, Cherryholmes (1988b) contends that this human solidarity, which is informed by his critical pragmatism, involves making epistemological, ethical, and aesthetic choices and translating them into discourse-practices.

The experience of curriculum introduced above is orchestrated in such a way that improvisation and spontaneity enhance the educational experience. Like improvisational jazz, zydeco, or cajun music, one sound or beat leads to another, forming an eclectic mixture of instruments and rhythms. Success in improvisational music and curriculum has one fundamental requirement, according to David Smith (1991): " ... The group members must be committed to staying 'with' each other, constantly listening to subtle nuances of tempo and melody, with one person never stealing the show for the entire session" (p. 198). In education, this community solidarity requires giving of one's self over to conversation with young people and building a common shared reality in a spirit of self-forgetfulness in order to discover oneself in relation to the entire community experience. This is true not only in music, but for Smith and others who explore qualitative inquiry, it is especially true in curriculum studies in the postmodern era (Smith, 1991).

Qualitative inquiry and research cannot be planned using modern concepts of objectivity, nor can it be imposed uniformly upon students with statistical certainty. Phenomenologists, who are at the forefront of much qualitative curriculum inquiry, insist that the subjective encounter creates authentic understanding— and it may happen unexpectedly. Just as daydreams and nightmares may surprise the imagination, so does the aesthetic encounter. A sunset, a storm, a song, a passionate relationship, a word of praise, or even a dramatic tragedy may spark understanding and engender a synthetical experience. In order to understand qualitative inquiry, educators must remove the blinders of modernity and look at curriculum through different kaleidoscopic lenses. Curriculum leaders must begin by replacing inspectional and clinical models with phenomenological, autobiographical, and metaphorical reflection that utilizes multi- and extrasensory phenomena and perceptions simultaneously to expand our understanding of the whole educative moment contemporaneously. Only in this way will we move toward the postmodern aesthetic curriculum.

Orchestration requires that teachers and students enter a new zone of cognition and self-reflection where the whole experience is greater than the sum of discrete individual activities. An art critic, for example, does not measure percentages of colors mixed on the painter's palate. Rather, the critic as connoisseur evaluates the impact of the unique balance of color in the entire context of the painting as used by the artist to achieve a synthetical and empathetic relationship with the viewer. A wine connoisseur may sniff the cork, swirl the wine in a glass, and take a sample taste. However, the connoisseur does not "grade" a wine on texture, smell, taste, and visual quality in isolation. The final product, whether a painting or a fine wine, is a masterpiece if all the sense experiences cohere and engender a synthetical experience. Elliot Eisner has advanced this concept in his research in educational evaluation. Eisner (1991) writes:

> [Connoisseurship] is a matter of noticing, and noticing requires perceptivity. *Perceptivity* is the ability to differentiate and to experience the relationships between, say, one gustatory quality in the wine and others. Like the interplay of sounds in a symphonic score, to experience

> wine is to experience an interplay of qualitative
> relationships. Wine connoisseurship requires an
> awareness of not only qualities of taste but also qualities of
> appearance and smell. The color at the edge of a red wine
> when the glass is tipped is indicative of its age, the
> browner it is, the older. The ways in which its "legs" hang
> on the inside of the glass says something about its body.
> The perfume or nose of a wine is another quality that
> counts. . . . Our connoisseurship of wine is influenced by
> more than our ability to differentiate the subtle qualities of
> wine we taste and to compare them in our sensory
> memory with other wines tasted. It is also influenced by
> our understanding of the conditions that give rise to these
> qualities. . . . Enologists now are highly trained in the
> chemistry and the science of winemaking, yet in the end,
> the making of wine is an art. (pp. 64–65)

The art of winemaking, like the art of teaching, requires that we
experience qualitative nuances of wines and classrooms. It also
requires judgments about the qualities experienced. Ultimately,
the aesthetic experience, and not a formula or lesson plan, is the
true measure of quality. Eisner concludes that educational
inquiry will be more complete and informative when we
increase the range of ways we describe, interpret, and evaluate
curriculum and instruction. The inclusion of aesthetic and
qualitative approaches to inquiry, along with the development of
connoisseurship as a teacher competency, will "contribute to the
improvement of educational practice by giving us a fuller, more
complex understanding of what makes schools and classrooms
tick" (Eisner, 1991, p. 8).

Eisner's connoisseurship moves curriculum and
evaluation away from modern notions of prescriptive
behaviorism where teachers and students simply enact or
implement preconceived notions of teaching and knowledge—
such as the accountability evaluation instruments for teachers
and promotion exams for students that are being implemented in
many states. However, Eisner is really a transitional figure in the
emerging aesthetic curriculum field. Postmodernism will
deconstruct the concept of connoisseurship with its notion of
expertise and shift the aesthetic judgment to a multiplicity of
voices and subcultures.

The complexity of understanding aesthetic experiences is difficult for those of us living in a modern mechanistic society where connoisseurship and qualitative evaluation, much less postmodern multiplicity and eclecticism, do not conform to the logic of positivism, behaviorism, rationalism, and structural analysis. However, postmodernism provides an aesthetic vision where multiplicity replaces binary hierarchies and subjectivity replaces pastiche. Here synthetical experiences can be understood like Gadamer's "fusion of horizons," where the individual is not subsumed or imitated but integrated with the hermeneutic circle.

The beginning of my personal journey to understand this postmodern aesthetic perspective occurred unexpectedly in the Metropolitan Museum of Art in New York City during a high school trip. Our teacher took us to the museum to view a retrospective exhibit of the history of art through the eyes of several painters from medieval times through abstract expressionism. I walked hurriedly through the art of the ages with my high school friends, anxious to get to the end so that we could move on to our pizza lunch. As we made our way into the final gallery, a huge canvas covering an entire wall startled us. The canvas was filled with swirls of color, particles of glass and dirt, random drippings from paint brushes, and splashes from buckets of paint. We all laughed at this mess, and we mused aloud why it would be included in a major art exhibit. We rushed to the exit to meet our chaperon for lunch. As I reached the exit, a magnetic pull from the painting caused me to freeze. I realized that I had to go back into the gallery and investigate this strange painting, so I asked my teacher to let me stay in the museum. He agreed, but my friends urged me to come out. The tug-of-war ended as I sent them ahead and returned to the painting.

I walked alone and stood face to face with myself before Jackson Pollock's *Autumn Rhythm*. The intensity of the emotions of this artist touched a nerve in my adolescent confusion. I sensed the pain of the artist's struggles and suffering, which seemed to parallel my own inner turmoil. Pollock's frustration with social structures reverberated with my own indignation about the Vietnam War, racism, and social injustice. Jackson

Pollock's battle with alcoholism leaped from the canvas and caused me to reflect on my own family's struggle with this disease. I did not "know" Jackson Pollock at the time, but I came to experience his emotions as I encountered *Autumn Rhythm*. Just as "knowing" in biblical literature refers to intercourse, there was a bond of intimacy that intensified as I stood with Pollock's painting.

Hundreds of people must have come and gone while I spent an hour or more in the room. However, time stood still for me. I was not a painter; I had never formally studied art. I had never heard of Jackson Pollock, but I became the artist through his painting as his journey and my journey were united in a synthetical moment. When I reluctantly left the museum and caught up with my friends, I could not explain the mysterious events that occurred as I stood before *Autumn Rhythm*.

Jackson Pollock continues to influence my life and my education. I experienced a phenomenological moment of revelation and personal understanding that, like the beauty and intensity of nature in autumn, defines my life. Studying the technical details of the abstract expressionist style of painting or the biography of Jackson Pollock could never have replaced that synthetical moment in the Metropolitan Museum of Art. However, following my encounter with *Autumn Rhythm* I have devoured every book available on these topics. This demonstrates a central dimension of qualitative aesthetic inquiry in the postmodern curriculum: the experience of disturbance, perturbation, contemporaneousness, or synthetical moments will inspire students to read, to research, to explore, to learn, to meditate, and to expand their understanding of the initial experience. It will also ignite a passion for justice and compassion.

The aesthetic dimension of the postmodern curriculum is clearly reflected in this story about *Autumn Rhythm* and Jackson Pollock. Knowledge is not logically ordered and waiting to be discovered, rather it is constructed in experiences of the whole body and being. "The intellect may raise all kinds of questions—and it is perfectly right for it to do so—but to expect a final answer from the intellect is asking too much of it, for this is not in the nature of intellection. The answer lies deeply buried under the bedrock of our being" (Suzuki, Fromm, and DeMartino, 1960, pp. 48–49). *Autumn Rhythm* did not provide answers to my intellect, rather it touched the bedrock of my being and initiated a search for meaning and understanding, not only about art history, abstract expressionism, and Jackson Pollock but most significantly about the purpose of life, the reason for suffering, the tragedy of alcoholism, and the relationship between inner confusion and turmoil. My visit to the Metropolitan Museum of Art, it turns out, was not simply a retrospective art lesson, it was a border crossing, a seminal moment, a synthetical event—a postmodern curricular experience—that initiated a lifelong journey into the realm of contemporary art and postmodern living. This experience created a context within which the future study of art has been appealing, satisfying, lifegiving, and educational.

These curriculum landscapes and experiences of transformative pedagogy challenge the educational community to reevaluate the traditional understanding of the learning environment. Even a traditionalist like Mortimer Adler (1982) writes: "Our concern with education must go beyond schooling. . . . Education is a lifelong process of which schooling is only a small part. . . . Schooling should open the doors to the world of learning" (p. 9–11). The postmodern world demands awareness of the environment and openness to the deep ecology of learning: "The forests speak out, the oceans beckon, the sky calls us forth, the plants want to share their story, the mind of the universe is open to all of us, the planet wants to instruct. Educators, through their methods and their content, can either open wide the doors to this wonder or narrow the doorways to offer only a partial view which they can then control" (LePage, 1987, p. 180). Andy LePage argues that participation in the environment is far more educational than passive observation. Participation in new environments and expanded horizons provides students and teachers with insights into alternative strategies for living, and therefore expanded possibilities for the future. These possibilities, in turn, offer a vision of hope to people who otherwise would be unaware of alternatives. In this sense, aesthetic theories also inform social and political theories of education, as Landon Beyer proposes.

Attention to the alternatives that provide hope is called "wide-awakenness" by the philosopher of education Maxine Greene. She argues for a strong emphasis on arts and humanities in education to promote this wide-awakenness and self-understanding that emerge from synthetical moments. Greene turns to the poet Henry David Thoreau for inspiration. According to Greene (1978), "Thoreau writes passionately about throwing off sleep. He talks about how few people are awake enough for a poetic or divine life. He asserts that to be awake is to be alive" (p. 162). David Orr (1992) also turns to Thoreau for understanding: "Thoreau did not research Walden Pond, rather, he went to live 'deliberately'" (p. 125). Thus, *Walden* becomes a mosaic of philosophy, poetry, natural history, geology, folklore, archeology, economics, politics, and education for Thoreau, and in this sense aesthetics leads to wholeness. Orr (1992) explains: "Thoreau's subject matter was Thoreau; his goal, wholeness; his tool, Walden Pond; and his methodology, simplification" (p. 125). This is the antithesis of the modern curriculum that artificially separates subject matter, isolates and analyzes discrete parts, and obfuscates simple beauty. Orr (1992) concludes:

> Aside from its merits as literature or philosophy, *Walden* is an antidote to the idea that education is a passive, indoor activity occurring between the ages of six and twenty-one. In contrast to the tendencies to segregate disciplines, and to segregate intellect from its surroundings, *Walden* is a model of the possible unity between personhood, pedagogy, and place. For Thoreau, Walden was more than his location. It was a laboratory for observation and experimentation; a library of data about geology, history, flora, fauna; a source of inspiration and renewal; and a testing ground for the man. *Walden* is no monologue, it is a dialogue between a man and a place. In a sense, *Walden* wrote Thoreau. His genius, I think, was to allow himself to be shaped by his place, to allow it to speak with his voice. (p. 125–126)

This, too, is the postmodern curriculum: the inspiration of nature and poetry; the unity of self, pedagogy, and place; becoming through encounters with place; and uncovering the voice of self-expression. Qualitative inquiry engenders this postmodern curriculum.

While the technological influences of modern society on the curriculum are increasing feelings of hopelessness and powerlessness, qualitative inquiry has the potential to create what Greene calls a "different kind of breathing" and a sense of "wide-awakenness." This is essential for postmodern transformation. The debilitating modern alternatives to wide-awakenness are characterized as a "culture of silence" by Paulo Freire (1970) that allows for the uncritical absorption of only official (i.e., state, school, expert) renderings of life; as a "society of formless emotion" by Susanne Langer (1957) that has neglected the education of feeling; and as "technical rationality" by Donald Schon (1983) and Donald Oliver and Kathleen Gershman (1989) that depends on instrumental problem solving by the application of scientific theory and techniques devoid of reflection-in-action and deep personal knowing with the whole body. Education must explore new landscapes of learning if transformation, liberation, and hope are to replace the decadence, inertia, and decay of modernity. Freire, Langer, Barone, Schon, Oliver, Gershman, Beyer, LePage, Greene, Orr, and Eisner, among others, warn of the harmful consequences of our continued attachment to modern models of rationality that avoid artistic, intuitive, and nonrational ways of knowing. Eisner (1985) writes:

> Knowledge is considered by most in our culture as something that one discovers, not something that one makes. Knowledge is out there waiting to be found, and the most useful tool for finding it is science. If there were greater appreciation for the extent to which knowledge is constructed—something made—there might be a greater likelihood that its aesthetic dimension would be appreciated. (p. 32)

David Ray Griffin documents the ecological and social disasters that lurk ahead if our worldview does not shift from a modern to this postmodern aesthetic vision. Griffin (1988a) warns: "A great deal is at stake. We must collectively move from mechanistic and dualistic worldviews and positivist and other antiworldviews to an ecological worldview" (p. 102).

Art is one of the primary places where an ecological mode of learning with emphasis on knowledge construction occurs. An adequate aesthetic pedagogy might enable contemporary learners to break with assimilative power and reconstitute certain works of art as occasions for convergence, synthetical moments, understanding of the self, and social critique. The individual's encounter with art can be an occasion for transformation, transcendence, and praxis, and thus a critical dimension of the postmodern curriculum.

The artistic landscape as an occasion for learning is actually a revolutionary development in the philosophical understanding of art. It is a kind of theory that focuses upon the response to a work of art in order to account for it and to account for the importance of the aesthetic mode in human life. It is important to distinguish how these phenomenological assumptions contrast with the traditional ontological philosophy of art, which deals with beings as they are in themselves regardless of the way they are apprehended or of the fact that they are apprehended at all.

Phenomenology, on the other hand, is based on the assumption that we cannot speculate about what beings are in themselves. Rather, the emphasis should be placed on *possibility* and *becoming* as a goal of the curriculum, for human consciousness can never be static. Jean-Paul Sartre argues that human consciousness (being-for-itself) can never become a substance or an objective thing (being-in-itself), and this is why possibility must be the focus of educational inquiry. Hence, each new experience adds to the accumulated meaning of experience for each individual and sets the stage for present and future possibilities. While the present is conditioned by the past, every moment is also pregnant with future possibilities for change and new directions. The aesthetic experience can inspire new personal realizations, as John Dewey (1934b) in *Art as Experience* explains:

> A work of art, no matter how old or classic is actually not just potentially, a work of art only when it lives in some individual experience. A piece of parchment, of marble, of canvas, it remains self-identical throughout the ages. But as a work of art it is re-created every time it is aesthetically

> experienced. . . . The Parthenon, or whatever, is universal
> because it can continue to inspire new personal
> realizations in experience. (pp. 108–109)

Pablo Picasso (1971) has also described artistic creation in a
similar way:

> A picture is not thought out and settled beforehand. While
> it is being done it changes as one's thoughts change. And
> when it is finished it still goes on changing according to
> the state of mind of whoever is looking at it. A picture
> lives a life like a living creature, undergoing the changes
> imposed on us by our life from day to day. This is natural
> enough, as the picture lives only through the man who is
> looking at it. (p. 268)

Picasso and Dewey reflect one of the important phenomenological dimensions of postmodern aesthetics: events find their meaning in subjective encounters where knowledge is constructed and
reconstructed in every new situation. In this sense, a work of art
truly exists only in the encounter. If locked in a darkened vault, a
painting is simply an aggregate of materials. Art, like the
curriculum, is the process of becoming and recreating in each
new situation. Phenomenology seeks description of how the
world is experienced by persons, or for Martin Heidegger, a
method or science of the phenomenon of consciousness. The
purpose is not just description of phenomena, but the
understanding of what lies behind them, their *being* or ontology.

Phenomenological understanding of curriculum replaces
the modern obsession with standardized interpretation of
literature and fine arts (especially in humanities departments,
ironically), predetermined methodologies and styles for writing,
painting, and researching, and universal master narratives that
can be applied to knowledge acquisition. For Maurice Merleau-
Ponty (1962) perception is primary, as in the actual feelings of
amputated limbs perceived by amputees—called the phantom
limb. Ozmon and Craver (1990) explain: "Abstract truth is not
self-evident in perception, but perception has with it the
potential for arriving at the truth in a more subtle fashion as it is
sensed or experienced rather than as it is filtered through the
philosophical dogmatisms and assumptions of the past" (pp.
246–247).

Yvonna Lincoln (1992), in an essay on curriculum inquiry and the humanistic tradition, expands on this concept of phenomenological perception and relates it to lived experience:

> Phenomenology enjoys a status today as a soundly conceived philosophical school, the bent of which is to return experience to the lived rather than the instrumental or conceptual world and to view the conceptual world as one given meaning and mediated by the lived, present being and temporal experience.... Phenomenologists are themselves increasingly concerned with the abstractions represented by the scientific, technological, and instrumental approaches to curriculum that prevailed during the first half of this century. The notion of the curriculum as a set of concepts, ideas, and facts to be mastered; students as empty vessels to be filled with those concepts; and pedagogy as a set of techniques to be acquired by teachers is often rejected by contemporary curricularists. (p. 91)

Max van Manen and other contemporary phenomenologists support this rejection of traditional techniques. There is a growing body of evidence and a set of moral suasions that students themselves are capable of rich inner lives, that their experience is worth eliciting and building on, and that pedagogy is a form of interactive relationship rather than a bag of tricks to be assembled in the teaching process (van Manen, 1988).

The development of phenomenology as applied to artistic-aesthetic expression has roots in cubism and flourishes with abstract expressionism of the twentieth century. These movements are in contrast to the High Renaissance, and they are foreign to painters such as Raphael. The traditional understanding of art in the Renaissance held that content is predetermined, and that the artist must focus on the form through which content is conveyed. Raphael utilized art apprentices to help paint his canvas or mural from the cartoon. This would be considered anathema to phenomenologists, who comprehend form and content as congruent. Ronald Padgham (1988) writes: "The content in the new theory is the individual in the process of becoming; becoming that which he [or she] has not yet been, but that which he [or she] is capable of becoming" (p. 377).

Maxine Greene applies this understanding of form and content to education and contends that involvement with the arts and humanities has the potential for provoking reflectiveness. She challenges educators to devise ways of integrating arts into what is taught at all levels of the educational enterprise. This has direct implications for social and moral issues in postmodern curriculum and in art education. Greene (1978) explains the implications as follows: "I would like to believe that the concerns of art educators are akin to those I have described: to enhance qualitative awareness, to release imagination, and to free people to see, shape, and transform. I would hope for the kinds of curricula that permit an easy and articulated transaction between making and attending" (p. 74).

The congruence of form and content is revealed in such works as *Nude Descending a Staircase* by Duchamp in 1912. The illusion of movement is created in the cubist painting exactly as a camera would capture it in frames many years later. Picasso's sculptures likewise reveal a vision of what had never been seen before, for no one before Picasso had seen the now obvious similitude between the pointed saddle and handlebars of a bicycle and the visage of a bull in *Guernica* (Greene, 1978). Furthermore, abstract expressionists like Pollock reveal the intensity of their emotional responses in paintings like *Autumn Rhythm*, where the experience of the observer becomes a communion with the artist. Twentieth-century artists have frequently discussed the existential and phenomenological nature of their methodology. Ronald Padgham contends that there is no right or wrong way to teach, just as there is no right or wrong way to paint. There is only one's natural way. Padgham (1988) states: "To discover one's natural way necessitates self-discovery or consciousness of self" (p. 367). Jackson Pollock (1971) explains how this process evolves:

> When I am in my painting, I am not aware of what I am doing. It is only after a short get acquainted period that I see what I have been about. I have no fears about making changes, destroying the image, etc. Because the painting has a life of its own, I try to let it come through. It is only

> when I lose contact with the painting that the result is a
> mess. Otherwise there is pure harmony, an easy give and
> take, and the painting comes out well. (p. 548)

This experience in turn leads to new expressive qualities in the
observer's world.

The phenomenological understanding of experience and
wide-awakenness that leads to transformation is found in many
diverse works such as Stravinsky's *The Rite of Spring*, Picasso's
Geurnica, Faulkner's *The Bear*, and Joyce's *Portrait of the Artist as a
Young Man*. Greene (1978) continues:

> Lacking wide-awakenness, I want to argue that
> individuals are likely to drift, to act on impulses of
> expediency. They are unlikely to identify situations as
> moral ones or set such cases; it seems to me, it is
> meaningless to talk of obligation: it may be futile to speak
> of consequential choice. (p. 43)

The result of this postmodern paradigm shift in education and
art can create a renewed sense of hope. Social change becomes
possible because individual transformation is a process that can
be experienced in the community of artists and aesthetic
educators. Social progress occurs as individuals change, not
when institutions change. Postmodern curriculum scholars
contend that attentiveness to the moral dimension of existence
should permeate classrooms, and teachers should be clear about
how to ground their own values. We are no longer in a situation
where character-training, values clarification, and systems of
rewards and punishment will make children virtuous, just, and
compliant. "We recognize the futility of teaching rules, of
preaching pieties, or presenting conceptions of the good. Moral
education, rather, must be as specifically concerned with self-
identification in a community as it is with judgments persons are
equipped to make at different ages" (Greene, 1978, p. 47).

Form and content should no longer be seen as separate;
they are congruent in the postmodern curriculum. For the
educator, inquiry and reflection merge with lecturing. Thus, not
a pedagogical, an aesthetic, or a theological dualism is any
longer sufficient or viable. The content of the curriculum is the
individual in the process of becoming that which he or she has

not yet been but that which he or she is capable of becoming. The various disciplines become part of the form and content, and a congruence is achieved.

The congruence of form and content is not only a phenomenological experience, it also has eschatological implications. Once the congruence is understood, then the limitations of time and space begin to diminish. They melt into the landscape like the watches in Salvador Dali's painting *The Persistence of Memory*. Experiences are no longer frozen in time. Learning elicits new experiences that encourage a futuring—a going beyond the present state of malaise. Teachers who themselves are submerged, who feel in some sense "finished" like the chairs or blackboards in their rooms, lack the moral persuasion to inspire students to critical questioning, to nurture aesthetic experiences, or to connect learning to creative thinking. Unfortunately, there is often nothing occurring in many classrooms: no talking, no questioning, no thinking, no exploring, and thus no convergence or synthesis. Teachers must be in touch with their own inner landscapes—their own aesthetic experiences—in order for learning to become a process of discovery, learning, and self-understanding.

Qualitative aesthetic experiences involve critical reflection. It is a kind of knowing called praxis: a knowing that becomes an opening to possibilities and empowerment. Greene (1978) calls it "a poem about one human being's self-formation, recaptured through a return (in inner time) to an original landscape, the place where it all began" (p. 15). This experience of returning is not only necessary for wide-awakenness, but also for autobiographical wholeness and self-reflection. It even goes beyond the aesthetic encounters discussed above. The emphasis has shifted from the external to the internal and artists seek an inner experience that creates an interconnectedness. Otherwise, enthusiasm and hope will be lost. Without that awareness and that hope teachers find it unimaginably difficult to cope with the demands of children in the schools today. Like Horace Smith in Theodore Sizer's (1984) book *Horace's Compromise: The Dilemma of the American High School*, teachers will "neither have the time nor energy, nor inclination to urge their students to critical reflection:

they themselves have suppressed the questions, and avoided
backward looks" (p. 38).

This, then, is the implication of aesthetics for the
postmodern curriculum: transformation and learning are
stimulated by a sense of future possibilities and sense of what
might be. Building community and enabling personal
awakenness are crucial in this process. Maxine Greene (1978)
moves toward the postmodern curriculum as she advises:

> I would lay stress upon talking together, upon the mutual
> exchange that expresses lives actually lived together, that
> forges commonalities. I would work for the kind of critical
> reflection that can be carried on by persons who are
> situated in the concreteness of the world, by persons
> equipped for interrogation, for problematization, and for
> hermeneutic interpretation of the culture—of the present
> and the past. (p. 107)

This can be accomplished: schooling flourishes in some places
because of emphasis on this type of community building. Once
engaged in the journey, the traveler no longer remains isolated
and separated from the dreams and visions that give sustenance
for exploration and praxis. A postmodern transformative
pedagogy is most clearly seen as the engagement of this journey
by students and teachers who are confident that the
consummation of education is liberation and synthesis.

An awareness and sensitivity toward many
environments—physical, psychological, spiritual, and social—is
an integral part of the postmodern proposals that inform the
postmodern curriculum. Participation in aesthetic environments
provides the educational community with alternative strategies
for living and expanded possibilities for the future. Because
postmodern curriculum understands the future as that which
brings to completion what has already been set in motion, the
alternative possibilities offer a vision of hope for schools and
society. This vision would remain idealized and romanticized
were it not for the dimension of aesthetic understanding and
hope called "wide-awakenness" by Maxine Greene, "fusion of
horizons" by Hans-Georg Gadamer, "praxis" by Paulo Freire,
"reflection-in-action" by Donald Schon, "connoisseurship" by
Elliot Eisner, "becoming" by Ronald Padgham, "experience" by

John Dewey, "rich inner lives" by Max van Manen, "synthetical moments" by William Pinar, and "contemporaneousness" by Michel Serres.

Although characterized in many unique, ironic, and even contradictory ways, the aesthetic dimensions of learning in postmodern curriculum emphasize the primacy of experience, the merging of form and content, the recursion and convergence of time, the celebration of the self-conscious individual, and the understanding of phenomenological experience. This perspective on curriculum offers the individual a process for growing and becoming. It also offers schools an opportunity for critical reflection that is open to what has not yet been but what is also absolutely possible. Without this vision, teachers and students will have neither the time nor the energy, neither the hope nor the endurance, to move beyond the modern technological models and toward the emerging postmodern curriculum. Aesthetics, the fine arts, and qualitative inquiry are integral to the creation of landscapes of learning and synthetical moments of self-understanding for curriculum development in the postmodern era. In fact, aesthetic phenomena may ultimately be the only justification for our curriculum theorizing, even for our very existence, according to Friedrich Nietzsche (1968) when he writes in *The Birth of Tragedy*: "We have our highest dignity in our significance as works of art—for it is only as an aesthetic phenomenon that existence and the world are eternally justified" (p. 52).

CHAPTER ELEVEN

Time Management and Chaos in the Infinite Cosmos

> We do not conceive of sudden, radical, irrational change as built into the very fabric of existence. Yet it is. And chaos theory teaches us, Malcolm said, that straight linearity, which we have come to take for granted in everything from physics to fiction, simply does not exist. Linearity is an artificial way of viewing the world. Real life isn't a series of interconnected events occurring one after another like beads strung on a necklace. Life is actually a series of encounters in which one event may change those that follow in a wholly unpredictable, even devastating way. That's a deep truth about the structure of our universe. But, for some reason, we insist on behaving as if it were not true.
>
> *Michael Crichton, Jurassic Park (1990) (p. 171)*

I was recently asked to conduct a one-hour seminar for the Louisiana Leadership Academy, an ongoing certification program for principals. The designated topic was "time management." Not having any particular expertise or interest in this topic, I was reluctant to accept the invitation. However, the seminar director was a friend, and he convinced me that I could say something interesting to a group of school administrators, especially since I had been a principal for many years. For the next several weeks I was preoccupied and anxious about this presentation. I felt certain that the principals would be expecting a practical program with suggestions for improving their organizational skills in order to reduce the pressure of their demanding schedules, and I was not sure of the best method of conducting the seminar in order to address their very real day-to-day concerns.

Frustrated and uncertain, I immersed myself in time management literature for several days. I read *Seven Habits of Highly Successful People* by Stephen Covey (1989), *The One Minute Manager* by Kenneth Blanchard and Spencer Johnson (1981), *Organize Yourself!* by Ronnie Eisenberg (1986), and the classic ethnography used in many leadership courses, *The Man in the Principal's Office* by Harry Wolcott (1973). I reviewed the time management methods that I had used myself as a principal, such as organizational flow charts, five-year plans, delegation to department heads, computerized appointment schedules, comprehensive and detailed handbooks, a binder filing system, informative newsletters, and master calendars. As I prepared for this seminar all the exhaustion of my career as a principal came rushing back into my memory. I remembered that no matter how well a school was organized, the unexpected and unpredictable were the daily norm: bomb threats on exam days; parents and board members bursting into the office with a new idea or a complaint; malfunctioning telephones, heaters, air conditioners, and toilets; emergency discipline meetings; crying secretaries, crying teachers, crying students; head lice outbreaks in first grade; early dismissals for inclement weather on football playoff games; outstanding teachers who are transferred in the middle of the year; food fights in the lunchroom. Donald Schon called this "managing messes." I was exhausted remembering these incidents and the last minute planning that was a constant part of school administration. I also remembered the barrage of complaints, especially from teachers, whenever the school schedule was disrupted. Time was viewed as a precious commodity to be allocated judiciously.

School administrators know that randomness and chaos more accurately define their lives than predictability and stability, and yet modern bureaucrats continue to frustrate educators by organizing schools around the modern conception of time as controllable and manageable. As I was preparing for this time management seminar, I also happened to be reading an article from the journal *New Scientist* and several books on chaos theory and the new sciences including *The Tao of Physics* by

Fritjof Capra (1975), *The Reenchantment of Science: Postmodern Proposals* edited by David Ray Griffin (1988), *Order Out of Chaos: Man's New Dialogue with Nature* by Ilya Prigogine and Isabelle Stengers (1984), *Chaos: Making a New Science* by James Gleick (1987), *A Brief History of Time: From the Big Bang to the Black Holes* by Stephen Hawking (1988), *The Cosmic Blueprint: New Discoveries in Nature's Creative Ability to Order the Universe* by Paul Davies (1988), and, most significantly, *The Structure of Scientific Revolutions* by Thomas Kuhn (1970). The contrast between the two sets of readings was dramatic and disturbing.

Thomas Kuhn reminded me that one of the tasks of the historian of science is to "describe and explain the congeries of error, myth, and superstition that have inhabited the more rapid accumulation of the constituents of the modern science text" (1970, p. 2). The more I reflected on chaos theory, and the more I recognized the problematic nature of organization in modern schooling, the clearer it was that I would have to change the focus of my preparation for this time management seminar. Reading the following conclusion in Kuhn's book confirmed my conviction: "In both political and scientific development the sense of malfunction that can lead to crisis is a prerequisite to revolution" (p. 92). The sense of malfunction and crisis in education was abundantly clear, and thus Kuhn's hypothesis raised the possibility of a paradigm shift in the organization and curriculum of the schools in my mind. Chaos theory and the new sciences provided metaphors as well as a scientific basis for a different understanding of time and education, and this became the focus of my presentation with the administrators. It was a seminar that those present will certainly remember—for better or for worse!

Chaos theory, according to William Doll, gives meaning and substance to the language of disequilibrium, reflective intuition, surprise, puzzlement, confusion, zones of uncertainty, non-rationality, and metaphoric analysis. Doll (1991) writes: "Metaphoric analysis is hardly possible within a model structured around behavioral objectives, competency based performance, accountability, mastery learning, and effective teaching" (cited in Caine and Caine, 1991, p. 19). It is the disequilibrium itself that provides opportunities for creative tension and self-reflection. "Chaos" was first coined by physicist Jim Yorke. As Yorke says, "We tend to think science has explained how the moon goes around the earth. But this idea of a clocklike universe has nothing to do with the real world" (cited in Briggs, 1992, p. 12). John Briggs (1992) describes chaos as a natural state of the universe, and he uses weather as an example: "With its variability, general dependability, and moment to moment unpredictability, weather infiltrates our schedules, sets or undermines our plans, affects our moods, and unites us with the environment and each other. Weather is also an example of a mysterious order in chaos" (p. 13). In 1961 at MIT Edward Lorenz discovered a disturbing fact. He realized that the mere accumulation of more information about variables related to the weather such as wind speed, humidity, temperature, lunar cycles, and even sunspots do not help to increase the accuracy of long-range weather forecasts. Dynamic and complex systems like weather, he discovered, are composed of many interacting elements, and the slightest perturbation has a significant impact on future patterns. Following Lorenz, researchers have examined all dynamic systems from the human brain to electrical circuits for evidence of chaos. Our interest here is the curriculum and the classroom, where chaos theory and complexity can help us to understand the postmodern vision that challenges the static and controllable universe of classical physics.

Chaos theory provides support for the aesthetic, political, gendered, racial, cultural, theological, and ecological postmodern proposals that we have seen throughout part two of this book. We therefore conclude part two by exploring the new sciences and their relationship to curriculum development, perhaps the most revolutionary research to support the postmodern paradigm shift that is underway.

Prigogine and Stengers have challenged the traditional social science approach to research in part because the mechanistic view of reality is being called into question in almost every field of scientific endeavor. New discoveries are unfolding in the universe that contradict the absolute principles of the classical sciences and the scientific method. Complexity replaces certainty. Prigogine and Stengers (1984) have demonstrated that systems in equilibrium and disequilibrium behave differently, and that order can emerge out of chaos. James Gleick (1987) and Paul Davies (1988) contend that there is an emerging science of complexity that is built in part on the fact that hidden in apparent chaos are complex types of order. The postmodern curriculum encourages chaos, nonrationality, and zones of uncertainty because the complex order existing here is the place where critical thinking, reflective intuition, and global problem solving will flourish. The standardization of rote memorization, conformity, control, and time management, following from the faculty psychology movement of the nineteenth century and the scientific management movement of the twentieth century, restrict learning to a one-dimensional level imposed uniformly upon students and teachers alike. In order to move away from standardization into complexity and this new zone of cognition, educators must adopt a new postmodern vision.

How is this postmodern vision possible within a bureaucratic paradigm committed to the principles of modernity? James Lovelock (1979) in his Gaia hypothesis provides an example based on the image of the Earth from the moon:

> The new understanding has come from going forth and looking back to the Earth from space. The vision of that splendid white flecked blue sphere stirred us all. It even opened the mind's eye, just as a voyage away from home enlarges the perspective of our love for those who remain there. . . . We now see the air, the ocean and the soil are much more than mere environment for life; they are a part of life itself. . . . There is nothing unusual in the idea of life on Earth interacting with the air, sea and rocks, but it took a view from outside to glimpse the possibility that this combination might constitute a single giant living system. (cited in Tucker, 1993, p. 11)

Lovelock contends that the vision of the Earth from the moon began a paradigmatic change in the relationship between human persons and the environment. In the same sense, a vision of curriculum development from the perspective of the new sciences can create a paradigm shift in our educational practices that will replace the linear, objective, and time management models that have dominated our thinking. If this seems to be an exaggeration, consider the emphasis we place on managed time in schools: class schedules and bells to differentiate time blocks; researchers who measure time on task, wait time between questions, and the relationship between the transition time and the academic performance of students; structured practice times, feeding times, and dismissal times; discipline plans that take away time in time-out rooms; timed tests and examinations; and duty times, planning times, and meeting times for teachers. Time is understood to exist as an independent metaphysical reality capable of being managed and organized for maximum efficiency.

Newtonian models and mechanistic systems on which modern educational paradigms are constructed ignore the developments in the sciences that indicate that social systems are interactive and open ended, and that time is an integral part of the reality. Both space and time are entities that are interwoven into matter. Paul Davies (1990) observes: "Space and time are a part of the plan of the physical universe; they are not just the stage on which the great drama is acted out, but are a part of the cast. We have to talk about the creation of space and time as well as matter and energy. . . . The world was made with time and not in time" (p. 11). Einstein set the stage for understanding space-time with his theory of relativity and his writings on electromagnetic radiation of atomic phenomena in quantum theory, both published in 1905. Einstein strongly believed in nature's inherent harmony, and he sought to find a unified foundation of physics by constructing a common framework for electrodynamics and mechanics, the two separate theories of classical physics. This is known as the special theory of relativity.

Relativity unified and completed the structure of classical physics, and it also drastically changed traditional concepts of space and time. The foundation of the Newtonian worldview is now suspect. In Einstein's theory of relativity, space is not three dimensional and time is not a separate entity. Both are intimately connected in a four-dimensional continuum called space-time. It is now impossible to understand time outside the context of space, and vice versa. Capra (1975) explains:

> There is no universal flow of time, as in the Newtonian model. Different observers will order events differently in

time if they move with different velocities relative to the observed events. In such a case, two events which are seen as occurring simultaneously by one observer may occur in different temporal sequences for other observers. All measurements involving space and time thus lose their absolute significance. In relativity theory, the Newtonian concept of an absolute space as the stage of physical phenomena is abandoned, and so is the concept of an absolute time. Both space and time become merely elements of the language a particular observer uses for describing the observed phenomenon. (pp. 50–51)

Einstein expanded on the special theory of relativity to include gravity in 1915 with the publication of his proposal of the general theory of relativity. While the special theory of relativity has been demonstrated by innumerable experiments, the general theory remains the object of investigation. However, it is widely accepted in the study of astrophysics and cosmology. In the general theory the force of gravity has the effect of "curving" space and time, and thus abolishes the concept of absolute time and space. Capra (1975) concludes: "Not only are all measurements involving space and time relative; the whole structure of space-time depends on the distribution of matter in the universe, and the concept of 'empty space' loses its meaning" (p. 52). Einstein set the stage for the emergence of the new physics and new ways of understanding the universe. Chaos theory and complexity in the postmodern era are informing all disciplines, including curriculum development and educational leadership.

Complex systems can improve in the midst of turmoil. Curriculum models based on modern visions of Newtonian physics have attempted, like a clockwork universe, to impose uniformity. Every lesson, every goal and objective, must conform to predetermined principles, cultural forms, social structures, or curricular guides. The postmodern curriculum, on the other hand, is based on a new science: a complex, multidimensional, kaleidoscopic, relational, interdisciplinary, and metaphoric system. These complex systems in science and education challenge the second law of thermodynamics, which sees the universe as running down as entropy increases. Paul Davies contends that there is no claim that the second law of thermodynamics is invalid, only that it is inadequate because it applies only to closed systems that are isolated from their environments. Davies (1990) writes: "When a system is open to its environment and there can be an exchange of matter, energy, and entropy across its boundaries, then it is possible to simultaneously satisfy the insatiable desire of nature to generate more entropy and yet have an increase in complexity and organization at the same time" (p. 10). Thus, the universe as a whole can be seen as a closed system while subsystems of the universe remain open to their environments. This is a crucial element of postmodernism: radical eclecticism necessitates an openness to diverse subcultures and environments that can increase in complexity. In the same sense, the curriculum is now seen as an open system that exists in complexity. After observing open and closed systems and their environments, the French Jesuit paleontologist Pierre Teilhard de Chardin (1959) wrote: "We are now inclined to admit that at each further degree of combination something which is irreducible to isolated elements emerges in a new order. . . . Something in the cosmos escapes from entropy, and does so more and more" (cited in Davies, 1990, p. 10).

Something in the classroom and in the curriculum must also escape from entropy. William Doll, in *A Post-Modern Perspective on Curriculum*, contends that just as the physical sciences in the seventeenth century led society into modernity, the new physics is ushering in postmodernity. Doll (1993) turns to Werner Heisenberg's uncertainty principle to support his claim. In traditional modern physics scientists believe that if they can improve their measurements and calculate with infinite precision, absolute understanding of the universe and its physical properties would follow. Heisenberg disagreed, and he demonstrated that it does not matter how accurate the instrument or measurement because the act of measuring changes the outcome of the measurement process itself. Teachers have always instinctively known this to be true. The presence of an observer in the classroom measuring effective teaching changes the dynamics of the lesson and alters the class being observed.

The Heisenberg uncertainty principle examines the subatomic world and contends that if we choose to measure one quantity (e.g., the position of the electron), we inevitably alter the system itself. Therefore, we cannot be certain about other quantities (e.g., how fast the electron is moving). Since an interaction is involved in every measurement, and since measurements are involved in observations in modern science and education, some physicists contend that the act of observation changes the system. While this applies to the interaction of particles in quantum physics, a few scientists are also beginning to extend this principle to the realm of consciousness as well. Further, because some particles exist so briefly, they are not considered to be real, but "virtual." Thus, the universe as we know it is ultimately based on chance and randomness at the subatomic level. Can quantum physics inform postmodern curriculum? Let us explore further.

In classical physics, everything is known and can be measured. In quantum physics, uncertainty is built into the metaphysical reality. Position and velocity of an electron cannot be measured simultaneously, not because the observer is not looking carefully but because there is no such thing as an electron with a definite position. Electrons are "known" only in their relationship to other electrons. Electrons do not orbit the neutron like a planet, as most physics books reported until recent years. Rather, an electron exists in a cloud like a twin. Neither a particle nor a wave, the electron is described more by its relationship and potentiality instead of its actuality. Each electron, in a sense, enfolds in itself the universe as a whole and hence all its other parts, emphasizing internal relatedness. In the postmodern curriculum it does not make sense to evaluate lessons, students, and classrooms based on predetermined plans, outcomes, or standards, for like the elusive electron, relationships and potentialities explain their existence—and not predetermined structure. Fritjof Capra (1975) explains:

> The exploration of the subatomic world in the twentieth century has revealed the intrinsically dynamic nature of matter. It has shown that the constituents of the atom, the sub-atomic particles, are dynamic patterns which do not exist as isolated entities but as integral parts of an

inseparable network of interactions. These interactions involve a ceaseless flow of energy manifesting itself as the exchange of particles; a dynamic interplay in which particles are created and destroyed without end in a continual variation of energy patterns. The particle interactions give rise to the stable structures which build up the material world, which again do not remain static, but oscillate in rhythmic movements. The whole universe is thus engaged in endless motion and activity; in a continual cosmic dance of energy. (p. 211)

Reading this passage reminds me of the motion and energy of classrooms and schools. If the universe on the quantum level and on the cosmic level is not rigid and fixed, why does our vision of curriculum, schooling, and research remain fixated on the metaphor of classical modern physics? William Doll (1993) contends that our current school curricula are not merely based on a scientific-efficiency model (Kliebard, 1986) "but have their foundations in seventeenth- to nineteenth-century modernist thought" (p. 158). The "naturalness" of this thought needs to be questioned, for what is self-evident in one paradigm becomes absurd in another. "In an intellectual time frame, Copernicus and Einstein represent the extreme boundaries of the modern paradigm, with Descartes and Newton as the medians. But, of course, as with any extremes, Copernicus and Einstein also represent the bridges between paradigms, one with the pre-modern the other with the post-modern" (Doll, pp. 21–22).

What is this postmodern paradigm in the sciences that is revolutionizing curriculum theory and other disciplines? David Ray Griffin believes that it is a reenchantment. At the root of modernity and its discontents is a disenchanted and mechanistic worldview that denies to nature the qualities of subjectivity, experience, and feeling. Griffin (1988a) writes: "Because of this denial, nature is disqualified—it is denied all qualities that are not thinkable apart from experience" (p. 2). A postmodern organic understanding of life provides the basis for a reenchantment of science that will support a new vision of the cosmos. Stephen Toulmin in his important book, *The Return to Cosmology: Postmodern Science and the Theology of Nature*, contends that we must think about the cosmos as a single integrated system where all things in the world—human, natural, and divine—are related in an orderly fashion. This cosmic interrelationship—quantum interconnectedness—is central to the postmodern curriculum. David Bohm (1988) explains:

> Because we are enfolded inseparably in the world, with no ultimate division between matter and consciousness, *meaning and value are as much integral aspects of the world as they are of us.* If science is carried out with an amoral attitude, the world will ultimately respond to science in a destructive way. Postmodern science must therefore overcome the separation between truth and virtue, values and fact, ethics and practical necessity. To call for this non-separation is, of course, to ask for a tremendous revolution in our whole attitude to knowledge. But such a change is necessary, and indeed long overdue. Can humanity meet in time the challenge of what is required? (pp. 67–68)

Likewise, can curriculum development meet the challenge of what is required? Why is it so difficult to move beyond the modern paradigm in curriculum development to this postmodern vision?

One of the reasons for our difficulty with moving to a postmodern vision is our modern attachment to practical solutions to resolve immediate problems. Classical physics provides the structures for addressing these types of concerns. In our daily experience we can function in what has been called the "zone of middle dimension," where classical physics can still be useful. On a daily basis we can deliberately remain oblivious to the quantum and cosmic phenomenon. Unaware of this dimension of "space-time," we can convince ourselves that classical physics, traditional management practices, and modern curriculum development paradigms, if perfected, can solve the ecological, sociological, and educational crises of our time. We fail to recognize complexity and the interrelatedness of actions. Postmodernism challenges us to enter a new zone of cognition. Although the "zone of middle dimension" may have been useful in the modern era, the negative consequences of ignoring the quantum and cosmic dimensions of the physical universe threaten the survivability and viability of life. Postmodern visions of space-time must be infused into our management and curriculum development paradigms. A Kuhnian revolution is truly underway, and educators cannot afford to ignore these postmodern developments.

What is this paradigm and new conception of curriculum as chaos? First, it is not destructive and purposeless. William Doll (1993) explains chaos concisely in reference to a phase space diagram of a nonlinear system, commonly called a Lorenz attractor, after Edward Lorenz, who first used this type of graph to show a systems view of weather patterns:

> First, chaos is not a wild, random abandon. Far from it; the pattern is quite orderly but complex. Chaos refers to this complex ordering. It is not possible to predict with complete accuracy where the next point on the trajectory will be (no two trajectories repeat exactly), but neither do the points fly beyond the bounds of the diagram. Two, the trajectories have both "bounds" and a center "attractor" area. Neither of these are precisely defined, but as the trajectories fly out from the center area they are attracted back, only to fly out again. The system, in its dynamic tension between moving out and back, has an overall coherence. Three, on occasion, any given point on the trajectory will "flip over" from one "owl's eye" or "butterfly wing" to the other. These "flip over" events are certain to happen over time but unpredictable for any given moment. One cannot say when such a flipping will occur, only that it will. The pattern is random, but it is a pattern. (p. 93)

Reread this passage from Doll's text again, substituting the classroom for the phase space diagram. Think of student experience when reading about flip-over events. Replace chaos in your mind with a dynamic interchange in the classroom during which many students are eager to contribute. Chaos in the classroom is such an event. First, there is a central attractor—thematic unit, an experiment, or a short story. Second, the discussion will move back and forth from one point to another without predictability—but all the questions and comments are contained within the framework of the lesson theme. Third, flip-over events in the classroom are unpredictable and may lead to a dynamic integration of new ideas into the curriculum.

In summary, postmodern curriculum challenges the clockwork universe of classical physics, which was developed before thermodynamics. It also challenges the picture of the cosmos as nothing but a random collection of particles acted upon by blind forces and capable of being controlled by artificial structures. Newton gave us a picture of a uniform universe in which every particle moved according to strictly defined laws of motion where all events were the result of the unwinding of a gigantic mechanism. Time had no real significance because the state of the universe at all times and in all places is precisely determined. This is a sterile cosmology in which time is just a parameter and does not offer any opportunity for change, flux, unfolding, or chaos. It creates an ideology of false security. In the postmodern sense time management is impossible because the universe is not created in time and space but with time and space.

The date for my seminar on time management arrived. I was assigned the last session in the afternoon. The back of the room was filled with exhausted administrators who had been required to give up a Saturday for "leadership points." No one sat in the front. We did not even begin on time! I started the seminar by relating a story of my experience attending a rural black church over the past several years. Musicians and choir members come to the sanctuary one at a time, robe, and prepare their instruments and materials. Parishioners arrive and greet each other and talk about community activities. Slowly, steadily, yet unnoticeably, a level of energy begins to fill the church. The volume of interchange rises as the piano begins to be played louder. The choir members gradually gather and softly clap their hands. And then suddenly the celebration begins! All the music and clapping come together in a thunderous explosion of energy. Unlike most other churches, no one comes to a microphone to call for attention, or to announce the page number of the first hymn, or even to offer greetings. These things happen spontaneously in this African-American church, for everyone is present and open to the complexity of the moment in the midst of apparent confusion. There is no need to ask people to rise and open books to sing, for the congregation is intuitively immersed in the music of the moment. Here, the service takes on a life of its own. No one looks to watches to determine the starting time of the service. As one gentleman told me, "It starts when everyone is ready." Sometimes the preacher speaks for minutes, sometimes hours, but he knows when to fall silent and when to raise his voice. The congregation speaks with him in a double-voiced chorus of "Amens" and "Praise be Jesus!" The pastor and the people are not separate; they operated in a dynamic harmony.

This is an example of the interrelationships that must also pervade curriculum development in the postmodern era. The curriculum must build to a crescendo in an environment of unified space-time. Random and improvisational events build on each other and create a symphonic community experience (see Wheatley [1992]). There is order in the chaos of postmodern curriculum development. Some administrators left my seminar disappointed; they did not receive a list of new time-saving practices to organize their professional lives. Others left the seminar refreshed; they experienced an understanding of life-saving insights that would change their conception of space-time. Curriculum development in the postmodern era is a cosmic vision accessible to those educators willing to see order emerging from the chaos of life.

PART THREE

Curriculum Development in the Postmodern Era

CHAPTER TWELVE

Postmodern Education
Kaleidoscopic Sensibilities

The kaleidoscope is distinct from the telescope that uses lenses and mirrors to gather the light emanating from distant objects in order to observe them more precisely. It is also different from the microscope that renders minute objects distinctly visible. The kaleidoscope, in contrast, produces a succession of symmetrical designs using mirrors to reflect the constantly changing patterns made by bits of colored glass at the end of a tube. The kaleidoscope creates constantly changing images and yet is always symmetrical within its own context. The telescope condenses what is fixed and charts a perceived unchanging universe. The microscope enlarges and isolates in order to categorize. Postmodernism is like the kaleidoscope; this book has been an attempt to create kaleidoscopic sensibilities. The designs were constantly changing and becoming something new, and yet all of them remained interrelated. Unlike telescopic attempts to condense and microscopic attempts to enlarge, postmodernism celebrates the diverse and complex understandings within each unique context.

The complexity of the kaleidoscopic postmodern vision cannot be reduced to a single definition or a new master narrative. It must be experienced within its own context. The nature of postmodernism requires what we described in chapter eleven as chaos. John Briggs (1992) presents an appropriate metaphor for curriculum development: "Complex natural phenomena such as weather can't be stripped down, cleaned off, and studied under glass in a laboratory. An individual tree is the result of a vast, shifting set of unique circumstances, a kaleidoscope of influences such as gravity, magnetic fields, soil composition, wind, sun angles, insect hordes, human harvesting, other trees, [and] continuously active forces, far too numerous to determine in detail" (p. 14). And so it is with postmodern curriculum development, a kaleidoscopic phenomenon that is the result of a vast, interrelated web of ideas, texts, personalities, architectural structures, stories, and much more.

This chapter will begin to connect the web of ideas discussed in the preceding chapters with the milieu that teachers face in the traditional school setting, especially in light of the dominance of restructuring reform movements in recent years. We will explore the ways that schools can create kaleidoscopic sensibilities as they experience curriculum in the postmodern era. John Dewey's question as to whether schools are a function of society or society is a function of schools undergirds our discussion. This chapter will point the way for educators to be eclectic and kaleidoscopic without succumbing to the malaise and relativism that paralyzed school reform movements and curriculum development programs in the modern era.

As we have seen throughout this book, the transition from the structures of modernity to a postmodern global society is in process. Donald Oliver and Kathleen Gershman (1989) assert: "We are at the end of an age, so that its metaphors and symbols no longer explain where we have been nor inform us about what next to do" (p. 7). Economic, ecological, environmental, ethical, and educational equilibrium are all being called into question. As we have seen, chaos is evident (Gleick, 1987; Davies, 1988; Doll, 1993). This is distressing to many educators and confusing to others. Is the chaos to be celebrated as an indication of a postmodern self-reorganization of the open system cosmology of the new physics (Prigogine and Stengers, 1984)? William Doll (1993) writes: "A process whereby chaos and order are enfolded within each other, uniting to form a more complex, comprehensive, and sometimes 'strange' new order [is] the new vision . . . of a post-modern view" (p. 88). Kathleen Hayles (1990) writes about the concept of chaos bound inextricably to order, as in the yin and the yang in Eastern thought.

In contrast to this view, some ask if chaos is evidence of social decline and moral decay in contemporary men and women who refuse to accept the perennial truths of the closed system universe of modernity. Allan Bloom (1987) warns: "The crisis of liberal education is a reflection of a crisis at the peaks of learning, an incoherence and incompatibility among the first principles with which we interpret the world, which constitutes the crisis of our civilization" (p. 346). Turmoil is pervasive; however, its long-term impact is still unfolding. Will renewal emerge from our malaise and anguish or is hope finally and irrevocably irrelevant? However, if hope is not terminal, then perhaps the process of writing the modern postmortem on hope is itself the genesis of the resurrection of a new paradigm of curriculum development for the postmodern era. As we have seen throughout part two, philosophy, theology, social theory, gender studies, political theory, and literature offer many rich sources of reflection on this concept, thus providing hope for a curriculum that will be instructive for the postmodern global society.

The modern educational structures created in the spirit of Frederick Taylor's scientific management, Ralph Tyler's curriculum rationale, Abraham Maslow's hierarchy of needs, Benjamin Bloom's domains of learning, B. F. Skinner's behaviorism, Jerome Bruner's early work in cognitive structures, and the systems of other patriarchs of contemporary curriculum development still dominate our rhetoric and practice on all levels of schooling. In fact, all teachers have certainly been exposed to these theories throughout their formal teacher training. However, the demoralization of educators, disenfranchisement of students, and the dissatisfaction of stakeholders in educational systems are all indications that something is terribly wrong. These theories, despite their contributions to previous generations, have proved to be impotent in the face of growing turmoil in the modern world. Schools are too often characterized by departmental isolation, racial and gender divisiveness, political maneuvering, violent crime, professional jealousy, decaying and environmentally hazardous infrastructures, and economic stagnation. There are some efforts to develop cooperative research and interdisciplinary scholarship on some campuses, but unfortunately these minimal efforts are discouraged by the very structure of the education bureaucracy and the competitive nature of schooling in general. The threat of budgetary cutbacks, bureaucratic reorganization, explosive and confrontational structures, suffocating accountability programs, and performance evaluations loom ominously on the horizon for educators. Many tenured teachers and professors publicly criticize the bureaucracy while languishing in their own malaise. Curriculum committees spend their time reviewing course proposals, clarifying goals and objectives, and debating changes in the state curriculum guides or university catalogues oblivious to the contemporary curriculum discourses that have been introduced throughout this book. Creative energies are most often directed toward income-producing activities, competitive athletics, and social events, while important but fiscally unproductive and/or politically controversial projects languish for lack of interest or support. Discipline, violence, and drugs are most often cited as the critical issues facing teachers and students in the schools. How can curriculum renewal, particularly the call for transcending the structure of the disciplines and creating a curriculum for the postmodern era, proceed under these conditions?

The first important step is for educators to reflect on the global perspective that is influencing crises in education in the United States. Global transformations in the 1990s have brought the promise of freedom from totalitarian regimes to some societies (e.g., the Balkans and South Africa), repression of democratic movements in others (e.g., China's Tiananmen Square), renewal of ethnic brutality in many countries (e.g., Bosnia-Herzegovina and Rwanda), and massive starvation and impoverishment as the result of political instability in still others (e.g., Somalia). Some countries have simultaneously experienced both the exhilaration of liberation and the anguish of emergent racism (e.g., Germany) and economic decline (e.g., Russia). Traditional democracies have witnessed an explosion of violent crime and racial unrest (e.g., the United States and England). Recent kidnappings in Colombia and Nicaragua have put judges and politicians at risk and threatened the functioning of the judicial process. Global terrorism, environmental degradation, economic recession, religious intolerance, institutional racism and sexism, psychological paralysis, and chemical addiction have reached epidemic proportions. We can no longer pretend that these issues are outside the domain of curriculum development. They are at the heart of curriculum inquiry.

Schooling in the 1990s from primary classrooms to graduate schools has experienced parallel turmoil. Teachers are demoralized and administrators are immobilized, leading many to retreat to the comfort zone of self-righteous ideological certainty. Students and teachers at risk of physical harm divert their energy from learning to survival. In this environment, tangible evidence of structural and curricular transformation is rare, despite rhetoric about academic freedom, cultural literacy, political correctness, accountability, interdisciplinary studies, site-based management, national assessment, professional standards, mastery teaching and learning, back-to-the-basics, assertive discipline, cognitive learning, outcomes-based education, schools of excellence, and the like. It appears as though the educational reforms proposed are totally unrelated to the problems facing the global community. Has humanity anesthetized ethical visions and repressed social justice? Is this absurd phenomenon further evidence of the end of hope?

Recent scholarship indicates a movement toward global standardization in curriculum, suggesting that a single concept of contemporary society may be moving toward global dominance. This phenomenon of curricular similarity is not restricted to developed countries, where one might expect to find some degree of standardization. Curricular differences between developing and developed countries are not as great as one might expect (Raymond, 1991). This should not be surprising. Franchises, subdivisions, strip malls, international commerce, information cyberspace, satellite media, mass culture, tourism, and interstate freeways have depersonalized communities and made cities and schools indistinguishable from one another. In an ironic twist, the congestion at prominent natural and historical landmarks is so overwhelming and threatening to the preservation of the monuments themselves that governments have closed some original landmarks and created simulated versions nearby for tourist consumption. Thus, tourists in London from India may take their picture with wax figures of Gandhi, the royal family, or the Beatles at Madame Tussaud's Museum. Japanese tourists may experience a taste of the old

American Wild West at EuroDisney in France. The authentic is repressed while the imitation becomes the new reality, and modern men and women are oblivious to the difference. Postmodernism refers to this as hyperreality, contending that reality has collapsed exclusively into images, illusion, and simulations. The model is more real than the reality it supposed-ly represents. Jean Baudrillard (1983) writes: "Hyperreality is that which is already produced" (p. 146). Our dreams, Carl Jung reminds us, are closer representations of the self because they are unencumbered by the suppression and denial that dominate our waking hours in modern society. Modern life is really an imitation. Modern curriculum development is an illusion. We must attend to our dreams and awaken postmodern sensibilities.

Contemporary society, like education, has reached the apex of modernity, an absurd psychodrama of self-destruction. Startled and frightened by the modern experience, people retreat from global consensus to the protection of a "minimal self" (Lasch, 1984) impervious to the interconnectedness of human communities and the interdependence of all phenomena (Bergson, 1950). Modernity does not offer a vision of order in chaos, a whole to part relationship, or a global experience in the local context. It should not be surprising then that teachers and students in such a climate would also find security in a "minimal curriculum" that isolates disciplines and departments, separates knowledge from the learner, seeks meaning apart from context, judges learning on memorization, and immortalizes the competitive victor. The commitment of modernity to Cartesian dualism and bifurcated structures is pervasive. However, a postmodern vision will thrive only once there is a clear understanding of the negative impact of the modern milieu on the human spirit that has been rent asunder.

Reflecting the prevailing social trends, educators appear to be blinded to the epochal nature of global transformations as they employ modern strategies to alleviate the pain of the by-products of social upheaval. Modern technology does not address the educational problems we face, despite the fact that modern technology has provided us with some important achievements. The spiritual, aesthetic, historical, sociopolitical, ethical, racial, gendered, and cultural dimensions of the human community, as we discussed throughout part two of this book, must be incorporated into our understanding of curriculum. Understanding curriculum, from this point of view, must take precedence over traditional curriculum development and program planning. As we saw in chapters three and four, the process of running the race, *currere*, rather than the racecourse itself should be the focus of the curriculum.

A clear articulation of a postmodern process vision of curriculum development that includes the concept of *currere* is urgently needed, and this vision could be a prophetic statement for a world in turmoil and denial. The fragmentation of society and individual persons, as also reflected in the fragmentation of disciplines and departments in schools, is a central concern of the emerging postmodern era. The disciplinary structure of the curriculum is comfortable to students, faculty, and administrators not only because it is familiar but also because many have not experienced, or even considered, a postmodern alternative. Interdisciplinary, aesthetic, and multidimensional alternatives must be incorporated into schooling. This book has been an attempt to expose more educators to the postmodern possibilities being proposed in the 1990s. Postmodern voices are abundant in the arts, sciences, and humanities.

As an example of the enormity of the problem we face, I will relate the story of a recent student in a philosophy of education class. I will call him Jim. During the first class session we moved our desks from rows to a circle. I spent some time discussing linear and circular thinking (M. A. Doll, 1993), technical knowing and grounded, ontological knowing (Oliver and Gershman, 1989), hermeneutics and nonlinear teaching (W. Doll, 1993), analysis versus intuition (Bergson, 1950), experience and education (Dewey, 1938), seminar methodologies, process philosophy (Griffin et al., 1993), and the medicine wheel in native American cultures (Regnier, 1992) in order to establish a theoretical basis for the circular classroom milieu. (From experience, most students in my classes are initially uncomfortable with seminar circles because they have seldom, if ever, experienced them before.) I told the students that I would expect them to contribute in some way to the seminar discussion each week, but that they would be free to choose the method and timing of their participation. About half the students responded immediately. The circle was liberating for them. Others remained silent and skeptical for a few class sessions but gradually began to express their philosophical views and questions once a bond of trust had been established. However, by the fifth session Jim had yet to say a word despite the fact that this was his final course before receiving his specialist degree. At the sixth class session an "ah-ha" moment occurred. A verbose and articulate student interrupted the class and said, "I am very concerned about something, and I wish we could discuss it as a class." I agreed (reserving my enthusiasm for the moment). She continued, "At the first class session you asked us all to participate. I feel as though I am monopolizing the conversation because I notice that a few students never get to speak. I would like the class to let me know if I am talking too much." Then she turned to Jim and asked, "Jim, you have not said anything. Am I monopolizing your time?"

Jim responded, "No. I enjoy your comments. I am thirty years old. I have been in school my entire life—elementary, high school, BA, MEd, and now a specialist degree. No one has ever asked me to discuss my philosophy before, and I have never taken a class in a seminar circle. Please keep talking because I am afraid, and I do not know what to say."

Jim's autobiographical reflections, received without criticism, opened the door to further conversations about educational methodologies, linear and process thinking, postmodern philosophies, and *currere*. A discernible transformation began. Of course a potential danger that my students point out to me is that they can no longer sit in lecture halls and absorb "inert ideas" (Whitehead, 1929) without frustration. They claim that I have "ruined them" for the traditional Tylerian curriculum development model of the disciplines in the university.

As an interesting aside to this story, early in my first semester in the university a note was written on the board by another professor. It stated, "Whoever moves the desks in a circle each week, please put them back the way they belong." There is a definite and pervasive perception among elementary, secondary, undergraduate, and graduate education faculty members, at least in my experience, that the traditional modern classroom structure is sacred—that somehow it "belongs" a certain way. I sometimes worry that one week I will enter my classroom and the desks will once again be bolted to the floor! Just as postmodernism has its roots in architecture (Jencks, 1986, 1988), so too might our postmodern educational proposals for schooling have to begin with architecture. The longer we continue to build schools like prisons, offices, factories, and shopping malls without psychological, ecological, and sociological sensitivity, the longer we will perpetuate a bankrupt modern curriculum ideology.

A credible curriculum for the postmodern world must keep an eye toward the trends and issues discussed above. We must rigorously investigate global understandings of curricular programs, policies, practices, and philosophies, but not for the purpose of reforming and refining them. The postmodern vision must transcend and transform the traditional bureaucratic approach to curriculum development. However, the primary focus must remain keenly centered on the particular context of local educational communities, and specific cultural concerns, as well as individual autobiographies as noted throughout this book. Both the global and the local are important, and they must not be bifurcated. An integrated understanding of the individual and society is of critical importance. George S. Counts in *The Social Foundations of Education* made the following important observation, "The historical record shows that education is always a function of time, place, and circumstance. In its basic philosophy, its social objective, and its program of instruction, it inevitably reflects in varying proportion the experiences, the conditions, and the hopes, fears, and aspirations of a particular people or cultural group at a particular point in history" (cited in Gutek, 1993, p. 88).

The long-standing and almost perennial philosophical debate between those who argue, like Mortimer Adler and Robert Hutchins, that education is a universal process that reflects a monolithic conception of human nature, and those, like Counts, who insist that education must be culturally relevant to particular situations and societies can be instructive to our discussion of the transformation of curriculum development in the postmodern era. We must be careful not to become polarized at either end of this debate. The more appropriate position recognizes the interdependence of the global condition and the local context. Perhaps Alfred North Whitehead (1929, 1933) in *Aims of Education* and *Adventures of Ideas* best explained this concept of interdependence. As education moves from the individual story in his initial stage of romance, through the process of finding commonalities and differences in his second stage of precision, to his final stage of generalization, Whitehead (1933) understands that the commonalities and connections signify that a "harmony of the whole is bound up with the preservation of the individual significance of detail" (p. 264). Thus individual pluralism in specific contexts gives strength to the whole edifice of education. I would call this kaleidoscopic community sensibility; Charles Jencks calls it radical eclecticism. Jencks (1992) succinctly explains why postmodernism must be radically eclectic:

> We must be aware . . . that a complete sublation, or Hegelian dialectic which resolves contraries, is not always the result or goal of post-modernism: parts, sub-assemblies, sub-cultures often keep their unassimilated identity within the new whole. Hence, the conflicted nature of the pluralism, the radical eclecticism of the post-modern style. (pp. 14–15)

In the spirit of Whitehead's analysis and Jencks' radical eclecticism, some initial guiding principals for an integrated global and local vision for curriculum development in the postmodern era will be discussed below.

First, a process approach to education is capable of engendering a significant reconceptualization of the nature of schooling globally as well as the experience of education locally because it respects the unique development of the individual and recognizes the interrelationship of all experiences. The emergent nature of this reconceptualization rejects hierarchical, authoritarian, patriarchal, and hegemonic ideologies, as well as models of curriculum committed exclusively to educational outcomes outside process and context. We must begin with the autobiographical (Pinar, 1876) and the "intuition of duration" (Bergson, 1950, p. 27) and then support and encourage individuals to make connections to broader concepts. Dewey (1938) and Whitehead (1929) demonstrated that this process can be rigorous and scientific without sacrificing the experience of the individual. For example, one of my graduate students teaches an oral history project at a local high school. Students volunteer for this experiential social studies class. Two meetings per week are held at a local antebellum plantation museum, two meetings on the high school campus, and one day is used for community research. The goal of the class is to allow students to construct an oral history in the community that can be used at the museum. A particular concern of the project organizers is that the names of the plantation owners are noted throughout the museum, but the enslaved Africans are only mentioned on one plaque as having resided in the "slave quarters." The names of the enslaved people are known in the community, and the students are trying to reconstruct and reinterpret the history of the plantation through interviews and artifacts. This is an example of a postmodern curriculum that incorporates the historical, aesthetic, racial, autobiographical, and philosophical issues presented throughout part two. It is uniquely local in character but global in its impact.

Second, the modern behavioristic emphasis in schooling, as exemplified in the unrelenting commitment to behavioral objectives, learning hierarchies, "value-neutral" empirical-analytical methodologies, goals and objectives, rote memorization, and competitive learning environments is not only outmoded but also detrimental to the emergence of an appropriate global postmodern educational experience. Whitehead (1929) protested against this modern perpetuation of "inert ideas." He wrote in *Aims of Education*, "Students are alive, and the purpose of education is to stimulate and guide their self-development. . . . Teachers should also be alive with living thoughts. The whole book is a protest against dead knowledge, that is, against inert ideas" (p. v). In order for classrooms to reflect Whitehead's vision, teachers must be lifelong learners and students must be leaders of instruction. A hermeneutic circle must be formed in classrooms where the discourse is shared, empowering, emerging, and tentative. This is a dramatic break with modern bureaucratic curriculum paradigms. Is there a method for implementing a new postmodern paradigm? Yes, one teacher, one student, and one classroom at a time. Postmodernism cannot be imposed uniformly, but it can provide the philosophical support for a change in consciousness that will necessarily lead to new practices. This is called evoking, a postmodern alternative to re-presenting or representation. Evoking is assumed to free one's analysis of objects, facts, descriptions, generalizations, experiments, and truth claims from absolute master narratives. Educators must evoke rather than impose representations.

Third, a constructive postmodernism as understood by David Ray Griffin (1988a), William Doll (1993), and Donald Oliver and Kathleen Gershman (1989), among others, as distinct from deconstructive or critical postmodernisms, offers an important emerging approach to understanding curriculum. Poststructural and deconstructive philosophies are also making an important contribution to our understanding of language, especially as language reflects and influences worldviews. Educators in the postmodern era are not reticent to engage both poststructuralists and constructivists, males and females, and a diversity of all people of all colors, races, and spiritualities in dialogue and to incorporate language analysis and process philosophy into our curriculum proposals. For example, Patti Lather (1994) distinguishes between "close reading which constructs a realist tale; a structural reading which constructs a critical tale; a situated reading which constructs a reflective tale; and a poststructural reading which constructs a deconstructive tale" in order to help educators move beyond empirical-analytical reading methodologies to a more empowering poststructuralism. Madeleine Grumet (1988) offers a phenomenological approach to reading and language that "celebrates the presence of an absence" in the educational experience. Grumet (1988) writes: "Meaning is something we make out of what we find when we look at texts. It is not the text" (p. 142). Lather and Grumet demonstrate that postmodernism is eclectic and kaleidoscopic, and that it should move beyond the oppressive structures of modernity. The postmodern curriculum challenges us to get on with the business of providing concrete options and inspiring hope in the midst of global social and educational crises.

Fourth, the curriculum itself must be viewed primarily as *currere* (Pinar and Grumet, 1976) and support the context necessary to move from romance through precision to generalization (Whitehead, 1929). Our educational proposals must also attend to the problem of alienation, destruction, decadence, and evil (Griffin, 1976; Noddings, 1989; Jencks, 1992) so as to avoid the pitfalls of facile utopianisms prevalent in some critical political analyses, while at the same time being careful not to succumb to a nihilistic existentialism devoid of spirituality and aesthetic values as found in some philosophies (Stanley, 1992). Administrators and teachers must be attentive to language, especially as it is politically, socially, and historically embedded. Our language must be inclusive on all levels of communication.

Fifth, and finally, as we have seen in part two, there is important curriculum scholarship that incorporates hermeneutics (Haggerson & Bowman, 1992), phenomenology (Greene, 1978; Grumet, 1988b; van Manen, 1990, 1993), social psychoanalysis (Kincheloe & Pinar, 1991), liberation theology (Kincheloe et al., 1992), process theology (Griffin, 1988b; Griffin, Beradslee, & Holland, 1989), spiritualities (Hammerschlag, 1988, 1993; Griffin, 1988b; Purpel, 1989), race (McCarthy, 1990; Castenell & Pinar, 1993), feminism (Noddings, 1989, 1992; Miller, 1990; Pagano, 1990), and specific cultural issues that will support efforts to understand curriculum for global transformation and expose postmodern proposals to a wider audience. The transformation of curriculum will be most fruitful if cooperative research includes a variety of these contemporary voices.

In presenting these five short summary comments, I am reminded that curriculum scholars must avoid the temptation to construct a traditional metaphysics and epistemology to justify a postmodern view of curriculum development. Bergson (1950) writes that "metaphysics is the science which claims to dispense with symbols" (p. 24). Oliver and Gershman (1989) expand on this thought:

> It is obvious to us that we have come to confuse those issues which require the deepest kind of ontological knowing with issues that might be clarified and resolved

> through technical knowing. This confusion permeates
> education. We come to see problems of curriculum
> selection (what is worthwhile knowing and how to learn
> it) as translatable into a technical field of study through
> which one can identify the appropriateness of bits of
> explicit information, or the value of a certain skill. This
> confusion in the selection of modalities of knowing we
> would call the technical fallacy. (p. 15)

While the nature of the human person, knowledge
construction, spirituality, and ethics should be included in our
postmodern proposals, this must be accomplished by utilizing a
process approach within the context of democratic community
experience. In other words, we must arrive at a vision of
curriculum for the postmodern era using the very process
proposed for global curriculum educational transformation,
described throughout part two, and not resort to the technical
fallacy as described by Oliver and Gershman. If postmodern
curriculum truly offers an alternative for schooling in the 1990s,
it must emerge in a context employing the very principles
proposed. If not, then postmodernism degenerates into another
ultramodern project. Oliver and Gershman's ontological
knowing, which is expressed through mystical experience,
reflection, metaphor, poetry, drama, liturgy, dreams, and music
rather than the analytic and linear language of technical
knowing, is perhaps the preferable model to ensure faithfulness
to the postmodern context.

These general concepts offer a glimpse into the thinking
that underlines the perspective of postmodern curriculum
scholars in the 1990s. These are not absolute principles, nor do
they attempt to form a coherent philosophical paradigm. They
are simply pivotal ideas in the schema of an approach to
curriculum that could contribute to the transformation of
education in the postmodern era.

The postmodern curriculum reminds us that debates about
the canon, goals, and objectives of the curriculum, while
considered by some as important to the process of clarifying the
content and structure of the educative events planned by school
districts and universities, are of limited value in our efforts to
improve education and society. In fact, the competitive nature of
these debates engenders futility because it often results in

polarization and protracted confrontation. If curricular concerns are limited to dialogue about the canon, content of course descriptions, methods of quantitative evaluation, and sequence of course offerings, we have effectively eliminated the discussion of postmodern approaches to understanding curriculum that move beyond disciplinary structures as proposed throughout this book.

Curriculum debates must be redirected to the understanding of curriculum, the construction of the individual in relation to educative moments, the development of autobiographical, aesthetic, intuitive, and proleptic experience, and the socio-cultural and sociopolitical relations emerging from an understanding of the individual in relation to knowledge, other learners, the world, and ultimately the self. In short, we must move from the modern paradigm of curriculum development in the disciplines to the postmodern paradigm of understanding curriculum in various contexts. In this sense, curriculum development becomes kaleidoscopic. It is always shifting perspectives and constantly reflecting new and liberating visions of learning and living. This is the postmodern hermeneutic process of uncovering layers of meaning, deconstructing master narratives, affirming women's ways of knowing, creating ecological sustainability, uncovering the wide-awakenness of the aesthetic vision, engendering poststructural sensitivities, and ultimately experiencing hope in the educational journey. The postmodern curriculum, in all its kaleidoscopic perspectives, offers an opportunity for education to move beyond moribund modes of analysis to a new understanding of curriculum development in the postmodern era.

CHAPTER THIRTEEN

A Postmodern Postscript
Proleptic Prolegomena

We are a people in whom the past endures, in whom the present is inconceivable without moments gone by. The Exodus lasted a moment, a moment enduring forever. What happened once upon a time happens all the time.

Abraham Joshua Heshel

There is no such thing really as was, because the past is.

William Faulkner

The present holds within itself the complete sum of existence, backwards and forwards, that whole amplitude of time which is eternity.

Alfred North Whitehead

The true present is nothing else but the eternity that is immanent in time. The believer is the one who is entirely present.

Jurgen Moltmann

Time, space, and causation are like the glass through which the absolute is seen. . . . In the absolute there is neither time, space, nor causation.

Swami Vivekananda

To impose upon becoming the character of being—that is the supreme will to power. . . . That everything recurs is the closest approximation of a world of becoming to a world of being.

Friedrich Nietzsche

The ideal of using the present simply to get ready for the future contradicts itself. Hence the central problem of an education based on experience is to select the kind of present experiences that live fruitfully and creatively in subsequent experiences.

John Dewey

There must be another life, here and now, she repeated. This is too short, too broken. We know nothing, even about ourselves. We're only just beginning, she thought, to understand, here and there. She held her hand hallowed; she felt that she wanted to enclose the present and future, until it shone, whole, bright, and deep with understanding.

Virginia Woolf, The Years

The postmodern reply to the modern consists of recognizing that the past, since it cannot really be destroyed, because its destruction leads to silence, must be revisited: but with irony not innocently. . . . Irony, metalinguistic play, enunciation squared. Thus, with the modern, anyone who does not understand the game can only reject it, but with the postmodern, it is possible not to understand the game and yet to take it seriously. Which is, after all, the quality (the risk) of irony. There is always someone who takes ironic discourse seriously. . . . I believe that postmodernism is not a trend to be chronologically defined, but rather an ideal category or, better still, a *kunstwollen*, a way of operating.

Umberto Eco from The Postscript to The Name of the Rose

The preceding thoughts from literary, philosophical, theological, and postmodern figures create an image of time and space that is very different from the irreversible linear arrow and progressive sequence of modernity. Time is not an irreversible line on a trajectory where new and modern understandings are better than the outdated past. Postmodernism reconceptualizes time as duration, post-structuralism as eternal recurrence. On the one hand, time is a duration where the past is embedded in the present, as Henri Bergson contends. On the other hand, for Nietzsche, nothing abides, but all returns to be destroyed again and again. The *process* of becoming endures, but nothing in that process endures, except as repeated enduring states. Modern notions of being, Nietzsche contends, have arisen from discontent with becoming. Eternal recurrence is more than "mere" becoming, it reveals the eternal value of every moment. In both duration and eternal return, Bergson and Nietzsche reject modern notions of linear time in favor of the process of becoming that is so integral to postmodernism.

The crisis of modernity arises precisely because history and time are conceived of as linear and thus capable of being broken. If the present can be broken, it can also be conceived of as degraded and meaningless. Then the modern pathos is projected backward and forward, projecting this vision on every present—past, present, and future. Postmodernism reconnects space-time with individuals and society in order to transcend this modern embedded pathos. James Macdonald (1988) writes: "The impetus for choosing and becoming in us is not something that need be externally imposed; but it is rather a process of helping others see possibilities and helping them free themselves from going beyond this present state of embedded existence" (p. 163). Postmodern schooling must reconnect students and teachers, space and time, meaning and context, the knower and the known, humanities and sciences, and especially past, present, and future. What modernity has rent asunder, postmodernity reevaluates as radically eclectic by embracing the fragmented beauty. Postmodernism celebrates the process of becoming and the interdependence of eternal becoming. The following story explains my journey toward understanding this postmodern concept of becoming that is integral to the reconceptualization of curriculum and instruction in the 1990s, which is impossible to envision through the lenses of modernity.

A remarkable thing happened to me in early October 1955; apparently I died. However, I did not become aware of this event until a balmy spring afternoon in New Orleans in 1989 while returning home from a party hosted by several professors and graduate students. By coincidence I made several unconscious wrong turns and ended up on the old Airline Highway rather than Interstate 10. I had not been on the Airline since my childhood, long before the interstate was built. As I approached a cemetery, a rush of memories flooded my being. I remembered sitting in the back of my father's Chevy Impala as a child. He turned to my mother and whispered, "That is where I buried the baby."

As with many families in the 1950s, we never talked about tragedy and painful memories. Many years later I overheard some older cousins talking about a baby brother named Timothy James who had died in distress shortly after birth and was taken by my father to be buried. My father himself died years later, but his faint whisper to my mother from thirty years previous came back to me on this tropical Louisiana afternoon in 1989. I was mystically drawn to the cemetery for the first time in my life. I felt awkward as an adult inquiring at the desk about my brother's grave from 1950s, especially since I was not certain that it was actually located in this cemetery. After many interruptions by grieving families making funeral arrangements and secretaries who could not locate Timothy James Slattery in the computerized records, I almost gave up my search. I was anxious to return home, but the transcendent lure of the cemetery was urging me on. I asked if there were, perhaps, any Slattery graves from the early 1950s in this cemetery, assuming that I may have remembered my father's whisper inaccurately. After an interminable wait, the secretary returned with news of a Slattery baby plot, but none with the name Timothy James. I rushed from the office and made my way to what would be one of the most jolting encounters of my life.

I arrived at the children's burial section, guarded by an angelic statue, to discover the plot: the inscription on the tombstone read *George Patrick Slattery, Jr.* In that moment all of time and history merged; life and death disappeared. I laughed, I cried, I prayed, and I thought about my brother, Timothy, my deceased father, George Patrick Slattery, Sr., and myself, George Patrick Slattery, Jr. We were all somehow mysteriously united in that tomb. Eventually, I grabbed some paper from my car and began to write a poem that began, "What child is buried in my brother's tomb? Who came forth from my mother's womb? Am I the child marked for life? Or the one who entered the grave in strife?"

When I related this event the next day to another brother, Kevin, he was shocked to learn of this circumstance. He advised that I was probably Timothy and that my name had been changed to George Patrick Slattery, Jr., after our brother, the original George Patrick, Jr., had tragically died at birth. We were all infants at the time, and a change of names could have been easily accomplished without suspicion. Kevin insisted that our father, in the patriarchal southern tradition, always wanted a son to "carry" on his name, and thus the burial of the child had to be kept a secret since another son was to take his place. I had been marked for life and death, both on the tombstone and by name.

Further inquiries over the next few months began to unravel the mystery. However, as I often pondered my identity and the secret of the tombstone, I would listen to the Moody Blues sing, "Timothy Leary's dead, boy. No, no, no, no, he's outside, looking in!" If I were really Timothy, then yes, I was on the outside of the tomb looking in. The Cartesian distinction between life and death became blurred; metaphysics and identity took on a very different meaning as a result of this chance encounter.

This story affirms several commitments that I have as a postmodern educator and curriculum theorist. I have attempted to convey throughout this book my insights and intuitions about curriculum gleaned from years of experience, mystery, suffering, passion, and joy. First of all, I understand and affirm the postmodern rejection of metanarratives, for I am constantly amazed that the absolute certainty of the "truths" that have been concretized into facts in schooling have all deconstructed over time—even the certainty of my name and identity became elusive in 1989. Second, the artificial bifurcations of black and white, body and soul, sciences and humanities, male and female, gay and straight, teacher and student, winner and loser, honors and remedial, dream and reality, and even life and death, all prevent the emerging postmodern vision of the aesthetic synthesis, the hermeneutic community circle, ecological sustainability, kaleidoscopic sensibilities, and social justice from emerging. Dualistic thinking must be vigorously challenged in the postmodern curriculum and apparent opposites must be reintegrated into a creative tension of complementary and multifaceted dimensions of the whole as in the yin and yang of Eastern thought. Third, the interconnectedness of individual experiences in a global context that engender cosmic understandings is dramatically changing human consciousness. Poetry is the natural response to the mystery of the universe, not measurement and codification. For in poetry, narrative, and art we can understand the self as continuously being reconstructed in new and ironic ways in every social and cultural milieu. Fourth, in order to understand knowledge, I must experience intimacy. The knower cannot be separated from the known and meaning cannot be separated from the context that gives rise to the meaningful experience. Educators must reenvision their relationships with students and with each other and begin to find ways to affirm and validate every voice in the school community. The dominant power position of teachers and administrators must be replaced by empowerment models. These models are not simply site-based management, authentic assesssment, or cooperative learning groups. Rather, the very concept of the self in relation must evolve to a new realm of consciousness. This can be accomplished on all levels of schooling as teachers and students create empathetic, caring, holistic, and liberating practices. Fifth, and finally, the encounter at the tomb reinforces my understanding of the complexity of metaphysics; chaos and uncertainty principles are at work under the surface of our existence, physically, psychologically, and spiritually. In this sense a "quantum curriculum" (Bernard and Slattery, 1992) is needed to uncover the layers of meaning of the phenomena that could enrich our lives and our schooling practices. These practices must include attention to aesthetics, hermeneutics, phenomenology, poststructural analysis, multiculturalism, autobiography, theology, historicity, a postliberal and postrevolutionary political theory rooted in community and ecology, chaos theory and the new sciences, and liberatory perspectives of society.

The postmodern curriculum must ultimately understand time as proleptic. The past and the future are comprehensible only in the context of the present. The artificial bifurcation of time and the linear "arrow of time" must be challenged. Educators must infuse the curriculum not only with a proleptic philosophy, but most important a proleptic experience. Since the Christian cultural heritage is familiar to many, I will use a theological example to demonstrate such understanding. Proleptic eschatology has philosophical roots in the twentieth century writings of Ernst Bloch (1968, 1970, 1986), Henry Nelson Wieman (1969a, 1969b), Jurgen Moltmann (1967), and Carl Peter (1974). Moltmann and Peter explain that Jesus Christ, as the fullness of the Diety, entered historical time as both divine and human. Therefore, the Christ had an "end in view" experience of the resurrection prior to the actual event. Jesus Christ, for Christians of faith, had already experienced the resurrection in the timelessness of the eternal Godhead prior to his death on the cross.

This is not a strange new theology. The early Christian communities denounced many heresies in the centuries following the death of the historical Jesus, including Arianism, which was condemned by the Council of Nicaea. Originating with the Alexandrian presbyter Arius (d. 336 C.E.), Arianism taught that Jesus Christ could not be considered the "Son of God" except in some subordinate or inferior sense. The "Son" was not considered the same as "The Father," and thus there was a time when the "Son" did not exist. The Council of Nicaea contested this theology vociferously, arguing that Jesus the Christ was the same substance (*homoousios*) as God "the Father." Various forms of Arian theology were popular in the fourth century, C.E. Therefore, the Nicene Creed, still recited in many Christian churches today, repeated the *homoousios* several times to reiterate that Jesus Christ was "True God from true God." The creed also insists that the Christ was "Begotten, *not* made. *One in being* with the father. Through the Christ all things were made. For salvation Jesus came down from heaven."

The insistence here is that Jesus Christ is identical in being with the eternal Godhead. This theology is called proleptic because the future is not distant and separated from the present, rather it is embedded in the present. In a similar fashion in literary theory, prolepsis refers to events preceding the beginning of a novel or short story. Flashbacks, foreshadowing, and *déjà vu* are literary devices used to create a prolepsis. Bloch calls this the experience of the "already but not yet," Wieman calls it the "growth of creative interchange," Moltmann calls it the "eschaton, the horizon with God ahead," and Peter calls it "the lure of the transcendent benevolent future." In curriculum theory prolepsis is indicated by Gadamer's "fusion of horizons," Dewey's "social consequences of value," Greene's "landscapes of learning," Freire's "praxis," Pinar's "currere," Padgham's "becoming," Macdonald's "hermeneutic circle," W. Doll's "transformative recursion," Griffin's "sacred interconnections," Bergson's "duration," Nietzsche's "eternal return," and M. A. Doll's "dancing circle." These eschatological sensitivities suggest movement toward a postmodern proleptic curriculum theory. The proleptic experience seeks to infuse hope into the postmodern vision of schooling by giving meaning and purpose to the present occasions in education.

Why is proleptic hope so important? Students and teachers are limited by the concepts of hope perpetuated by modernity. The bifurcated choice of modernity is clear; either choose the apocalyptic vision of many fundamentalist religions and delay all hope to a distant life after death, or collapse all hope into the immediate gratification of the senses. The first is called futuristic or apocalyptic eschatology because the present is disconnected from the ultimate experience of salvation or utopia. The second is called realized eschatology because the past and future do not affect the present sense experiences, which contain the only metaphysical reality. Apocalyptic and futuristic eschatology have both deformed consciousness in the modern era and caused the repression and suppression of the complexity of the human dynamic. Realized eschatology reinforces the addictions and malaise of modern society.

Humanity desperately needs a postmodern alternative to these two dominant eschatologies that have blurred, and ultimately destroyed, the vision of the eternal recurrence and the interconnectedness of past, present, and future. A proleptic curriculum offers a postmodern vision of justice, complexity, compassion, ecological sustainability, spirituality, and internal relatedness. A proleptic understanding of the integration of time, place, and self is one of the most essential elements of curriculum development for the postmodern era (Slattery, 1989).

What is this proleptic vision for postmodern curriculum development? While definitions and master narratives of this emerging paradigm are to be resisted, this book has presented a vision of the postmodern curriculum that is radically eclectic, determined in the context of relatedness, recursive in its complexity, autobiographically intuitive, aesthetically inter-subjective, phenomenological, experiential, simultaneously quantum and cosmic, hopeful in its constructive dimension, radical in its deconstructive movement, liberating in its poststructural intents, empowering in its spirituality, ironic in its kaleidoscopic sensibilities, and ultimately, a hermeneutic search for greater understanding that motivates and satisfies us on the journey. With T. S. Eliot, "We shall not cease from exploring, and the end of all our exploring will be to arrive where we started, and know the place for the first time."

References

Adler, Mortimer J. (1982). *The paideia proposal: An educational manifesto.* New York: Macmillan.

America 2000: An educational strategy. (1991). Washington, DC: U.S. Government Printing Office.

Aoki, Ted Tetsuo. (1985). *Toward curriculum inquiry in a new key.* (Department of Secondary Education Occasional Papers Series, #2, rev. ed.). Edmonton: University of Alberta.

———. (1988). Toward a dialectic between the conceptual world and the lived world: Transcending instrumentalism in curriculum orientation. In W. F. Pinar (Ed.), *Contemporary curriculum discourses* (pp. 402–416). Scottsdale, AZ: Gorsuch, Scarisbrick.

———. (1992). Layered voices of teaching: The uncannily correct and the elusively true. In William F. Pinar & William M. Reynolds (Eds.), *Understanding curriculum as phenomenological and deconstructed text* (pp. 17–27). New York: Longman.

Aoki, Ted Tetsuo, Franks, D., & Jacknicke, K. (Eds.). (1987). *Understanding curriculum as lived: Curriculum Canada VII.* Vancouver: University of British Columbia.

Apple, Michael W. (1979). *Ideology and curriculum.* London: Routledge and Kegan Paul.

———. (1982). *Education and power.* Boston: Routledge and Kegan Paul.

———. (1985). *Teachers and texts: A political economy of class and gender relations in education.* New York: Routledge and Kegan Paul.

———. (1993). *Official knowledge.* New York: Routledge and Kegan Paul.

Apple, Michael W., & Christian-Smith, Linda (Eds.). (1991). *The politics of the textbook* (pp. 1–21). New York: Routledge and Kegan Paul.

Arendt, H. (1958). *The human condition.* Chicago: University of Chicago Press.

Armstrong, V. I. (Ed.). (1971). *I have spoken.* Chicago: Swallow Press.

Aronowitz, Stanley. (1992). *The politics of identity: Class, culture, social movements.* New York: Routledge, Chapman, and Hall.

Arons, Stephen. (1983). *Compelling belief: The culture of American schooling.* New York: McGraw Hill.

Bahmueller, C. F. (Ed.). (1991). *Civitas.* Calabasas, CA: Center for Civic Education.

Baldwin, James. (1971). Author's notes, Blues for Mister Charlie. In J. Glassner & C. Barnes (Eds.), *Best American plays.* New York: Crown.

———. (1988). A talk to teachers. In R. Simonson & S. Walker (Eds.), *Multicultural literature: Opening the American mind.* St. Paul, MN: Graywolf.

Barone, Thomas. (1993). Breaking the mold: The new American student as strong poet. *Theory into Practice, 32* (3), pp. 5–18.

Baudrillard, Jean. (1983). *Simulations.* New York: Semiotext (e).

Belenky, Mary Field, Clinchy, Blythe McVicker, Goldberger, Nancy Rule, & Tarule, Jill Mattuck. (1986). *Women's ways of knowing: The development of self, voice, and mind.* New York: Basic Books.

Bennett, William J. (1987). *James Madison high school: A curriculum for American students.* Washington, DC: U.S. Department of Education.

———. (1988). *James Madison elementary: A curriculum for American students.* Washington, DC: U.S. Department of Education.

Bereiter, Carl, & Scardamalia, Marlene. (1992). Cognition and curriculum. In Philip W. Jackson (Ed.), *Handbook of research on curriculum* (pp. 517–542). New York: Macmillan.

Bergson, Henri. (1946). *The creative mind: An introduction to metaphysics.* (M. L. Andison, Trans.). New York: Philosophical Library.

———. (1950). *Time and free will.* F. L. Pogson (trans.). London: Allen and Unwin.

Bernard, Hilly. (1994). Hermeneutics and education: Discourse/practice. Unpublished dissertation perspectus. New Orleans: University of New Orleans.

Bernard, Hilly, & Slattery, Patrick. (1992). Quantum curriculum. Dayton OH: *JCT* Bergamo Conference. Unpublished paper.

Beutow, H. A. (1988). *The Catholic school: Its roots, identity, and future.* New York: Crossroad.

Beyer, Landon E. (1988). Art and society: Toward new directions in aesthetic education. In W. F. Pinar (Ed.), *Contemporary Curriculum Discourses* (pp. 380–397). Scottsdale, AZ: Gorsuch, Scarisbrick.

Bird, Lois Bridges. (1993). The whole of whole language. In Ron Miller (Ed.), *The renewal of meaning in education* (pp. 129–147).

Blacker, David. (1993, March). Education as the normative dimension of philosophical hermeneutics. Paper presented at the annual meeting of the Philosophy of Education Society in New Orleans, LA.

Blanchard, Kenneth, & Johnson, Spencer. (1981). *The one minute manager.* New York: Berkeley Books.

Bloch, Ernst. (1968). Man as possibility. In R. Capps (Ed.), *The future of hope* (pp. 3–27). New York: Herder and Herder.

———. (1970). *A philosophy of the future.* New York: Herder and Herder.

———. (1986). *The principle of hope.* Oxford: Blackwell.

Bloom, Allan. (1987). *The closing of the American mind.* New York: Simon and Schuster.

Boateng, F. (1990). Combatting deculturalization of the African-American child in the public school system: A multicultural approach. In K. Lomotey (Ed.), *Going to school: The African-American experience* (pp. 73–84). Albany: State University of New York Press.

Bobbitt, Franklin. (1918). *The curriculum.* Boston: Houghton Mifflin.

Bohm, David. (1988). Postmodern science and a postmodern world. In David Ray Griffin (Ed.), *The reenchantment of science* (pp. 57–68). Albany: State University of New York Press.

Bonhoeffer, Deitrich. (1966). *The cost of discipleship.* New York: Macmillan.

———. (1971). *Letters and papers from prison.* New York: Macmillan.

Book of Mormon. (1961). Joseph Smith (Trans.). Salt Lake City, UT: The Church of Jesus Christ of Latter Day Saints.

Books, Sue. (1992). Literary journalism as educational criticism: A discourse of triage. *Holistic Education Review, 5* (3), 41–51.

Bowers, Chet A. (1987). *Elements of a post-liberal theory of education.* New York: Teachers College Press.

———. (1993). *Education, cultural myths, and the ecological crisis.* Albany: State University of New York Press.

Bowers, Chet A., & Flinders, David J. (1990). *Responsive teaching: An ecological approach to classroom patterns of language, culture, and thought.* New York: Teachers College Press.

Bowles, S., & Gintis, H. (1976). *Schooling in capitalist America.* New York: Basic Books.

Brameld, Theodore. (1956). *Toward a reconstructed philosophy of education.* New York: Holt, Rinehart, & Winston.

———. (1971). *Patterns of educational philosophy—Divergence and convergence in culturological perspective.* New York: Holt, Rinehart, & Winston.

Bridges, Thomas. (1991). Multiculturalism as a postmodernist project. *Inquiry: Critical thinking across the disciplines, 7* (4), pp. 3–7.

Briggs, John. (1992). *Fractals, the pattern of chaos: Discovering a new aesthetic of art, science, nature.* New York: Simon and Schuster.

Britzman, Deborah P. (1992). The terrible problem of knowing thyself: Toward a poststructural account of teacher identity. *CT: An Interdisciplinary Journal of Curriculum Studies, 9* (3) pp. 23–50.

Brownson, Orestes. (1839). *The Boston Quarterly Review.* In Michael B. Katz (Ed.), *School reform: Past and present.* Boston: Little Brown, 1971.

Burbules, Nicholas C. (1993a). *Dialogue in teaching: Theory and practice.* New York: Teachers College Press.

———. (1993b). Process philosophy and critical pragmatism. Paper presented at the APPE summer institute. University of the South.

Caine, Renate Nummela, & Caine, Geoffrey. (1991). *Making connections: Teaching and the human brain.* Alexandria, VA: ASCD Press.

Campbell, Joseph, & Moyers, Bill. (1988). *The power of myth.* New York: Doubleday.

Capra, Fritjof. (1975). *The Tao of physics.* Berkeley: Shambhala.

———. (1982). *The turning point: Science, society, and the rising culture.* New York: Bantam.

Carlson, Dennis. (1992). *Teachers and Crisis : Urban School Reform and Tteachers' Work Culture.* New York: Routledge.

Carmody, Denise L. (1991). *The good alliance: Feminism, religion, and education.* New York: University Press of America.

Carson, Terrance R. (1987). Understanding curriculum and implementation. In T. Aoki, D. Franks, & K. Jacknicke (Eds.), *Understanding curriculum as lived: Curriculum Canada VII.* Vancouver: University of British Columbia.

———. (1992). Remembering forward: Reflections on educating for peace. In William F. Pinar and William M. Reynolds (Eds.), *Understanding curriculum as phenomenological and deconstructed text* (pp. 102–115). New York: Longman.

Castenell, Louis, Jr., & Pinar, William F. (1993). *Understanding curriculum as racial text: Representations of identity and difference in education.* Albany: State University of New York Press.

Caswell, Hollis L., & Campbell, Doak S. (1935). *Curriculum development.* New York: American Book Company.

Center for a Postmodern World. (1990). Position paper on postmodernism. Claremont, CA: Claremont Graduate School of Theology, John Cobb, director.

Chazan, B. (1985). *Contemporary approaches to moral education: Analyzing alternative theories.* New York: Teachers College Press.

Cherryholmes, Cleo. (1988a). An exploration of meaning and the dialogue between textbooks and teaching. *Journal of Curriculum Studies, 20* (1), pp. 1–21.

———. (1988b). *Power and criticism: Poststructural investigations in education.* New York: Teachers College Press.

———. (1994). More notes on pragmatism. *Educational Researcher, 23* (1), pp. 16–18.

Christian-Smith, Linda. (1987). Gender, popular culture, and curriculum: Adolescence romance novels as gender text. *Curriculum Inquiry, 17* (4), pp. 365–406.

Cobb, John B., Jr. (1988). Ecology, science, and religion: Toward a postmodern worldview. In David Ray Griffin (Ed.), *The reenchantment of science* (pp. 99–113). Albany: State University of New York Press.

Coleman, James S., & Hoffer, T. (1987). *Public and private high schools: The impact of communities.* New York: Basic.

Collins, Patricia Hill. (1990). *Black feminist thought.* London: Harper Collins Academic.

Costner, Kevin. (Producer/Director). (1990). *Dances with wolves.* [Film]. Los Angeles: Orion.

Counts, George S. (1932). *Dare the schools build a new social order?* New York: John Day.

Covey, Stephen R. (1989). *The 7 habits of highly effective people.* New York: Simon and Schuster.

Cox, Harvey. (1984). *Religion in the secular city: Toward a postmodern theology*. New York: Simon and Schuster.

Daly, Herman E., & Cobb, John B. (1989). *For the common good: Redirecting the economy toward community, the environment, and a sustainable future*. Boston: Beacon.

Davies, Paul. (1988). *The cosmic blueprint: New discoveries in nature's creative ability to order the universe*. New York: Simon and Schuster.

———. (1990). Cosmogenesis. *Creation Spirituality, 6* (3), pp. 10–13.

Derrida, Jaques. (1972). Discussion: Structure, sign and play in the discourse of the human sciences. In R. Macksey & E. Donato (Eds.), *The structuralist controversy* (pp. 247–272). Baltimore: Johns Hopkins University Press.

———. (1981). *Positions*. Chicago: University of Chicago Press. (Originally published 1972).

Descombes, V. (1980). *Modern French philosophy*. New York: Cambridge University Press.

Dewey, John. (1897). My pedagogic creed. *The school Journal, 54* (3), pp. 77–80.

———. (1899). *The school and society*. Chicago: University of Chicago Press.

——— (1934a). *A common faith*. New Haven, CT: Yale University Press.

———. (1934b). *Art as experience*. New York: Minton, Balch, & Company.

———. (1938). *Experience and education*. New York: Macmillan.

———. (1985). *Democracy and education 1916*. Carbondale and Edwardsville: Southern Illinois University Press.

Diamond, Raymond T., & Cottrol, Robert J. (1983). Codifying caste: Louisiana's racial classification scheme and the Fourteenth Amendment. *Loyola Law Review, 29*, p. 255.

Doll, Mary Aswell. (1991). Dancing the circle. Address to the Cambridge School of Weston. June 8, 1991. Cambridge, MA.

Doll, Ronald C. (1992). *Curriculum improvement: Decision making and process* (8th ed.). Boston: Allyn and Bacon.

Doll, William E., Jr. (1993). *A post-modern perspective on curriculum*. New York: Teachers College Press.

Dreyfuss, G. O., Cistone, P. J., & Divita, C., Jr. (1992). Restructuring in a large district: Dade County, Florida. In Carl D. Glickman (Ed.), *Supervision in transition* (pp. 43–51). Alexandria, VA: ASCD Press.

Edgerton, Susan. (1993). Love in the margins. In Louis Castenell & William Pinar (Eds.), *Understanding curriculum as racial text: Representation of identity and difference in education* (pp. 55–82). Albany: State University of New York Press.

Eisenberg, Ronni. (1986). *Organize yourself!* New York: Macmillan.

Eisner, Elliot W. (1985). *The educational imagination: On the design and evaluation of school programs* (2d ed.). New York: Macmillan.

———. (1991). *The enlightened eye: Qualitative inquiry and the enhancement of educational practice*. New York: Macmillan.

———. (1993). Invitational conference on the hidden consequences of a national curriculum. *Educational Researcher, 22* (7), 38–39.

Eliot, T. S. (1971). *The collected poems and plays of T. S. Eliot: 1909–1950*. New York: Harcourt, Brace, and World.

Ellsworth, Elizabeth. (1989). Why doesn't this feel empowering?: Working through the repressive myths of critical pedagogy. *Harvard Educational Review, 59* (3), pp. 297–324.

Elmore, Richard F., & Sykes, G. (1992). *Curriculum Development*. New York: Macmillan.

Fanon, Frantz. (1967). *Black skin, white masks*. New York: Grove Press.

———. (1970). *A dying colonialism*. Harmondsworth: Pelican.

Faulkner, William. (1950). Speech of acceptance upon the award of the Nobel Prize for Literature. Stockholm, December 10. In James B. Meriwether (Ed.). (1965). *Essays, speeches, and public letters of William Faulkner* (p. 65). New York: Random House.

Fehr, Dennis Earl. (1993). *Dogs playing cards: Powerbrokers of prejudice in education, art and culture*. New York: Peter Lang.

Finn, Chester E., Jr. (1991). *We must take charge: Our schools and our future*. New York: Free Press.

Foucault, Michel. (1972). *The archaeology of knowledge and the discourse on language*. (Trans. A. M. Sheridan Smith). New York: Pantheon Books.

———. (1980). *Power/knowledge: Selected interviews and other writings, 1972–1977*. Colin Gordon (Ed.), Colin Gordon et al. (Trans.). New York: Pantheon.

———. (1982). *This is not a pipe*. Berkeley: University of California Press.

Fox, Matthew. (1992). *Sheer joy: Conversations with Thomas Aquinas on creation spirituality*. San Francisco: Harper.

Franklin, Barry M. (1986). *Building the American community: The school curriculum and the search for social control.* Philadelphia, PA: Falmer Press.

———. (1988). Whatever happened to social control?: The meeting of coercive authority in curriculum discourse. In William F. Pinar (Ed.), *Contemporary Curriculum Discourses.* Scottsdale, AZ: Gorsuch, Scarisbrick.

Freire, Paulo. (1970). *Pedagogy of the oppressed.* New York: Herder and Herder.

———. (1971). Conscientizing as a way of liberating. *Contacto* (March). See also *Liberation Theology,* A. T. Hennelly (Ed.), 1990. Maryknoll, NY: Orbis.

———. (1985). *The politics of education: Culture, power, and liberation.* South Hadley, MA: Bergin and Garvey.

Freire, Paulo, & Macedo, Donaldo. (1987). *Literacy: Reading the word and reading the world.* South Hadley, MA: Bergin and Garvey.

Fuller, P. (1985). *Images of God: The consolations of lost illusions.* London: Chatto and Windus.

Gadamer, Hans-Georg. (1975). *Truth and method* (G. Borden & J. Cumming, Ed. and Trans.). New York: Seabury.

———. (1976). *Philosophical hermeneutics* (David E. Linge, Ed. and Trans.). Berkeley: University of California Press.

Gadamer, Hans-Georg, & Derrida, Jacques. (1989). *Dialogue and deconstructionism: The Gadamer-Derrida encounter.* Albany: State University of New York Press.

Gaines, Ernest J. (1972). *The autobiography of Miss Jane Pittman.* New York: Bantam.

———. (1993). *A lesson before dying.* New York: Alfred A. Knopf.

Gibson, James J. (1979). *The ecological approach to visual perception.* Boston: Houghton Mifflin.

Gilligan, Carol. (1982). *In a different voice.* Cambridge, MA: Harvard University Press.

Giroux, Henry A. (1981). *Ideology, culture, and the process of schooling.* Philadelphia: Temple University Press.

———. (1983). *Theory and resistance in education: A pedagogy for the opposition.* South Hadley, MA: Bergin and Garvey.

———. (1988). *Schooling and the struggle for public life: Critical pedagogy in the modern age.* Minneapolis: University of Minnesota Press.

————. (Ed.). (1991). *Postmodernism, feminism, and cultural politics: Redrawing educational boundaries.* Albany: State University of New York Press.

————. (1992). *Border crossings: Cultural workers and the politics of education.* New York: Routledge.

————. (1993). *Living dangerously: Multiculturalism and the politics of difference.* New York: Peter Lang.

Giroux, Henry A., & McLaren, Peter. (1989). *Critical pedagogy, the state, and cultural struggle.* Albany: State University of New York Press.

Giroux, Henry A., Penna, Anthony N., & Pinar, William F. (1981). *Curriculum and instruction.* Berkeley: McCutchan.

Gleick, James. (1987). *Chaos: Making a new science.* New York: Viking Press.

Glickman, Carl. (1992). *Supervision in transition.* Alexandria, VA: ASCD Press.

Global Alliance for Transforming Education (GATE). (1991). Education 2000: A holistic perspective. *Holistic Education Review, 4* (4 [Supplement]), pp. 1–18.

Glock, C., & Bellah, R. (1976). *The new religious consciousness.* Berkeley: University of California Press.

Goodlad, J. I., Soder, R., & Sirotnik, K. A. (Eds.). (1990). *The moral dimensions of teaching.* San Francisco: Jossey-Bass.

Goodman, Jesse. (1987). Masculinity, feminism, and the male elementary school teacher. *JCT, 7* (2), pp. 30–60.

————. (1992). *Elementary schooling for critical democracy.* Albany: State University of New York Press.

Goodman, Ken. (1986). *What's whole in whole language.* Portsmouth, NH: Heinemann.

Gordon, Beverly M. (1989). The bootstrap ideology of educational reform: What the recent reports say about the current and future status of Blacks in higher education. In Christine M. Shea, Ernest Kahane, & Peter Sola (Eds.), *The new servants of power: A critique of the 1980s school reform movement* (pp. 87–102). New York: Greenwood.

Graham, Robert J. (1991). *Reading and writing the self: Autobiography in education and the curriculum.* New York: Teachers College Press.

Greeley, Andrew M. (1982). *Catholic high schools and minority students.* New Brunswick, NJ: Transaction.

————. (1992). A modest proposal for the reform of Catholic schools. *America, 166* (10), 234–238.

Greene, Maxine. (1978). *Landscapes of learning.* New York: Teachers College Press.

Griffin, David Ray. (1976). *God, power, and evil: A process theodicy.* Philadelphia: Westminster Press.

————. (1988a). *The reenchantment of science: Postmodern proposals.* Albany: State University of New York Press.

————. (1988b). *Spirituality and society: Postmodern visions.* Albany: State University of New York Press.

————. (Ed.). (1990). *Sacred interconnections: Postmodern spirituality, political economy, and art.* Albany: State University of New York Press.

Griffin, David Ray, Beradslee, W. A., & Holland, J. (1989). *Varieties of postmodern theology.* Albany: State University of New York Press.

Griffin, David Ray, Cobb, John B., Jr., Ford, Marcus P., Gunter, Pete A. Y., & Ochs, Peter. (1993). *Founders of constructive postmodern philosophy: Peirce, James, Bergson, Whitehead, and Hartshorne.* Albany: State University of New York Press.

Grumet, Madeleine R. (1988a). Bodyreading. In William F. Pinar (Ed.), *Contemporary curriculum discourses* (pp. 453–473). Scottsdale, AZ: Gorsuch, Scarisbrick.

————. (1988b). *Bitter milk: Women and teaching.* Amherst: University of Massachusetts Press.

————. (1988c). Women and teaching: Homeless at home. In William F. Pinar (Ed.), *Contemporary curriculum discourses* (pp. 531–540). Scottsdale, AZ: Gorsuch, Scarisbrick.

Gutek, G. L. (1993). *American education is a global society: Internationalizing teacher education.* New York: Longman.

Gutierrez, Gustavo. (1973). *Theology of liberation.* New York: Maryknoll Publishers.

Habermas, Jurgen. (1970). *Knowledge and human interests.* Boston: Beacon.

Haggerson, Nelson, & Bowman, Andrea. (1992). *Informing educational policy and practice through interpretive inquiry.* Lancaster, PA: Technomic.

Hall, Manley P. (1988). *Meditation symbols in Eastern and Western mysticism: Mysteries of the mandala.* Los Angeles: Philosophical Research Society.

Hammerschlag, Carl A. (1988). *The dancing healers: A doctor's journey of healing with native Americans.* San Francisco: Harper and Row.

———. (1993). *The theft of the spirit.* San Francisco: Harper and Row.

Hawking, Stephen W. (1988). *A brief history of time: From the big bang to black holes.* New York: Bantam.

Havel, Vaclav. (1992, March 1). The end of the modern era. *New York Times*, 141 (48,892), Sec. 4, p. E15.

Hayles, N. K. (1984). *The cosmic web.* Ithaca: Cornell University Press.

Heidegger, Martin. (1962). *Being and time.* (John Macquarrie and Edward Robinson, Trans.). New York: Harper and Row.

Henderson, James, & Hawthone, R. D. (1995). *Transformative curriculum leadership.* New York: MacMillan.

Hennelly, A. T. (Ed.). (1990). *Liberation theology: A documentary history.* Maryknoll, NY: Orbis.

Hirsch, E. D., Jr. (1987). *Cultural literacy: What every American needs to know.* Boston: Houghton Mifflin.

Hlebowiths, Peter W. (1993). *Radical curriculum theory revisited.* New York: Longman.

Hodge, Robert, & Kress, Gunter. (1988). *Social Semiotics.* Ithaca: Cornell University Press.

Howard, Roy J. (1982). *Three faces of hermeneutics.* Berkeley: University of California Press.

Huebner, Dwayne. (1975). Curriculum as concern for man's temporality. In W. F. Pinar (Ed.), *Curriculum theorizing: The reconceptualists.* Berkeley, CA: McCutchan.

———. (1976). The moribund curriculum field: Its wake and our work. *Curriculum Inquiry*, 6 (2), 2–11.

Hughes, Langston. (1973). The negro speaks of rivers. In R. Ellmann & R. O'Clair (Eds.), *The Norton anthology of modern poetry* (pp. 634–635). New York: W. W. Norton.

Hunter, Madeline. (1982). *Mastery teaching.* El Segundo, CA: TIP Publications.

Husserl, Edmond. (1964). *Phenomenology of internal time-consciousness.* Bloomington, IN: Midland.

Jackson, Philip (Ed.). (1992). *Handbook of research on curriculum.* New York: Macmillan.

James, S., Heller, D., & Ellis, W. (1992). Peer assistance in a small district: Windham Southeast, Vermont. In Carl D. Glickman (Ed.), *Supervision in transition* (pp. 43–61). Alexandria, VA: ASCD Press.

James, William. (1958). *Talks to teachers: On psychology; and to students on some of life's ideals.* New York: W. W. Norton.

Jameson, F. (1991). *Postmodernism and the cultural logic of late capitalism.* Durham, NC: Duke University Press.

Jardine, David W. (1992). Reflections on education, hermeneutics, and ambiguity: Hermeneutics as a restoring of life to its original difficulty. In William F. Pinar and William M. Reynolds (Eds.), *Understanding curriculum as phenomenological and deconstructed text* (pp. 116–130). New York: Longman.

Jeanrond, Werner. (1988). Hermeneutics. In J. Komonchak, M. Collins, & D. Lane (Eds.), *The new dictionary of theology* (pp. 462–464). Wilmington, DE: Michael Glazier.

Jencks, Charles. (1986). *What is post-modernism?* New York: St. Martin's Press.

———. (1988). *Architecture today.* New York: Harry N. Abrams.

———. (Ed.). (1992). *The post-modern reader.* New York: St. Martin's Press.

Jerusalem Bible, The. (1966). Garden City, NY: Doubleday.

Jones, Libby Falk, & Goodwin, Sarah Webster (Eds.). (1990). *Feminism, utopia, and narrative.* Knoxville: University of Tennessee Press.

Kesson, Kathleen. (1993). Critical theory and holistic education: Carrying on the conversation. In Ron Miller (Ed.), *The Renewal of meaning in education* (pp. 92–110). Brandon, VT: Holistic Education Press.

Kierkegaard, Søren. (1849). *The sickness unto death: A Christian psychological exposition for upbuilding and awakening* (H. V. Hong & E. H. Hong, Trans.). (1980). Princeton, NJ: Princeton University Press.

Kincheloe, Joe L. (1993). *Toward a critical politics of teacher thinking: Mapping the postmodern.* Westport, CT: Bergin & Garvey.

Kincheloe, Joe L., & Pinar, William F. (Eds.). (1991). *Curriculum as social psychoanalysis: The significance of place.* Albany: State University of New York Press.

Kincheloe, Joe L., Pinar, William F., & Slattery, Patrick. (in press). A last dying chord?: Toward cultural and educational renewal in the south. *Curriculum Inquiry.*

Kincheloe, Joe L., Slattery, Patrick, McLaren, Peter, & Oldenski, Tom. (1992, October). *Liberation theology*. Paper presented at the conference on curriculum theory and classroom practice, sponsored by *JCT: An Interdisciplinary Journal of Curriculum Studies* and the University of Dayton, OH.

Kincheloe, Joe L., & Steinberg, Shirley R. (Eds.). (1992). *Thirteen questions: Reframing education's conversations*. New York: Peter Lang.

———. (1993). A tentative description of post-formal thinking: The critical confrontation with cognitive theory. *Harvard Educational Review*, *63* (3), pp. 296–320.

Kincheloe, Joe L., Steinberg, Shirley, & Tippin, Debbie. (1992). *The stigma of genius: Einstein beyond modern education*. Durango, CO: Holobrook Press.

King, Coretta Scott. (1993). *My life with Martin Luther King, Jr.* (rev. ed.). New York: Henry Holt.

Kliebard, Herbert. M. (1986). *The struggle for the American curriculum: 1893–1958*. Boston: Routledge and Kegan Paul.

———. (1992a). *Forging the American curriculum: Essays in curriculum history and theory*. Boston: Routledge and Kegan Paul.

———. (1992b). Constructing a history of the American curriculum. In Philip W. Jackson (Ed.), *Handbook of research on curriculum* (pp. 157–184). New York: Macmillan.

Konikoff, Judy. (1993). An interview with Dr. Carl Brasseaux. LSU Baton Rouge, LA: Unpublished graduate research paper.

Kozol, Jonathan. (1967). *Death at an early age*. Boston: Houghton Mifflin.

———. (1975). *The night is dark and I am far from home: A political indictment of the United States public schools*. New York: Continuum.

———. (1991). *Savage inequalities: Children in America's schools*. New York: Crown.

Kuhn, Thomas. (1970). *The structure of scientific revolutions*. Chicago: University of Chicago Press.

Kung, Hans. (1988). *Theology for the third millennium: An ecumenical view*. New York: Doubleday.

Langer, Susanne K. (1957). *Problems of art*. New York: Charles Scribner.

Lasch, Christopher. (1984). *The minimal self: Psychic survival in troubled times*. New York: W. W. Norton.

Lather, Patti. (1989). Ideology and methodological attitude. *JCT: An Interdisciplinary Journal of Curriculum Studies, 9* (2), pp. 7–26.

———— (1991). *Getting smart: Feminist research and pedagogy with/in the postmodern.* New York: Routledge.

————. (1994). Gender issues in methodology: Data analysis in the crisis of representation. *Brochure for Conference held by AERA Winter Institute in Clearwater, Florida.*

Lemonick, M. D. (1992). Echoes of the Big Bang. *Time, 139* (18), pp. 62–63.

LePage, Andy. (1987). *Transforming education: The new 3 r's.* Oakland: Oakmore House.

Lerner, Gerda. (1986). *The creation of patriarchy.* New York: Oxford University Press.

Lincoln, Yvonna S. (1992). Curriculum studies and the traditions of inquiry: The humanistic tradition. In Philip W. Jackson (Ed.), *Handbook of research on curriculum* (pp. 79–98). New York: Macmillan.

———— (1994, March). Piety and purpose: Reclaiming élan for higher education. *Educational Researcher, 23* (2), pp. 35–36.

Lyotard, Jean François. (1984). *The postmodern condition: A report on knowledge.* Minneapolis: University of Minnesota Press.

Macdonald, James B. (1988). Theory, practice, and the hermeneutic circle. In William F. Pinar (Ed.), *Contemporary curriculum discourses* (pp. 101–113). Scottsdale, AZ: Gorsuch, Scarisbrick.

Maguire, Daniel C., & Fargnoli, A. N. (1991). *On moral grounds: The art/science of ethics.* New York: Crossroad.

Mann, Horace. (1848). Twelfth annual report of the [Massachusetts] Board of Education. In Lawrence Cremin (Ed.), *The republic and the school: Horace Mann on the education of the free man.* New York: Teachers College, 1957.

Marty, M. E. (1984). *Pilgrims in their own land: 500 years of religion in America.* Boston: Little Brown.

Maxcy, Spencer J. (1991). *Educational leadership: A critical pragmatic perspective.* New York: Bergin and Garvey.

Maxcy, Spencer J. (Ed.). (1993). *Postmodern school leadership: Meeting the crisis in educational administration.* Westport, CT: Praeger.

McCall, Nathan. (1993). *Makes me wanna holla.* New York: Random House.

McCarthy, Camron. (1990). *Race and curriculum.* London: Falmer.

————. (1993). Multicultural approaches to racial inequality in the United States. In Louis Castenell & William Pinar (Eds.), *Understanding curriculum as racial text: Representations of identity and difference in education* (pp. 225–246). Albany: State University of New York Press.

McCarthy, Camron, & Apple, Michael. (1988). Race, class, and gender in American education: Toward a nonsynchronous parallelist position. In Lois Weis (Ed.), *Class, race and gender in American education* (pp. 3–39). Albany: State University of New York Press.

McLaren, Peter. (1989). *Life in schools: An introduction to critical pedagogy in the foundations of education.* New York: Longman.

————. (1993, January). Multiculturalism and the postmodern critique: Towards a pedagogy of resistance and transformation. *Cultural Studies, 7* (1), pp. 118–146.

McLaren, Peter, & Dantley, Michael. (1990). Leadership and a critical pedagogy of race: Cornel West, Stuart Hall, and the prophetic tradition. *Journal of Negro Education, 59* (1), pp. 29–44.

McLaren, Peter, & Leonard, Peter. (Eds.). (1993). *Paulo Freire: A critical encounter.* London and New York: Routledge.

McNeil, J. D. (1990). *Curriculum: A comprehensive introduction* (4th ed.). Boston: Little Brown (Harper).

McNeil, Linda. (1986). *Contradictions of control: School structure and school knowledge.* New York: Routledge and Kegan Paul.

Megill, Allan. (1985). *Prophets of extremity.* Berkeley: University of California Press.

Merleau-Ponty, Maurice. (1962). *Phenomenology of perception.* London: Routledge and Kegan Paul.

Miller, Janet L. (1980). Women: The evolving educational consciousness. *JCT: An Interdisciplinary Journal of Curriculum Studies, 2* (1), pp. 238–247.

————. (1987). Women as teacher/researchers: Gaining a sense of ourselves. *Teacher Education Quarterly, 14* (2), pp. 52–58.

————. (1990). *Creating spaces and finding voices.* Albany: State University of New York Press.

————. (1992). Women and education: In what ways does gender affect the educational process? In Joe L. Kincheloe and Shirley Steinberg (Eds.), *Thirteen questions* (pp. 151–158). New York: Peter Lang.

Miller, John P. (1988). *The holistic curriculum.* Ontario: Canada: Ontario Institute for Studies in Education.

Miller, Page Putnam, & Thelen, David. (1993). Historians and archivists. *Chronicle of Higher Education,* 40 (16), December 8, p. B3.

Miller, Ron (Ed.). (1993). *The renewal of meaning in education: Responses to the ecological crisis of our time.* Brandon, VT: Holistic Education Press.

Moltman, Jurgen. (1967). *The theology of hope.* London: SCM Press.

Moran, Gabriel. (1981). *Interplay: A theory of religion and education.* Winona, MN: Saint Mary's College Press.

Moore, Mary Elizabeth M. (1989, October 15). The art of teaching from the heart: The heart of the matter. Paper presented at the School of Theology at Claremont, CA.

Morrison, Toni. (1989). Unspeakable things unspoken: The Afro-American presence in American literature. *Michigan Quarterly,* Winter, pp. 1–34.

Muhammad, Khallid. (1994). Nation of Islam speaker urges black students to "wake up." In *The Vermilion,* 90 (ix), University of Southwestern Louisiana Student Weekly (March 11), pp. 1–2. Lafayette, LA. Stephanie Fournet, editor-in-chief.

National Conference of Catholic Bishops (NCCB). (1972). *To teach as Jesus did: A pastoral message on Catholic education.* Washington, DC: U.S. Catholic Conference Publications Office.

Needleman, J. (Ed.). (1989). *Tao Te Ching by Lao Tsu.* Gia Fu Feng and Jane English (Trans.). New York: Vintage.

Newland, Bethene. (1993, November). Against "new age" teaching [Letter to the editor]. *Lafayette Advertiser,* p. E-5.

Newman, Joseph W. (1990). *America's teachers: An introduction to education.* New York: Longman.

Nietzsche, Friedrich. (1968). The birth of tragedy. In Walter Kaufmann (Trans. and Ed.), *Basic writings of Nietzsche* (3d ed.). New York: Modern Library.

Noddings, Nel. (1984). *Caring: A feminine approach to ethics and moral education.* Berkeley: University of California Press.

———. (1989). *Women and evil.* Berkeley: University of California Press.

———. (1992). *The challenge to care in schools: An alternative approach to education.* New York: Teachers College Press.

Oakes, Jeannie. (1985). *Keeping track: How schools structure inequality.* New Haven, CT: Yale University Press.

References

285

O'Gorman, R. T. (1987). *The church that was a school: Catholic identity and Catholic education in the United States since 1790.* Washington, DC: NCEA Catholic Education Futures Project.

Oliva, Peter F. (1992). *Developing the curriculum* (3d ed.). Boston: Harper Collins.

Oliver, Donald W., & Gershman, Kathleen W. (1989). *Education, modernity, and fractured meaning: Toward a process theory of teaching and learning.* Albany: State University of New York Press.

Ornstein, Allan C., & Levine, Daniel U. (1993). *Philosophical foundations of education* (5th ed.). Boston: Houghton Mifflin.

Orr, David W. (1992). *Ecological literacy: Education and the transition to a postmodern world.* Albany: State University of New York Press.

Osajima, Keith. (1992). Speaking silence. *JCT: An Interdisciplinary Journal of Curriculum Studies,* 9 (4), pp. 89–96.

Ozmon, Howard, & Craver, Samuel. (1990). *Philosophical foundations of education* (4th ed.). Columbus, OH: Merrill.

Padgham, Ronald. (1988). Correspondences: Contemporary curriculum theory and twentieth-century art. In William F. Pinar (Ed.), *Contemporary curriculum discourses* (pp. 359–379). Scottsdale, AZ: Gorsuch, Scarisbrick.

Pagano, Jo Anne. (1990). *Exiles and communities: Teaching in the patriarchal wilderness.* Albany: State University of New York Press.

Page, Reba. (1990). *Curriculum differentiation: Interpretive studies in the United States' secondary schools.* Albany: State University of New York Press.

———— (1991). *Lower-track classroom: A curricular and cultural perspective.* New York: Teachers College Press.

Pajak, Edward. (1989). *The central office supervisor of curriculum and instruction: Setting the stage for success.* Boston: Allyn and Bacon.

Percy, Walker. (1954). *The message in the bottle.* New York: Farrar, Straus, and Giroux.

————. (1960). *The moviegoer.* New York: Ivy.

Peter, Carl. (1974). Metaphysical finalism in Christian eschatology. *The Thomist,* 38 (January), pp. 125–145.

Phenix, Phillip. (1975). Transcendence and the curriculum. In William F. Pinar (Ed.), *Curriculum theorizing: The reconceptualists* (pp. 323–337). Berkeley, CA: McCutchan.

Picasso, Pablo. (1971). Conversations. In H. B. Chipps (Ed.), *Theories of modern art: A source book of artists and critics* (p. 268). Berkeley: University of California Press.

Pinar, William F. (1975). *Curriculum theorizing: The reconceptualists.* Berkeley, CA: McCutchan.

———. (1978). Notes on the curriculum field 1978. *Educational Researcher, 7* (8), pp. 5–12.

———. (Ed.). (1988a). *Contemporary curriculum discourses.* Scottsdale, AZ: Gorsuch, Scarisbrick.

———. (1988b). Time, place, and voice: Curriculum theory and the historical moment. In William F. Pinar (Ed.), *Contemporary curriculum discourses* (pp. 264–278). Scottsdale, AZ: Gorsuch, Scarisbrick.

———. (1994). *Autobiography, politics, and sexuality: Essays in curriculum theory, 1972–1992.* New York: Peter Lang.

Pinar, William F., & Grumet, Madeleine R. (1976). *Toward a poor curriculum.* Dubuque, IA: Kendall/Hunt.

Pinar, William F., & Reynolds, William M. (Eds.) (1992). *Understanding curriculum as phenomenological and deconstructed text.* New York: Longman.

Pinar, William F., Reynolds, William M., Slattery, Patrick, & Taubman, Peter Maas. (in press). *Understanding curriculum: An introduction to the study of historical and contemporary curriculum discourses.* New York: Peter Lang.

Pollock, Jackson. (1971). My painting. In H. B. Chipps (Ed.), *Theories of modern art: A source book of artists and critics* (pp. 540–556). Berkeley: University of California Press.

Prigogine, Ilya, & Stengers, Isabel. (1984). *Order out of chaos: Man's new dialogue with nature.* New York: Bantam.

Provenzo, Edward F., Jr. (1990). *Religious fundamentalism and American education.* New York: State University of New York Press.

Purpel, David E. (1989). *The moral and spiritual crisis in education: A curriculum for justice and compassion in education.* New York: Bergin and Garvey.

Raymond, C. (1991, March 6). New study finds convergence of school curricula worldwide. *Chronicle of Higher Education*, p. A8.

Regnier, Robert. (1992). The sacred circle: Foundation for a process pedagogy of healing. Paper presented at the Sixth Annual

Meeting of the Association of Process Philosophy of Education, Louisville, KY. April 24–26.

Reynolds, William. (1989). *Reading curriculum theory: The development of a new hermeneutic*. New York: Peter Lang.

Ricouer, Paul. (1981). *Hermeneutics and the human sciences*. J. Thompson (Trans. and Ed.). Cambridge, England: Cambridge University Press.

Robinson, J. M. (Ed.). (1977). *The Nag Hammadi Library*. San Francisco: Harper and Row.

Roman, Leslie, & Apple, Michael. (1990). Is naturalism a move away from positivism? In Eliot Eisner & Alan Peshkin (Eds.), *Qualitative inquiry in education* (pp. 38–73). New York: Teachers College Press.

Roman, Leslie, & Christian-Smith, Linda. (1987). *Feminism and the politics of popular culture*. London: Falmer.

Rorty, Richard. (1979). *Philosophy and the mirror of nature*. Princeton: Princeton University Press.

———. (1982). *Consequences of pragmatism*. Minneapolis: University of Minnesota Press.

———. (1989). *Contingency, irony and solidarity*. Cambridge: Cambridge University Press.

Ruether, Rosemary R. (1983a). *Sexism and God-talk: Toward a feminist theology*. Boston: Beacon Press.

———. (1983b). *To change the world: Christianity and cultural criticism*. New York: Crossroads.

Rushdie, Salmon. (1989). *The satanic verses*. New York: Penguin.

St. Julien, John. (1992, April). Explaining learning: The research trajectory of situated cognition and the implications of connectionism. Paper presented at AERA in San Francisco, CA.

———. (1994). Situated cognition. Louisiana State University, Baton Rouge: Unpublished doctoral dissertation.

Sarup, M. (1989). *An introductory guide to post-structuralism and post-modernism*. Athens: University of Georgia Press.

Saussure, Ferdinand de. (1959). *Course in general linguistics*. New York: McGraw-Hill.

———. (1974). *Course in general linguistics*. J. Culler (Ed.), and W. Baskin (Trans.). London: Falmer.

Saylor, J. G., Alexander, W. M., & Lewis, A. J. (1981). *Curriculum planning for better teaching and learning* (4th ed.). New York: Holt, Rinehart, and Winston.

Schleiermacher, Frederich D. E. (1978). Outline of the 1819 lectures. *New Literacy History*, 10 (1), pp. 1–16.

Schon, Donald A. (1983). *The reflective practitioner: How professionals think in action*. New York: Basic.

———. (1987). *Educating the reflective practitioner*. New York: Basic.

———. (1991). *The reflective turn*. New York: Teachers College Press.

Schubert, William H. (1986). *Curriculum: Perspective, paradigm, possibility*. New York: Macmillan.

Schubert, William, & Ayers, William (Eds.). (1992). *Teacher lore: Learning from our own experience*. New York: Longman.

Schwab, Joseph. (1970). *The practical: A language for curriculum*. Washington, DC: National Education Association.

Sears, James T. (1990). *Growing up gay in the South*. New York and London: Haworth Press.

———. (1992). *Sexuality and the curriculum*. New York: Teachers College Press.

Sears, James T., & Marshall J. Dan (Eds.) (1990). *Teaching a::d thinking about curriculm: Critical inquiry*. New York: Teachers College Press.

Serres, Michel. (1982). *Hermes: Literature, science, philosophy*. Baltimore: Johns Hopkins University Press.

Shakir, M. H. (Trans.). (1990). *The Our'an*. Elmhurst, NY: Tahrike Tarsile Qur'an.

Shea, Christine, Kahane, Ernst, & Sola, Peter. (1989). *The new servants of power: A critique of the 1980s school reform movement*. New York: Greenwood Press.

Shepard, Paul. (1977). Place in American culture. *North American Review*, Fall, pp. 22–32.

Short, Edmund C. (1991). *Forms of curriculum inquiry*. Albany: State University of New York Press.

Simons, Marlise. (1994, January 30). Cousteau says oceans vandalized. New York Times New Service. *Lafayette Sunday Advertiser*, 128 (129), p. A-6.

Sizer, Theodore. (1984). *Horace's compromise: The dilemma of the American high school*. Boston: Houghton Mifflin.

Slattery, Cheryl. (1989). "My mommy was pregnant but then she miscarried." Lafayette, LA: Unpublished manuscript.

Slattery, Patrick. (1989). Toward an eschatological curriculum theory. Baton Rouge: Louisiana State University. Unpublished dissertation.

―――. (1992a). Toward an eschatological curriculum theory. *JCT: An Interdisciplinary Journal of Curriculum Studies, 9* (3), 7–21.

―――. (1992b). Theological dimensions of the school curriculum. *Journal of Religion & Public Education, 19* (2–3), pp. 173–184.

Slattery, Patrick, & Daigle, Kevin. (1991, October). Curriculum as a place of turmoil: Deconstructing the anguish in Ernest Gaines' *Pointe Coupee* and Walker Percy's *Feliciana*. Paper presented at the conference on curriculum theory and classroom practice, sponsored by *JCT: An Interdisciplinary Journal of Curriculum Studies and the University of Dayton*. (1994, in press, *Curriculum Inquiry*).

Slattery, Patrick, & Slattery, Cheryl. (1993). Writing children's books in a language arts curriculum. *Journal of Children's Books in Ireland, 9* (December), p. 7.

Sloan, Douglas. (1983). *Insight-imagination: The recovery of thought in the modern world*. New York: Teachers College Press.

―――. (1993). Forward. In Ron Miller (Ed.), *The renewal of meaning in education* (pp. 1–5). Brandon, VT: Holistic Education Press.

Smith, David G. (1988). Experimental eidetics as a way of entering curriculum language from the ground up. In William F. Pinar (Ed.), *Contemporary curriculum discourses* (pp. 417–436). Scottsdale, AZ: Gorsuch, Scarisbrick.

―――. (1991). Hermeneutic inquiry: The hermeneutic imagination and the pedagogic text. In Edmund C. Short (Ed.), *Forms of curriculum inquiry* (pp. 187–210). Albany: State University of New York Press.

―――. (1965). *Philosophy of education*. New York: Harper and Row.

Sola, Peter. (1989). The corporate community on the ideal business-school alliance: A historical and ethical critique. In Christine M. Shea, Ernest Kahane, & Peter Sola (Eds.), *The new servants of power: A critique of the 1980s school reform movement* (pp. 75–83). New York: Greenwood.

Spring, Joel. (1990). *The American school: 1642–1990*. New York: Longman.

———. (1993). *Conflict of interests: The politics of American education* (2nd ed.). New York: Longman.

Stanley, William B. (1992). *Curriculum for Utopia: Social reconstructionism and critical pedagogy in the postmodern era.* Albany: State University of New York Press.

Stannard, David E. (1992). *American Holocaust: Columbus and the conquest of the new world.* New York: Oxford University Press.

Stark, R., & Brainbridge, W. S. (1985). *The future of religions: Secularization, revival, and cult formation.* Berkeley: University of California Press.

Stinson, Susan W. (1991). Dance as curriculum, curriculum as dance. In George Willis & William H. Schubert (Eds.), *Reflections from the heart of educational inquiry* (pp. 190–196). Albany: State University of New York Press.

Suzuki, D. T., Fromm, Erich, & DeMartino, Richard. (1960). *Zen Buddhism and psychoanalysis.* New York: Grove.

Tanner, Daniel, & Tanner, Laurel. (in press). *Curriculum development: Theory into practice* (3d ed.). New York: Macmillan.

Taubman, Peter Maas. (1993a). Canonical sins. In Louis Castenell & William Pinar (Eds.), *Understanding curriculum as racial text: Representation of identity and difference in education* (pp. 35–52). Albany: State University of New York Press.

———. (1993b). Separate identity, separate lives: Diversity in the curriculum. In Louis Castenell & William Pinar (Eds.), *Understanding curriculum as racial text: Representation of identity and difference in education* (pp. 287–306). Albany: State University of New York Press.

Taylor, Mark C. (1984). *Erring: A post-modern a/theology.* Chicago: University of Chicago Press.

Teilhard, Pierre de Chardin. (1959). *The divine milieu.* New York: William Collins and Sons.

Thompson, H. Ed, III, & Baldson, Ken (Eds.). (1993). *Sex and knowledge.* Saskatoon, Alberta: Hemlock.

Toffler, Alvin. (1990). *Powershift: Knowledge, wealth, and violence at the edge of the 21st century.* New York: Bantam.

Toulmin, Stephen. (1982). The construal of reality: Criticism in modern and post modern science. In W. J. T. Mitchell (Ed.), *The politics of interpretation* (pp. 99–118). Chicago: University of Chicago Press.

Toynbee, Arnold. (1947). *A study of history*. New York: Oxford University Press.

Troyna, Barry, & Hatcher, Richard. (1992). *Racism in children's lives: A study of mainly-white primary schools*. London and New York: Routledge.

Tucker, Mary Evelyn. (1993). *Education and ecology: Earth literacy and the technological trance*. Chambersburg, PA: ANIMA Books.

Tyler, Ralph. (1949). *Basic principles of curriculum and instruction*. Chicago: University of Chicago Press.

van Manen, Max. (1982). Edifying theory: Serving the good. *Theory Into Practice, 21* (1), pp. 44–49.

———. (1984). Action research as a theory of the unique. (Department of Secondary Education Curriculum Praxis Occasional Papers Series, #31). Edmonton: University of Alberta.

———. (1986). *The tone of teaching*. Richmond Hill, Ontario: Scholastic-Tab.

———. (1988). The relationship between research and pedagogy. In William F. Pinar (Ed.), *Contemporary curriculum discourses* (pp. 427–452). Scottsdale, AZ: Gorsuch, Scarisbrick.

———. (1990). *Researching lived experience: Human science for an action sensitive pedagogy*. London, Ontario: Althouse Press.

———. (1993). *The tact of teaching: The meaning of pedagogical thoughtfulness*. Albany: State University of New York Press.

Vygotsky, Lev S. (1978). *Mind in society: The development of higher psychological processes*. Cambridge, MA: Harvard University Press.

Wald, K. D. (1987). *Religion and politics in the United States*. New York: St. Martin's Press.

Watkins, William H. (1993). Black curriculum orientations: A preliminary inquiry. *Harvard Educational Review, 63* (3), pp. 321–338.

Watts, Alan. (1957). *The way of Zen*. New York: Vintage.

Weis, Lois. (1983). Schooling and cultural production: A comparison of black and white lived culture. In Michael Apple & Lois Weis, *Ideology and practice in schooling* (pp. 235–261). Philadelphia: Temple University Press.

———(Ed.). (1988). *Class, race, and gender in American education*. Albany: State University of New York Press.

West, Cornel. (1988). Postmodernism and black America. *Zeta Magazine, 1* (6), pp. 27–29.

———. (1990). The cultural politics of difference. *October*, 53, pp. 93–109.

Wexler, Philip. (1992). *Becoming somebody: Toward a social psychology of school*. (With the assistance of W. Crichlow, J. Kern, & R. Martusewich.) London: Falmer Press.

Wheatley, Margaret J. (1992). *Leadership and the new science: Learning about organization from an orderly universe*. San Francisco: Benett-Koehler.

Whitehead, Alfred North. (1929). *Aims of education*. New York: Free Press, Macmillan.

———. (1933). *Adventure of ideas*. New York: Macmillan.

———. ([1929], 1978). *Process and reality* [corrected edition]. David Ray Griffin and Donald W. Sherburne (Eds.). New York: MacMillan.

Whitson, Anthony J. (1988a). Adventures in monopolis: The wonderland of schooling in Arons' Compelling Belief. *Journal of Curriculum Theorizing*, 7(3), 101–108.

———. (1988b). The politics of "non-political" curriculum: Heteroglossia and the discourse of "choice" and "effectiveness." In William F. Pinar (Ed.), *Contemporary Curriculum Discourses* (pp. 279–331). Scottsdale, AZ: Gorsuch, Scarisbrick.

———. (1991). *Constitution and curriculum*. London: Falmer.

Wieman, Henry Nelson. (1969a). *The source of human good*. Carbondale: Southern Illinois University Press, Articus Books. (Originally published 1946).

———. (1969b). The revolution of our time. *Interchange* (March–April), Center for Creative Interchange.

Wiles, J., & Bondi, J. C. (1993). *Curriculum development: A guide to practice* (4th ed.). Columbus, OH: Merrill.

Wilhelm, Ronald. (1994). Exploring the practice-rhetoric gap: Current curriculum for African-American history month in some Texas elementary schools. *Journal of Curriculum and Supervision*, 9 (2), Winter, pp. 217–223.

Willis, George, & Schubert, William H. (Eds.) (1991). *Reflections from the heart of educational inquiry: Understanding curriculum and teaching through the arts*. New York: SUNY Press.

Willis, George, Schubert, William H., Bullough, Robert V., Jr., Kridel, Craig, & Holton, John T. (1993). *The American curriculum: A documentary history*. Westport, CT: Greenwood Press.

Willis, Paul. (1977). *Learning to labour*. Westmead, England: Saxon House.

Wilshire, Bruce. (1990). *The moral collapse of the university: Professionalism, purity, and alienation.* Albany: State University of New York Press.

Wise, Arthur E. (1979). *Legislated learning: The bureaucratization of the American classroom.* Berkeley: University of California Press.

Wolcott, Harry. (1973). *The man in the principal's office: An ethnography.* New York: Holt, Rinehart, and Winston.

Wolf, Denise Palmer. (1992). Becoming knowledge: The evolution of art education curriculum. In Philip W. Jackson (Ed.), *Handbook of curriculum research* (pp. 945–963). New York: Macmillan.

Zais, R. S. (1976). *Curriculum: Principles and foundations.* New York: Thomas Y. Crowell.

Subject Index

aesthetics, xi, 207–225, 230; and postmodern art, 23–24

America 2000 and *Goals 2000*, 71

architecture, 15, 176–178

autobiography, 50, 51, 55–56, 62–63, 77, 105, 130–131, 143, 149, 152, 165–166, 199, 252; and autiobiographical accounts, 45–46, 49–50, 52–55, 64–66, 134–135, 137, 166–167, 179, 213–215, 227–229, 239–240, 249–251, 261–263; and identity, 131–132, 138, 158, 263–264; and self, 114–115, 121, 123, 125–129, 134, 158–159, 171, 173–174, 177, 188, 190, 210–211, 216; and self-destruction, 248; and writing, 165

behaviorism and behavioral objectives, 64–65, 76–77, 78, 151, 172, 212, 253

Bildung, 113

Black History Month, 122–123

breathing, 82–83, 86–87, 217

Center for a Post-modern World, 19

chaos, 149, 227–240, 243–245; and complexity, xvii, 243–

244; *see also* physics

Christian Scriptures, 85–86; and exegesis, 111; and hermeneutics, 111

circle, 176–181, 184–186

Civitas social studies curriculum, 39–40

cognition, 180, 182–183

commorientes, 137

communautes de base, 70

cooperative models, 93–94, 97

connoisseurship, 211–212, 224

cosmology, 106, 109–110, 142

critical theory, 191–206

cultural literacy, 40, 133, 141–143

currere, 56–58, 77, 151, 161, 249, 255

curriculum, xv-xix, 1–12, 27–30, 130, 154, 173, 252–257; an analogy to medicial field, xv-xvi; and crises, xvii; and historical events, 60–62, 88–89; models, 4–5; and politico-religious debates, 3; and standardization, 247–248; and theory, 9, 11, 31, 129, 150, 152–154, 163; and traditional development models, xvi-

295

Name Index

CRITICAL EDUCATION PRACTICE

SHIRLEY R. STEINBERG
JOE L. KINCHELOE
Series Editors

CRITICAL EDUCATION PRACTICE,
VOL. 1

CURRICULUM DEVELOPMENT IN THE POSTMODERN ERA